# Time-Effective Psychotherapy

# Related Titles of Interest

For more information or to purchase a book, please call 1-800-278-3525.

▶

# Time-Effective Psychotherapy

## Maximizing Outcomes in an Era of Minimized Resources

**Steven Friedman**
*Harvard Community Health Plan*

**Allyn and Bacon**
Boston • London • Toronto • Sydney • Tokyo • Singapore

*Library of Congress Cataloging-in-Publication Data*

Friedman, Steven
    Time-effective psychotherapy : maximizing outcomes in an era of minimized
resources / Steven Friedman.
        p.    cm.
    Includes bibliographical references and index.
    ISBN 0–205–26119–1
    1. Brief psychotherapy.   2. Managed mental health care.
I. Title.
    [DNLM:   1. Psychotherapy, Brief—methods.   2. Physician's Practice
Patterns.   3. Time Management—methods.   4. Managed Care Programs—
United States. WM 420.5.P5 F899 1997]
    RC480.55.F76   1997
    616.89'14'068—dc20
    DNLM/DLC                                                      96–21219
    for Library of Congress                                          CIP

*To Donna and Sarah . . . with love*

A vision without a task is but a dream,
a task without a vision is drudgery,
a vision and a task is the hope of the world.

—*From a church in Sussex,*
*England, c. 1730*

# Contents

▶

# Preface

A book is a very personal product. This book is a personal account of my current thinking and clinical practices as they have evolved over a 20-year period. I like to think of my work as a kind of consultation that privileges people's requests and supports their dignity and sense of personal agency. This is not a therapy for people searching for insights through long-term psychoanalysis. The focus here is placed on helping people find solutions, in a time-effective way, to everyday problems of living.

I consider myself fortunate to have had a set of early training experiences that excluded immersion in rigid theoretical models and traditional pathologizing modes of diagnosis and treatment. My training in humanistic, eco-systemic perspectives and my background in experimental psychology led me to see the benefits of understanding and respecting the power of the social context to influence behavior and the value of maintaining a sense of curiosity and exploration in my work. I also developed a strong belief in the resources and capacities of people to create better lives for themselves. This is something I learned from my father, who always saw possibilities and helped me see that dreams and aspirations were the first step in getting there. My goal in doing therapy is respecting the complexities of people's lives while translating those complexities into simple ideas that can be acted on to enable change to occur.

Having, as long as I can remember, been an "efficiency freak," I found myself naturally looking for ways to move people along in therapy without creating unnecessary dependencies. Working over the past 10 years in an HMO setting further honed my skills in this direction.

This volume presents a set of principles and techniques that can be applied to the myriad array of problems that people present in therapy. However, my hope is that, more than being a simple description of ideas and practices, this book will stimulate you to find your own voice, one that defines who you are as a therapist. In the end it is not models and techniques that matter most, but rather your commitment, respect, and authenticity. Yogi Berra, the famous New York Yankee baseball player, when asked what he thinks about when he steps up to the plate, replied, "How can I think and hit at the same time?" While it is important to master a set of practices, at some point one has to put aside textbook guidelines and make the therapy process one's own. Maintaining a sense of curiosity and openness to your client's story and being faithful to your own voice will, in the end, make successful outcomes more possible. Bon Voyage!

S.F.

# Acknowledgments

The ideas in this book germinated in the course of my contact with the work of a number of innovative clinicians and thinkers in the field to whom I owe special gratitude: Milton Erickson, Carl Whitaker, John Weakland, Jay Haley, Lynn Hoffman, Steve de Shazer, Insoo Kim Berg, Bill O'Hanlon, Michael White, David Epston, Tom Andersen, and Ben Furman. All have had an impact on my practice over the years and serve as a virtual "reflecting team," offering ideas that continually broaden and enrich my clinical perspective.

I also wish to thank my team at Harvard Community Health Plan in Braintree, Massachusetts: Sally Brecher, Cynthia Mittelmeier, Madeline Dymsza, Robin Asher, and Chip Wilder, who provide a supportive and collaborative context in which to practice and learn. Steven Feinberg joined the team as a postdoctoral fellow and made an outstanding contribution. My clinical work significantly benefited from our weekly discussions. Cynthia Mittelmeier, Steven Feinberg, and Alan Rinzler deserve special appreciation for reviewing an early version of the manuscript, as does Donna Haig Friedman for her constructive ideas and suggestions.

Practicing psychotherapy in a managed care setting, as I have for over 10 years now, continually fosters my learning and professional growth. As a therapist, I have been challenged and inspired by the people with whom I work, colleagues and clients both. My colleagues in the mental health department at the Braintree Center of HCHP: Vicki Beggs, Rose Catalanotti, Stan Cole, Lauren Corbett, Ellen Frishman, Dan Gadish, Marge Lavin, Ted Powers, Jim Ritchie, Rob Schneider, Dan Teplin, and Ronnie Tilles, have been a source of learning and support, and for their friendship I am especially grateful. In addition, I want to acknowledge Margot Taylor Fanger, whose ideas about health and wellness have greatly influenced my own; Simon Budman, who has been a supportive colleague and teacher; and Michael Hoyt, consultant, confidant, and comrade in brief therapy.

Thank you also to those reviewers who shared their comments and opinions in the writing process: Ralph S. Cohen, Central Connecticut State University; Donald R. Nims, Western Kentucky University; and José B. Torres, University of Wisconsin-Milwaukee.

Finally, I want to express my appreciation to my wife Donna and my daughter Sarah for their patience and forbearance while I was immersed in this and other writing projects over the past 6 years. Their love, sensitivity, and support have made the completion of this work possible.

Some of the clinical examples in this work have been published elsewhere in somewhat different form. Chapter 4 contains clinical material that originally appeared in S. Friedman, S. Brecher, and C. Mittelmeier, (1995), "Widening the Lens, Sharpening the Focus: The Reflecting Process in Managed Care," in S. Friedman (Ed.), *The Reflecting Team in Action: Collaborative Practice in Family Therapy*, New York: Guilford Press. Chapters 6 and 7 contain material that originally appeared in the following sources: S. Friedman, (1993), "Escape from the Furies: A Journey from Self-Pity to Self-Love." in S. Friedman (Ed.), *The New Language of Change: Constructive Collaboration in Psychotherapy*, New York: Guilford Press; S. Friedman, (1992), "Constructing Solutions (Stories) in Brief Family Therapy," in S. Budman, M. Hoyt, and S. Friedman (Eds.), *The First Session in Brief Therapy*, New York: Guilford Press; and S. Friedman, (1994), "Staying Simple, Staying Focused: Time-Effective Consultations with Children and Families," in M. Hoyt (Ed.), *Constructive Therapies*, New York: Guilford Press. Chapter 8 contains material that originally appeared in S. Friedman (1996), "Couples Therapy: Changing Conversations," in H. Rosen and K. Kuehlwein (Eds.), *Constructing Realities: Meaning-Making Perspectives for Psychotherapists*, San Francisco: Jossey-Bass.

# About the Author

**Steven Friedman** is a family therapist at the Braintree, Massachusetts center of Harvard Community Health Plan. An active presenter of workshops and training on family therapy and time-effective therapy, Dr. Friedman serves on the editorial board of the *Journal of Systemic Therapies* and as a lecturer at the Massachusetts School of Professional Psychology. He is co-author (with Margot T. Fanger) of *Expanding Therapeutic Possibilities: Getting Results in Brief Psychotherapy* (1991), co-editor with Simon Budman and Michael Hoyt of *The First Session in Brief Therapy* (1992), and editor of *The New Language of Change: Constructive Collaboration in Psychotherapy* (1993) and *The Reflecting Team in Action: Collaborative Practice in Family Therapy* (1995).

# Introduction

You arrive at your office to hear the phone ringing. You pick it up. It's a reviewer from one of the managed care companies with whom you have a contract. The person on the other end wants to know why you need an additional three sessions to see Stephanie Jones and her family. You've seen Stephanie and her family on three previous occasions and your evaluation indicates that she is not suicidal or clinically depressed, simply upset and sad over her parents' impending divorce. You think, "Here we go again," having to justify treatment to an outsider, an "intruder." The reviewer wants to know if the therapy is "medically necessary" and whether you could handle things just as well using only one more session. You think to yourself that just a few years ago this would have not been necessary; you were free to negotiate the length of treatment with your clients without the oversight and intrusion of the client's insurance company. A new element has been added to the therapeutic system—the managed care company (MCC).[1]

As a clinician, with the best interests of your clients in mind, how will you justify the additional three sessions requested? Assuming a competency-based, goal-directed perspective, as will be highlighted in this book, the "intrusive" MCC will soon realize that your focused, outcome-oriented philosophy and attitude will lead to more rapid results. As the time-effectiveness of your methods becomes apparent, negotiating with the case manager will become less of a chore and more of a collaborative process.

In today's world, practitioners must not only contract with a variety of MCCs and learn a new vocabulary ("medical necessity," "capitation," "quality management," "preauthorization," "utilization review," etc.) but also must deal with a plethora of monitoring and reporting arrangements. Managed mental health care has meant extensive utilization review in which gatekeepers from the MCC monitor, review, and authorize needed services.

We live in a world of rapid change. As technologies have exploded, we have all become passengers on a fast-moving train where expectations for rapid responding have proliferated (see Figure I-1). Part of this rapidly changing world is our health care system. Managed health care, in the form of health maintenance organizations (HMOs), has grown significantly over the last several years in response to out-of-control costs that have become endemic to the health care industry (Califano, 1988). As part of health care, mental health services have also been significantly affected by these changes. Formerly a "cottage industry," mental health care in the United States is becoming industrialized. Issues of accountability, efficiency, and effectiveness play a larger role (Cummings, 1991; Patterson & Scherger, 1995). Attitudinal and behavioral shifts are required in moving from a "fee for service" to a "fee for efficiency" model.

Perceived shortcomings of the managed care movement include limits on needed services, a rationing of care, reduced flexibility for practitioners, and an overconcern with cost over quality. In times past, psychotherapists enjoyed the autonomy of "calling the shots" about how quality mental health care was defined and delivered. Today, as the consequences of unchecked costs have gained prominence, MCCs make the rules. Rather than seeing these changes as necessarily diminishing or devaluing the therapists' skills and practices, this can be seen as a time of challenge and change requiring a modification of skills. Instead of viewing their job as "survival" in the midst of a tidal wave of chaos or as a process of compromising professional integrity for economic expediency, clinicians can begin to hone their skills in gaining control over the processes that make therapy more time-effective.[2] In addition, in the coming

**FIGURE I-1.    Fast Philosophy to Go**

*Source: Boston Sunday Globe*, April 24, 1994; drawn by Berkeley Breathed. © 1994, Washington Post Writers Group. Reprinted with permission.

years we will be challenged to show how psychotherapy can reduce unnecessary utilization of medical services, for which there are already preliminary data (Follette & Cummings, 1967; Holder & Blose, 1987; Jones & Vischi, 1980; Mumford et al., 1984). Pointing up the need for innovative and focused therapeutic approaches, Cummings (1986) found that targeted treatment (matching the therapy to the client's problem) resulted in greater medical cost offset than more traditional, open-ended therapies. Such information can only support the benefits and efficacy of psychotherapy.

This book is about ways that psychotherapists can modify and enhance their skills to better meet the challenges of a changing mental health care marketplace using a competency-based, nonpathologizing approach. The framework proposed here reflects an attitude, or way of thinking about therapy, that emphasizes people's resources, strengths, capacities, and successes. Proactively developing skills in time-effective therapy will open the door not only to more positive therapeutic outcomes for our clients but also to an increased sense of personal integrity as we do quality work.

Not only do MCCs expect to see results, but clients do as well (see Figure I-2). In order to meet these goals, clinicians need to expand their existing repertoire of ideas and strategies in ways that open the door to more time-effective treatment. The guidelines and methods discussed in this book both help set the stage for change and offer the practitioner a hopeful and optimistic per-

*"Well, I do have this recurring dream that one day I might see some results."*

**FIGURE I-2.   Recurring Dream**

*Source: The New Yorker* Magazine, June 6, 1994. Drawing by Bruce Eric Kaplan; © 1994 The New Yorker Magazine, Inc.

spective about the change process itself. While being results-oriented, these approaches emphasize therapist individuality, creativity, and imagination.

## MEETING THE NEEDS OF A WHOLE POPULATION

Practicing in the era of managed care requires consideration for the needs of whole populations (Bennett, 1988; Sabin, 1991). Rather than giving priority to any one individual's needs, as in traditional fee-for-service practice, under this arrangement the practitioner not only is committed to the care of those he or she is already seeing, but also has a contractual responsibility to all those others in that population who may request services. In so doing, the practitioner must become comfortable allocating resources in the most judicious ways possible. The therapist's time becomes a precious resource that must be carefully rationed in providing for the needs of the whole population.

The predicted "third wave" of managed care will involve MCCs contracting with groups of practitioners who can be trusted to do time-effective therapy within a population-oriented framework (Cummings, 1991, 1995). As contracts move to become "capitated,"[3] clinicians will have to share responsibility with the insurance company in deciding how to best allocate resources. As these new health care partnerships become more and more prominent over the next decade, clinicians will be required to fine-tune their skills in brief psychotherapy.

## FROM PROBLEM TO POSSIBILITY

Most of us were trained to be "pathology detectors" looking for and then trying to "fix" dysfunction (Kowalski & Durrant, 1991). Many times our clients have also fallen prey to this view of their behavior, seeing themselves as deficient and incompetent. A focus on deficits, limitations, and dysfunction has the effect of further immersing both client and therapist in a whirlpool of pathology, passivity, and hopelessness. As we delve further into a "problem," we can easily feel overwhelmed and pessimistic about change. On the other hand, by becoming "competency detectors," therapists who look for and amplify the client's strengths and resources, the therapeutic process becomes a more hopeful and, as we shall see, a more time-effective enterprise. The competency-based view of therapy envisions the client as on a journey out of a problem-saturated world and into a world of increased autonomy and personal agency.

In this book a collaborative, competency-based framework is presented for generating time-effective outcomes with a diverse array of clients seeking service. Clinical examples offer a glimpse into the moment-to-moment therapy process, highlighting effective and hope-generating means to foster change.

## WHAT'S AHEAD

In Chapter 1, I present the basic assumptions and ideas that define competency-based practice, with special attention to the importance of therapist expectations and hope. The paradigm shift from problem to possibility is outlined, in a step-by-step process leading from the point of initial clinical contact to the achievement of a collaboratively constructed goal. Chapter 2 focuses on the importance of listening to and honoring the client's story in the initial interview. We shall see how, by integrating ideas from solution-focused thinking and the narrative approach, the initial interview can become more time-effective. Chapter 3 discusses ways to introduce tasks and homework that build on changes already started and offers ideas for effectively utilizing letter writing in therapy. Chapter 4 examines novel ways to integrate and apply models of team consultation and explores the ways an "audience" can significantly and positively affect the therapy process. Chapter 5 engages the reader in applying the ideas already discussed in finding time-effective ways to manage resources in a complex clinical situation. In each of these chapters, clinical examples are provided from the author's practice in a managed care setting.[4]

Chapters 6 through 8 present extended clinical interviews with an individual, a family, and a couple, respectively. Principles of time-effective therapy are highlighted. Practical exercises and questions for the reader are also included, making the material more interactive. In Chapter 9, the author responds to a set of specific questions on effective practice in managed care settings. Chapter 10 provides a summary and a framework for measuring outcome. In addition, ideas are outlined for staying sane and growing as a clinician in this new world of managed care. Each chapter concludes with a summary of key ideas, emphasizing the critical elements in doing time-effective therapy. A selected bibliography on competency-based therapy is included at the end of the book.

As managed health care continues to grow, so does the challenge of generating effective therapeutic outcomes under constraints of time and limited resources. Current economic realities and limits on insurance benefits require clinicians to develop a flexible repertoire of time-effective approaches, for dealing with the myriad array of problems presented in therapy. Population-based practice necessitates a shift of therapeutic set from seeing few people intensively to seeing many for briefer periods of time.

By reading this book, you will learn a competency-based approach that emphasizes:

1. A positive, optimistic, and hopeful mindset about change
2. A cooperative and collaborative relationship with clients
3. Client requests as the key to time-effective therapy
4. The initial interview as crucial to the change process
5. Client strengths, resources, and successes as building blocks for change

While the material presented here derives from work in an HMO, the ideas, attitudes, and techniques are applicable to any clinical setting. My hope is that the ideas outlined in this book will strengthen your abilities to utilize time more effectively in your daily clinical practice, while building upon your own philosophy, style, and ways of working. The managed care revolution, rather than being experienced as an intrusive force that undermines clinicians' control over the therapy process, can actually serve as a stimulus for positive change, for both our clients and ourselves. Managed care calls for a shift in attitudes away from clinical relationships characterized by continuous, long-term contact and dependency to models that emphasize intermittent contact and independent functioning. A sensitivity to time as a critical factor in therapy and a focus on generating successful outcomes will add significantly to psychotherapy's prominence and respect as a helpful and beneficial process that can effectively meet the needs of people in distress.

## NOTES

1. There are many forms of managed health care: *A staff model health maintenance organization* (HMO) offers a comprehensive array of medical services to a closed membership of subscribers who, on a yearly basis, pay a premium that covers all services. Usually a small "co-pay" fee (e.g., $5) is charged for each visit. Staff are salaried employees hired to provide services in multiple sites to this fixed population. In a *group model HMO* the organization contracts with a group of practitioners to provide medical services out of their own offices or in a group practice medical setting. The *Independent Practice Association* (IPA) is a group of practitioners working out of their own offices who are contracted to provide services on either a fee-for-service basis or on a capitated basis (see note 3). A *preferred provider organization* (PPO) provides financial incentives for patients to use a selected panel of doctors, although patients retain the freedom to use nonpreferred doctors and pay higher fees (after Austad & Hoyt, 1992).

2. The managed care revolution has significantly altered the way mental health services are delivered in the United States. While the perspectives outlined in this book will hopefully help you to refine your skills in doing therapy more time-effectively, they will only be efficacious if practiced within a sane and sensible managed

care system. As with other business operations, managed care companies can act responsibly with regard to their employees/providers and their customers or can act in more self-serving ways. As therapists, it is our job to advocate for policies that prevent corporate profit and "bean-counting" from totally driving the service delivery process. This requires mental health professionals to join with employers and consumers to challenge greedy for-profit managed care corporations whose goal is to economically undercut other managed care organizations. This undercutting process has the effect of driving quality managed care companies to further tighten their belts to stay competitive. Such a cost-driven strategy will ultimately fail as customer satisfaction drops and quality of care suffers. In order to maintain a sense of integrity in our work, clinicians need to advocate for systems that provide reasonable mental health benefits and rational structures for accountability.

3. In a fee-for-service structure, clinicians are better reimbursed when more services are provided. A capitated system works differently. The term "capitated" simply means that a provider group is given a fixed amount of money per subscriber with allocation of resources left to the provider group. Providers must judiciously manage resources to meet the needs of the entire population being served. If clinicians act from a purely economic position, for example, by withholding or restricting needed services, they will end up adding, rather than reducing costs, as withholding services only invites more costly treatments down the road. In a capitated system, therefore, clinicians are challenged to provide timely, high-quality service while managing costs.

4. Names and identifying information in the clinical illustrations presented have been changed to protect client confidentiality.

# ▶ 1

## The Journey from Problem to Possibility

*Deeds are the offspring of hope and expectancy.*
*—MILTON H. ERICKSON, M.D.*

*Father:* When he got home I wanted to ask him about where he lost the wallet, and he got very angry and sarcastic with me. We had a minor skirmish. He left the house, then came back, and we talked. Then I wound up giving him a hug before he left. We also had some words about my concerns [about his drug use].

*Therapist:* So you gave him a hug. What inspired you to do that?

Moment to moment in our clinical conversations we experience choice points at which we must decide where to direct our attention. Why in the above instance did the therapist decide to focus on the "hug" rather than on the "skirmish"? As we shall see in this book, an emphasis on strengths, on resources—on love, loyalty, and connection—can go a long way in supporting and maximizing change. Moving our attention from problems and the past to possibilities and the future will not only make our clinical work more effective and efficient, but also will enable our clients and ourselves to experience a greater sense of hope and self-efficacy. As you read this book, I would encourage you to think about the choice points you experience in therapy and to experiment with the ideas presented.

## A TYPICAL DAY IN A MANAGED CARE PRACTICE

Doing time-effective therapy requires agility and flexibility—the ability to think on your feet, to bring your creative energies into operation, and to juggle multiple and complex roles and realities. Take for example a recent day in my clinical life in an HMO: My first appointment is with a 14-year-old boy living with his mother and her gay lover. The 14-year-old is dealing with his mother's mood swings (she's on antidepressant medication) and his place in this household. He was actively suicidal for a period of time but is now doing better.

Following this, I meet for the first time with a single mother and her 15-year-old daughter. The daughter has just come out of a psychiatric hospital after a physical altercation between mother and daughter that led to the police being called. The mother is crying in my office about being treated by the police, courts and Department of Social Services as a "criminal" who doesn't care for her children. The daughter cries along with her. Both have been through hellish experiences in the past several months (including a sexual assault of the daughter by a neighbor) that have left the mother feeling guilty about her parenting. It's difficult to end the session because this is the first time this mother has had a chance to tell her story.

My next appointment is with a 60-year-old woman who is at the tail end of a 2-week psychiatric hospitalization and is seeing me as a transition out of the hospital. She has been depressed and confused, talks slowly, and tends to fixate on areas of her life that have not gone well.

Next up is a set of parents whose daughter went to court to file a child abuse petition against them. They are upset and worried about their daughter's behavior and angry that she would do such a thing. They want my help in controlling her.

In between these four appointments I talk on the telephone with the Department of Social Services in regard to the daughter who filed abuse charges against her parents and with three other clients. Later I will see a couple who have been living very separate lives and are considering a divorce, followed by a family in which the oldest son has been having stomach pains on school mornings. Next are a mother and daughter who initially came to see me about 6 months ago after the unmarried 18-year-daughter revealed she was pregnant. Today, two mothers come to my office with a beautiful 3-week-old baby. Mother and daughter are beaming, and the mother has successfully helped her daughter find an apartment and take steps toward increased independence.

In each of these situations, I must develop an alliance quickly and also actively engage with the participants in ways that both respect their requests for therapy and offer some ideas that can be helpful in the midst of their predicaments. In each clinical situation I must utilize and capitalize on the strengths and resources of the client(s) and tailor my approach to the client's unique situation.

All therapies, including the practice of time-effective psychotherapy, require sensitivity, patience, compassion, and an ability to listen for subtleties (Lipchik, 1994). Applying a set of principles blindly without attending to these aspects of the therapeutic relationship will lead inevitably to clinical dead-ends. Simply utilizing a set of methods without tailoring your approach to each unique clinical situation will leave both you and the client feeling frustrated. Therapist flexibility is vital. The steps in the therapy process cannot be neatly and algorithmically mapped out. As Milton Erickson emphasized, each therapy encounter must be *invented* based on that client's presentation. Therapy, being a recursive process, requires meeting clients at their points of readiness and shifting gears in light of the subtleties of the clinical conversation (Friedman, 1993a). As Eve Lipchik (1994) so articulately points out:

> The effectiveness of this type of therapy . . . depends on therapists' respecting and responding to idiosyncrasies of clients and their situations. The process must be expeditious, but not rushed; methodologically consistent, but not standardized; efficient but never impersonal; sharply focused but not oblivious to hidden messages from clients. (p. 39)

The goal of this book is not to provide a set of formulas for doing brief therapy but rather to articulate a set of attitudes and values that can most effectively and flexibly facilitate the therapy process to address clients' goals. While some of the work presented here may seem "simple" in its implementation, the reader should be aware that a significant amount of training and experience is necessary to do this work effectively. As Berg and de Shazer (1993) point out: "Simplicity takes a lot of self-discipline" (p. 22). What is required is letting go of many of the time-honored assumptions we have accepted as true—for example, that more therapy is better; that emotional catharsis, in and of itself, is healing; that exploration of the past is necessary for change to occur; that "real" change requires time; that one "symptom" will replace another if the "core" issues are not resolved; and that "digging deeper" means better therapy.[1] Although these traditional ideas have been with us for a long time, there is no empirical support for their validity. In fact, some of these assumptions have been responsible for unnecessarily prolonging the process of therapy.

To do therapy time-effectively, clinicians must free themselves from these traditional presuppositions and adopt a more flexible set of working assumptions about the process of change. As we shall see, developing skills in time-effective therapy requires a shift in focus and attitude from assessing and treating pathology and dysfunction to building on client strengths and resources. The attitudes and assumptions that form the basis for possibility therapy are the primary focus for this chapter. Before we head into this territory, however, let us look at the challenges that managed care presents to clinicians.

## THE CHALLENGES OF MANAGED CARE

The ways we deliver mental health services have been changing rapidly. The private practitioner offering clinical services without some connection to managed care is becoming more rare. Today a large and growing percentage of people belong to health maintenance organizations (HMOs) of one kind or another. The familiar fee-for-service world that therapists have traditionally known is becoming extinct. To survive and thrive in this changing world, clinicians must adapt and refine their skills so that they can not only be partners in the changing health care delivery system but also maintain their integrity with respect to the quality of services they provide.

Today's clinician is challenged to take seriously the client's presenting problem or request, to search for ways to prevent costly psychiatric hospitalizations, to develop strategies and techniques for effectively and efficiently helping people reach their goals with minimal dependency on use of institutional services or resources, to be sensitive to outcome and "consumer satisfaction," and to function at the interface of the client and the insurance company.

In the "managed care triangle" (after Friedman, 1990: see Figure 1-1) the needs of several constituencies converge. Each component of the triangle has a set of values and expectations. The *managed care company* (MCC) is primarily interested in containing costs by decreasing utilization of services, satisfying members' requests to be seen (rapid access), and maintaining high levels of member satisfaction with the services provided. Drawing on a set of principles about what constitutes quality care, the *therapist* is concerned with having time available to develop both a clinical relationship and a focus, such that the members' goals can be achieved in a timely fashion. The *customer* or member is looking for relief or resolution in regard to a predicament, dilemma, conflict or upset he or she is facing. Members also bring expectations and beliefs about how service should be provided (e.g., on a weekly basis) and what they are entitled to under the managed care plan to which they subscribe.

How these values and expectations are managed is reflected in the degree of tension that exists in the triangle. Each stakeholder in the system must be sensitive to the needs, values, and expectations of the other players. As we shall see in Chapter 5, a delicate balancing operation is required in

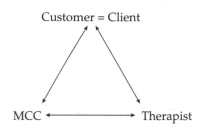

**FIGURE 1-1    The Managed
Care Triangle**

providing quality mental health care while working under the constraints and expectations of managed care realities. This triangle is constantly in flux and requires vigilant monitoring during the course of treatment. Rather than simply the clinician and the client in the room, we now have the MCC as a third "partner."

At times, therapists need to educate utilization review (UR) people about the process of psychotherapy. It is sometimes necessary, for example, to help the reviewer understand that a limit of one to three sessions in a particular clinical situation may not be a reasonable way to do therapy. We do not need to see ourselves as passive victims of an intrusive and uncaring MCC.

In the best of circumstances, treatment planning should be a negotiated process including all parties: therapist, UR person, and client. The clinician can serve as an advocate for the client and for the sensible practice of psychotherapy. How do we as clinicians manage the press for cost containment without compromising our principles and values about what constitutes good-quality care? If the press for cost containment outweighs the therapist's beliefs about what constitutes quality care, increased risk to the client and a loss of integrity by the therapist result. Therefore, the therapist is pressed to become an advocate for mental health services needed by clients.

In addition, clinicians need to further hone their skills so that they can allocate time and resources in ways that maximize positive outcomes. In a staff model HMO, which puts a premium on rapid service delivery, the clinician is faced with a continuous flow of new clients seeking service. Clinical demands are constantly high. A significant degree of creativity is required to manage one's practice in a cost-effective way while providing quality care.

In my own 30-hour-per-week practice in a staff model HMO, I see about 130 new clients each year. Considering that I've been doing this work for over 10 years now, I have built up a substantial panel of clients, any one of whom could call me to resume treatment at any time. As a result, I must continually juggle my time and resources to meet the needs of those I'm currently seeing as well as considering my responsibility to a larger population of people (HMO "members") to whom I am also accountable.

As one might imagine, this balancing operation requires significant flexibility in practice. One of the counterintuitive paradoxes of brief therapy is that you don't need to work fast to make progress, or, as the expression goes, it's possible to "make haste slowly." When you listen carefully to the client's story, focus on the client's competencies, strengths, and capabilities, and develop skills in focused clinical conversation, changes can occur quite rapidly. In the next section we explore this possibility paradigm, a competency-based and time-effective approach that effectively meets the challenges of practicing in managed care settings.

## COMPETENCY-BASED PRACTICE: PRINCIPLES AND ASSUMPTIONS

Many of the ideas outlined in this book derive from the innovative and pioneering work of Milton H. Erickson, who was uniquely committed to utilizing people's competencies in expeditiously creating a context for change. Building on this foundation, the work presented is conceived of as competency-based (Friedman & Fanger, 1991), combining aspects of solution-focused (Berg & Miller, 1992; de Shazer, 1988, 1991; Furman & Ahola, 1992; Hoyt, 1994b; O'Hanlon & Weiner-Davis, 1989) and narrative thinking (Parry & Doan, 1994; White, 1995; White & Epston, 1990). The goal of this work is to offer clients both new perspectives on their dilemmas and predicaments and new options for action. The process of therapy is one of generating collaborative conversations that connect our observations with the ongoing narratives of the client's life.

### *Psychotherapy in Transformation*

The field of psychotherapy has been undergoing a transformation from an emphasis on objective realities to a social constructionist view (Friedman [Ed.], 1993; Gilligan & Price, 1993; McNamee & Gergen, 1992). "Our worlds, rather than reflecting a fixed objective reality, are constructed and defined contextually in social and community discourse" (Friedman, 1993d, p. xiii). Rather than a belief in an objective set of truths or developmental norms or structures, the view taken here is that reality is constructed in our day-to-day conversations and interactions with one another primarily through the medium of language. The ways we perceive ourselves and the world are organized and maintained through the stories we tell ourselves as a function of our interaction with others. The conversational process with its meaning-generating potential opens the door to new constructions of personal reality

(Anderson, 1993; Anderson & Goolishian, 1988). Problems, rather than being seen as tangible structures, are viewed as stories that have been constructed and have developed meaning over time in a person's life. Therapy becomes a collaborative process for re-authoring stories in ways that offer hope for the future:

> Our dialogues with ourselves and with others come to define our views and determine our actions. We are "storied" animals. As [we shall see] the stories we come to tell about ourselves become lenses that shape the ways we process new information . . . . Since meanings are inherently negotiable and ambiguous, the conversational process has the potential to "render [both the client's and thera pist's] world newly strange. (Bruner, 1986, p. 24); Friedman, 1995, pp. 353–354.

Predicaments presented for therapy are viewed as threads of stories that have become self-determining, that have come to define for the individual or couple or family both the present and the future. Because these stories imply certain futures, they exert powerful influences on our present thinking and behavior (Schnitzer, 1993). It becomes the job of the therapist to look for and access alternative stories, ones that contradict the problem-dominated one and offer hope and possibilities (White & Epston, 1990). By so doing, the therapist sets the stage for people to notice aspects of their lives and relationships that help define new, more empowering life stories. Strengths and resources become woven into the development of new narratives that generate hope and create a context for change.

Rather than embracing the metaphors of medical practice: disease, patients, etiology, symptoms, diagnosis, cure, and so forth, the narrative metaphor offers us a hopeful, useful and nonpejorative language system that opens space for change. As Efran, Lukens, and Lukens (1990) point out: "By making distinctions we bring things into existence . . . [and] each set of distinctions creates new action possibilities" (p. 35). The dominant cultural story of psychotherapy has emphasized the diagnosis of illness and pathology, the unveiling of deficits and dysfunctions, and the search for causes or etiology. This culturally dominant frame includes words to describe people in distress that are generally pejorative and blaming (e.g., "narcissistic," "borderline," etc.), generating a "vocabulary of human deficit" (Gergen, 1991, p. 35) that has grown in the past century. "When we look for pathology we usually find it; We conclude it is the "true" representation of the person rather than the product of our lens. [and, in addition] . . . focusing primarily on dysfunction does not provide us with a map for moving toward new behaviors" (Waters & Lawrence, 1993, pp. 58, 60). In contrast to the medical model, the approach taken here is based on a different set of distinctions, ones that lead to a more hopeful set of action possibilities.

## *Widening the Lens, Sharpening the Focus*

In this book we'll explore an integrative, competency-based model that expands therapeutic possibilities and directs attention to defined outcomes. The work can be understood as encompassing two processes: a widening of the therapeutic lens to embrace multiple perspectives and ideas about the client's dilemma and a sharpening of focus that funnels these ideas into workable action plans. The therapist shifts between widening the lens— opening space for new narratives and ideas—and sharpening the focus on solutions and action steps.

Initially the therapist develops a cooperative stance by listening to the client's story and becoming curious about it. During this process the therapist begins to generate alternative stories, stories that offer the client new possibilities for viewing his or her life and relationships. A collaborative process ensues whereby therapist and client work as a team to develop meaningful solutions that respectfully incorporate the client's goals and wishes. This construction of goals is a negotiated process in which a clear outcome is defined and a series of action steps developed.

Clients bring to the provider's office a set of narratives or stories about their lives and relationships. These narratives define the clients' world views. The clinician, by listening carefully to the clients' presentations, opens the door to a world in which clients feel they are heard and their experiences validated. Most people who present us with their predicaments or dilemmas are struggling to make sense out of uncertainty. They have developed cognitive constructs that both define and limit the views they have about their situation. Because people's lives are invariably complex, the clinical encounter can easily become a vague, interminable process leading clients and therapist on a meandering journey over a complex terrain. It is therefore incumbent on the provider to direct the inquiry in ways that both validate the clients' predicaments and open space for new ideas. The structure outlined here, in the spirit of a warm, listening stance, offers the provider direction in collaborating with clients to produce a positive outcome in a time-effective manner. Table 1-1 outlines the shift in thinking in moving from a problem-focused to a possibility-focused consultation process. Each aspect of this process will be discussed at various points in the book.

## COMPARING PERSPECTIVES

The following section offers an opportunity to compare two interviews, one that takes a problem-focused perspective and one that takes a possibility-oriented view. As you listen in on these conversations, imagine yourself as the client. What effect would each of these conversations have on your feelings

**TABLE 1-1    Paradigm Shift: From Problem to Possibility**

| | |
|---|---|
| Belief in an objective reality/truth | Reality as socially constructed |
| Therapist is expert/analyst | Consultant is partner/catalyst |
| Therapist's voice privileged | Client's voice privileged |
| Client labeled/categorized | Each client is unique; consultant maintains position of curiosity |
| Teach the client the therapist's assumptions and language | Learn the client's assumptions; use client's language |
| Client = problem | Client oppressed/subjugated by the problem |
| View client as resistant, misguided, naive, blind | View client as doing the best he or she can; coping, resilient |
| Ask what is wrong and why | Ask what is wanted and how |
| Explore historical causes, who or what is to blame | Open space for new options; introduce new ideas; construct future actions; look for "exceptions," access resources; amplify successes |
| Good therapy is hard work, painful and long | An effective consultation can be brief and hope-generating |
| Clinical process is private, mysterious, "behind closed doors" | Clinical process is open; incorporates audiences, witnesses (e.g., reflecting team) |
| **Outcome** | |
| Cure/failure | Problem resolved/dissolved/viewed in new way; or recycle |

Adapted from S. Friedman & M. T. Fanger (1991), *Expanding Therapeutic Possibilities: Getting Results in Brief Psychotherapy* (San Francisco: The New Lexington Press/Jossey-Bass) and K. Tomm (1990, June), "Ethical Postures That Orient One's Clinical Decision Making" (presentation at American Family Therapy Academy, Philadelphia).

of efficacy, on your mood, and on your sense of hopefulness and optimism about change?

## Problem-Focused Interview

*Therapist:* Hello, I'm Dr. Charles. What brings you here today?

*Client:* I've been feeling very sad and depressed lately. My mother died a few weeks ago and my son recently left for college. I've been crying a great deal and have had trouble getting to work in the morning or focusing on tasks at work.

*Therapist:* How long have you been feeling this way?

*Client:* About 4 or 5 weeks now.

*Therapist:* How are you sleeping?

*Client:* Not well.

*Therapist:* Do you wake up at night or have trouble falling asleep?

*Client:* I usually have trouble falling asleep and then wake up very early in the morning.

*Therapist:* How has your appetite been?

*Client:* I think I've lost some weight over the past few weeks and I guess I'm not eating as much.

*Therapist:* Would you describe for me what you experience when you have these periods of sadness or depression?

*Client* [tearful]: I simply find myself crying, feeling sorry for myself, and feel like I can't put one foot in front of the other. I've even had thoughts like "If I got hit by a car and died, it would be okay." I know it's silly, but those thoughts have come to mind.

*Therapist:* Have you ever acted in any way to hurt yourself?

*Client* [crying]: I've never done anything to hurt myself and I don't really think I would.

*Therapist:* Have you experienced other times when you've felt this way?

*Client:* Maybe 5 or 6 years ago, when my husband lost his job.

*Therapist:* Does anyone in your extended family have a history of depression?

*Client:* Well, my father did have an alcohol problem and he always seemed to be depressed.

*Therapist:* Your sadness, difficulties sleeping, and recent loss of appetite tell me that you are probably experiencing a depression that could benefit from a trial of medication.

*Client* [continues crying]: Do you think that would help?

*Therapist:* I do think it would help, considering how you're feeling right now. I can set up an appointment for you to see Dr. Jones, who is a psychiatrist and can explain more about medications that can be helpful to you.

*Client:* Do you really think I need medicine to help me cope?

*Therapist:* The medication would simply be an aid in helping you to begin to have more energy and would help with the sleep also. We could also meet to talk about the things that have been bothering you lately.

*Client:* I'd like to think about it a bit before going ahead with the medicine.

*Therapist:* I wonder what's getting in the way of seeing Dr. Jones; It would only be for a consultation. You would be free to say "yes" or "no" to any recommendation for medication.

*Client:* I think I'd rather wait on this . . . .

*Therapist:* Would you like to make another appointment to come back?

*Client:* Can I call you if I feel the need?

*Therapist:* Of course, here's my card.

Now, let's take the same clinical situation from a possibility perspective.

## Possibility-Focused Interview

*Therapist:* Hi, I'm Dr. James. I'm interested in hearing what brings you here today and the ways you think we can best use the time we have together?

*Client:* I've been feeling very sad and depressed lately. My mother died a few weeks ago and my son recently left for college. I've been crying a great deal and have had trouble getting to work in the morning or focusing on tasks at work.

*Therapist:* What prompted you to call at this point?

*Client:* I realized that I don't want to go on this way, feeling down and crying all the time. I need to get my life back on track. It takes me twice as long to get ready in the morning.

*Therapist:* What kind of work do you do?

*Client:* I'm a stenographer and paying attention is very important. I've just been so distracted lately.

*Therapist:* What would be a positive sign that you were getting back on track?

*Client:* Being able to focus at work and maybe sleeping better at night. I've even had thoughts about dying, like "If I got hit by a car and died, it would be okay." I know it's silly, but those thoughts come to mind.

*Therapist:* Are these thoughts new?

*Client:* Yes. I've had them on and off for about a week or so.

*Therapist:* Have you ever done anything to hurt yourself?

*Client:* No. And I really don't think I would.

*Therapist:* How confident are you that you wouldn't hurt yourself—let's say a "10" is the most confident and a "1" is the least confident?

*Client:* I'd say a "9.5."

*Therapist:* What kinds of things do you do that prevent you from falling under the influence of these thoughts?

*Client:* I tell myself things will get better. Sometimes I'll call a friend or take a walk around the block.

*Therapist:* Have you ever experienced these feelings before?

*Client:* Yes, when my husband lost his job several years ago.

*Therapist:* How did you manage to get back on track at that point?

*Client:* I talked with several friends, and my minister was very helpful.

*Therapist:* Losing your mother sounds like a major blow, and then having your son go off to college just seems to have added to your sense of loss. I'm wondering about what you could do now that would help you feel more on track, considering that your mother's death was quite recent and having a child leave for college is a major life transition?

*Client:* I'm not sure.

*Therapist:* Sometimes people need time to grieve a loss and need to give themselves permission to fully experience the loss rather than fighting it or trying to avoid it. I wonder which option would be better for you—giving yourself permission to grieve or taking action to get yourself focused again? And maybe both are possible. What do you think?

*Client:* That's an interesting way to look at it. I guess maybe I am rushing things, expecting to recover so quickly. I'm used to being in control of my life and it's upsetting to feel so out of control [begins to cry].

*Therapist:* I'm curious about how you have managed to get yourself to work each day in light of how you've been feeling. A lot of people would have simply pulled the covers over their head and called in sick.

*Client* [smiling]: I've always been a dedicated worker, and I've been able to function relatively well at work even though, as I said, I find myself more distracted at times.

*Therapist:* Do you think it might be helpful to talk with your minister again, as you did several years ago?

*Client:* That might be a good idea.

*Therapist:* I wonder whether we could develop a plan where you allow yourself 15 minutes in the morning and maybe 15 minutes in the evening to think about and allow yourself to experience the recent losses. If a sad thought comes up during the day, you can simply save it for the evening. In this way you would be giving yourself permission to grieve but in a way that would be less interfering with your daily life. There is nothing wrong with letting down and crying considering what has happened recently. Obviously, it would be better to schedule this time rather than have the sadness intrude into your work or your sleep. From what you've told me I'm not surprised that you are sad. What do you think?

*Client:* I guess I have been too tough on myself.

*Therapist:* I wonder if you would like to set up another appointment? If so, we could check in on some of the ways you've found to give yourself permission to grieve and how this has helped you focus at work.

*Client* [looking brighter]: I think that might be helpful. Okay.

*Therapist:* In how many weeks would you like to set the next appointment, considering that you are going to need some time to try out this plan?

*Client:* Maybe 2 or 3 weeks.

*Therapist:* That sounds fine. One final thought: Sometimes people notice that there are times when they are feeling better in the week. I wonder if you might begin to notice those times and what you're doing that contributes to feeling better, like the kinds of things you were mentioning before, like calling a friend or taking a walk. You might notice other things you do between now and when we meet again that keep depression from pulling you down. Let's set something up then.

What differences exist between these two interviews? In the first (problem-focused) the "expert" clinician asks a series of questions whose goal is to arrive at a "definitive" diagnosis (in essence, focusing on pathology—what is wrong with the person). In the second (possibility-focused) the therapist acts as a consultant, a collaborator who works *with* the client in sorting out her predicament and developing a reasonable plan of action to deal with it. The therapist views the client as a resourceful and competent partner who is capable of getting her life back on track. In the problem-focused interview the client is viewed as a passive recipient of the therapist's knowledge and of medication. In the possibility-oriented interview the client is viewed as an active participant in creating change. In the former the client is told what is the best alternative; in the latter she is viewed as an expert with her own set of resources who is capable of taking action outside of the therapy context.

A story told by Stephen and Carol Lankton (1986) highlights the importance of therapist assumptions in guiding the therapy process:

> There was this old man who was sitting on the side of a hill. And some passerby came with a back pack over his back. And the passerby saw the old man looking over the city and said, "Hey old man, what kind of people live in that city down there that you are looking at?" And the old man said, "Well, tell me stranger, what kind of people live in the city from which you came?" The passerby said, "Well, it's funny you should ask me that. They were backstabbing, backbiting, untrustworthy people . . . I had to leave the city. They were terrible people. They were liars and con artists. It was dis-

gusting." And at that the old man said, "I'm sorry, but I'm afraid you are going to find the people in this city to be just like the people you left." The next day another passerby came and saw the old man sitting on the side of the hill looking at the city. And he said, "Hey old man, what kind of people live in that city down there?" And the old man said, "Well, what kind of people lived in the city that you left?" And he said, "It's odd that you should ask me about that. I was just thinking about how sad I am to have to leave. They were so kind and tender and warm and they would give you the shirt off their back. They were always willing to help a friend. I was sorry to have to go." And the old man said, "Well, I am pleased to tell you, you are going to find the people in this city to be just the same." (pp. 50–51)

We are categorizing and differentiating animals who try to make sense of our worlds (Bateson, 1972; Efran, Lukens, & Lukens, 1990). We group information into categories that allow us to have a structure from which to deal with the world consistently. These descriptions of events in the world, while allowing us to categorize and organize information, also restrict our view, closing off other categories and ways of describing the same information. Even in the face of contradictory evidence, humans have the tendency to focus on information that confirms our already held views and perceptions and to ignore or reject information that contradicts our views.

This process of categorization is evident in the way we practice therapy. In the field of psychotherapy, isn't it odd that analysts always seem to find intrapsychic issues that need exploration, that biologically oriented psychiatrists always seem to discover evidence for chemical imbalances and endogenous conditions, that strategic family therapists always seem to find a function in the family for the identified patient's symptom, and so on? In the same way, by seeing the world through psychiatric diagnostic categories and by defining people in terms of deficits and dysfunctions, we create a world of pathology.

People tend to generate "totalizing descriptions" (White & Epston, 1990) of their lives that dominate self-perceptions. These descriptions often define the self in negative and pejorative terms based on a set of historical experiences. For example, a person who has struggled with alcohol dependence may define him- or herself as an "alcoholic." Although the self is multifaceted (Gergen, 1985), the client may choose one aspect of self that becomes large and prominent in its capacity to ensnare the client in a web of influence and domination. The therapist's job becomes one of "deconstructing" these totalizing descriptions and re-authoring new descriptions or stories that open the door to new possibilities (White, 1995; White & Epston, 1990).

The deconstructing process involves "shrinking" the prominent element so that it becomes simply one possible way of viewing self rather than a

defining element. The re-authoring process involves highlighting less prominent stories (i.e., other elements of self) that contradict the problem-saturated view. The therapist must look for and amplify the contradictory stories
that the client presents that reduce the prominence of the dominant story. In
addition, the client needs to become more aware of those elements of self
that have not come under the influence of the dominant story.

It is the therapist's job to help the client view the world in new ways, to
develop the flexibility to seek out and notice information in his or her life
and relationships that contradicts this problem-saturated view. In so doing,
the client develops an expanded schema, or representation, one that defines
the self as having multiple possibilities rather than being defined by one single, dominating description. By being alert and attentive to stories of competency and success, the possibility therapist engages clients in an active
process of self-examination that offers hope and a sense of liberation from
old, constraining stories about their lives.

## A Practical Exercise

Let's a try a little experiment that can help you get in touch with your own
competencies and skills. Find a relaxed and comfortable position. This exercise will work best if you think about the questions with concrete examples
in mind. What I'd like you to do is imagine yourself with a client (an individual, a couple or a family). You are sitting in your office and feeling overwhelmed, passive, and stuck. You are having that old feeling again, one that
unfortunately surfaces from time to time, one that Michael White (1991)
describes as "wishing there was a therapist in the room." Let yourself experience the feelings you have as you sit with this client. What is happening?
What is being said? What is the tone of the interaction? What demands do
you feel? What is getting in the way of your feeling effective? As you think
about these questions, keep the focus on yourself rather than the client. As
you envision yourself in this situation, generate an animal metaphor that
best captures your feelings and attitude.

After spending a few minutes imagining yourself in this situation, shake
off these images (e.g., by moving around in your chair) and imagine yourself
sitting with another client with whom you are feeling effective, relaxed, and
self-assured. What is happening here? What are you doing that is contribut-
ing to your relaxed and comfortable state? Again, allow yourself a moment
to generate another animal metaphor that best fits your attitude in this situation. Now, take a few minutes to write down (1) what you experience when
you feel stuck and ineffective and (2) what you are doing that makes the
therapy process feel effective and useful. Finally, note those assumptions
and skills that help you to create a positive state, one that maximizes your
effectiveness.

It is these mobilizing assumptions that need to be nurtured in doing time-effective clinical work. As we look at some of the assumptions and values that form the basis for doing time-effective therapy, please keep in mind your own beliefs and values about therapy and remember the "animal" you want to be as you find yourself in various clinical situations.

## CLINICAL ASSUMPTIONS AND VALUES

The following are the assumptions and values that define competency-based practice. These ideas form a flexible framework or foundation for approaching, in a time-effective manner, the predicaments and difficulties that clients present in therapy.

*Approach the client with a naive, curious, open, and inquisitive mind.*

Those familiar with experimental psychology may remember the ambiguous figure represented in Figure 1-2. If you look closely, you can see two different pictures, one of an older woman, the other of a younger woman. To identify each of these pictures, you must adjust your perspective and break free from a fixed view. A time-effective therapist must be able to flexibly shift perspectives in being open to multiple possibilities and perceptions. Maintaining a sense of curiosity and openness is vital in doing effective brief therapy. It is very easy to adopt totalizing descriptions (White & Epston, 1990) of people that lead your thinking toward pathology and pessimism.

For example, you might get a referral to see a couple from a colleague who sees one of the partners individually. This colleague tells you that the partner he sees "has a personality disorder" and is "very narcissistic." What should you do with this information? Although it is common shorthand to refer to people in these ways, I have found it only serves to reduce my openness and skew my thinking in ways that are not helpful. I've learned to "forget" such descriptions and come at the clinical situation as fresh and naive as possible. Why be naive, you might ask. Aren't trained and experienced professionals supposed to use their analytical skills in making sense of the information they have? Being naive favors optimism (Weick, 1984), and being optimistic favors a curiosity and respect that can create powerful momentum for change. Later in this chapter more will be said about the importance of maintaining a set of hopeful expectations in therapy.

The following excerpt from an initial interview with a couple (from Friedman, 1993c) demonstrates the importance of maintaining a sense of curiosity and inquisitiveness in the therapy process, in ways that bring forth

**FIGURE 1-2    Older Woman–Younger Woman Visual Illusion**

*Source:* Drawn by cartoonist W. E. Hill; originally published in *Puck*, Nov. 6, 1915.

the clients' expertise (or indigenous knowledge) about their lives. We come into the interview after about 10 minutes.

*Husband:*  I just wanted to point out that when Edith scheduled this appointment we were really . . . at dead-ends.
*Wife:*  We were really desperate.

*Husband:* We were really mixed up about the whole thing.

*Therapist:* That was how long ago?

*Wife:* About a month or so.

*Therapist:* But you're saying that things have changed in the meantime?

*Husband:* We've talked a lot out. But there still are little things that could end up blowing up. See, I don't like to argue, number one . . . . Now we're getting deep into the thing.

*Therapist:* Well, let's not get too far into it yet.

*Husband:* Things have gotten patched up and we're getting along very well for the past 2 weeks.

*Wife:* We hit rock bottom.

*Husband:* We said, look, let's try to deal with this . . . .

*Therapist:* So you took some steps that moved things from where they were, which you were calling rock bottom, to someplace better.

*Wife:* Yes.

*Therapist:* What I'm interested in hearing about first is what each of you has done to get to where you are now. How did you get from the place you were when you were calling for the appointment to the place you are now, the better place, and what's better?

*Wife:* He kinda brought me back to my senses. He was trying to let me know he loves me . . . and that we have a lot of years behind us . . . the children need us, and to try to think more positively. I was thinking everything was black, everything was negative. But I had to get to a point to open up and be willing to try again, too.

*Therapist:* How did you do that? Because that isn't easy, to go from that point where you were feeling hurt, isolated, closed up, to open yourself up again, to possible hurt again. So how did you manage to do that?

*Wife:* I love him. I will always love him.

*Therapist:* So you had that going for you. What else helped you open yourself up?

*Wife:* We're both from divorced families and know what that's like.

*Therapist:* Can you tell me more about how you opened yourself up to being back in touch with Mal?

*Wife:* First of all, it was a real roller coaster ride. We were sleeping in separate bedrooms. I sort of detached myself from the whole thing. Then I reached the point where I said, we'll just lead separate lives. But I couldn't do that. We always ended up arguing. I was so frustrated and angry. I didn't know how to act around him anymore. I needed to get myself stable. He was so calm and here I was, like argh! [Demonstrates her frustration.]

*Therapist:* So getting yourself calm helped you?

*Wife:* Yes. I started feeling worn out. I wasn't getting anywhere. And then he started talking more positively. "We have an appointment with the marriage counselor, let's just wait . . . . I think it's a good thing." Before he didn't want to come to see a marriage counselor.

*Therapist:* So that gave you some hope?

*Wife:* It did.

*Therapist* [to husband]: What's your sense of what moved things from the point they were at to someplace better? [Here the therapist is offering the husband an opportunity to highlight the steps he and his wife took that led to an increased sense of confidence in the future.]

[The therapist then introduces "scaling questions" (Berg & de Shazer, 1993; de Shazer, 1994) as a medium for talking about change.]

*Therapist:* What kind of confidence levels do you have about the changes you've made since calling for the appointment? If "0" was no confidence and "10" was you were very confident, where would you place yourselves on that scale?

*Wife:* We're ready to go again. So we're like newlyweds now.

*Therapist:* Putting that into perspective, what kind of confidence do you have in the changes you've made?

*Wife:* I'd probably say that I'm at an "8" right now.

*Husband:* Me, too.

*Therapist:* Wow! . . . You said there have been other periods when things have swung downward and then up again. Are there reasons for feeling more confident now than after those periods?

*Husband:* Things are different now [less stressful than in the past in terms of work, schedules, children, etc.]. We've also sat down and discussed that we need time away.

*Therapist:* But when you say an "8," what is it that makes you feel more confident that things that have been talked about will actually happen?

*Wife:* Well, we had a weekend planned. But at the last moment my husband canceled. We were at a real bad point and I thought it would do us good.

*Husband:* We had been fighting and I didn't want to go away . . . .

*Therapist:* That was early on in this period?

*Wife:* Yes, that was when things were rocky. But I ended up going away with the children . . . . A couple of days ago he said, "We do need time away alone." We started talking about that. So I do feel confidence, but it's not a "10," it's an "8." We are very giving people and we end up putting other things in front of our relationship—our children, our jobs, and other things. We think our relationship will be okay on the shelf, but you can't do that.

*Therapist:* Tell me, what would it take to get from the "8" to the "10" or even to a "9.5"? What would need to happen that you would say, "I'm even more confident now"?

*Wife:* I don't know. That's why we came to you.

*Therapist:* But I think you have some ideas. Because you already made some steps that moved things from somewhere around a "0" up to an "8," which is a lot.

*Wife:* Right.

*Therapist:* What needs to happen now to further bolster your confidence, and make you feel less uncertain and worried about the future?

Notice how the therapist, in this example, doggedly stayed curious about and focused on this couple's efforts to make changes in their relationship. Rather than assume an expert role, the therapist simply accessed the clients' resources by amplifying those steps taken that led to change. Focus was on movement from the past to the present.

As a therapist, where might you go next with this interview? How might you structure the remainder of this session? What suggestions would you make to this couple? As it turned out, this was a single-session therapy in which the couple decided not to schedule another appointment. A conversation with the wife 6 months later revealed that the couple found this one session "very helpful in getting us back on track." My work with this couple involved supporting the gains they had already made and then discussing the steps needed to maintain those gains. An attitude of respect and curiosity about their efforts to improve their relationship, reflected in the questions asked, was the cornerstone to an effective and efficient therapeutic process.

> *Take seriously (respect) the client's request and keep your focus on the goal. Develop a cooperative and collaborative relationship with the client. Construct limited and achievable goals that maximize opportunities for successful outcomes.*

The collaborative therapist "co-constructs goals and negotiates direction in therapy, placing clients in the driver's seat as experts on their own predicaments or dilemmas" (Friedman, 1995, p. 355). The therapist serves as a consultant or catalyst rather than an expert or analyst (Bennett, 1989). In many instances, therapy goes on longer than necessary because neither the client nor the therapist realizes that the original goals have been met. Research (Bischoff & Sprenkle, 1993) has demonstrated that the closer the client and therapist come to agreeing on the nature of the "presenting problem," the lower the rate of client "dropout." Heinssen, Levendusky, and Hunter (1995) also reported increased compliance with treatment goals and more positive outcomes for an inpatient population when the clients were involved, at the outset, in a *collaborative* process of goal setting. It is therefore extremely important to find out what the client wants to accomplish in therapy.

## Defining a Well-Constructed Request

This is a request-based therapy, dependent on the goals of the client. For change to occur, people need to have a request or wish. What is important to the client? If a therapist or outside agency takes responsibility (i.e., mandates change), the client is less likely to take responsibility (Cade & O'Hanlon, 1994). When a therapist tries to talk a client into changing, the only position left open for the client is to defend the "no change needed" position. What does the client want to get out of therapy? Even clients mandated to treatment may have useful and workable goals (e.g., "to get the court off my back," " to get visitation with my children," "to get my parents to stop bugging me"). What the therapist needs to find out is what the client is willing to be a "customer" for (Berg, 1989; Berg & Miller, 1992). What does the client want from this consultation? Berg's concept of "customers, complaints, and visitors" (1989) provides a valuable structure for considering interventions and will be discussed more fully in Chapter 2.

Let's look at what defines a well-constructed request. There are five factors that can serve as useful criteria for designing therapeutic goals (Berg & Miller, 1992; Friedman & Fanger, 1991):

1. The goal needs to be salient (relevant) to the client.
2. The goal is best kept small and manageable.
3. The goal needs to be specific, observable, and framed in behavioral terms.
4. The goal should be stated in positive language (what the client *wants*, rather than what he or she *doesn't want*).
5. The goal must be realistically achievable with the necessary resources available.

Instead of focusing on what the client needs to move away from, interest is directed to what the client wants to move toward. As we shall see, a number of techniques are useful in helping the client generate a set of workable goals. For starters, rather than getting sidetracked by what is *not* working (which is often how clients initially talk about the "problem"), it is important to have the client state, in positive terms, what he or she wants to see more of. Let's look at a brief excerpt from an initial session with a couple to see how this works.

*Therapist:* One question I wanted to ask before we get started—have things gotten better over these 2 weeks [since the appointment was set] or are they about the same?

*Wife:* About the same, I guess.

*Husband:* A little better.

*Wife:* Yeah.

*Husband:* I think they've gotten better.

*Wife:* Yeah. We're communicating a little more.

*Therapist:* What has changed that has improved things?

*Wife:* He doesn't aggravate me as much.

*Husband:* I've been working a little harder [on the relationship].

*Therapist:* What have you [husband] been doing that's been helping the relationship?

*Wife* [to husband]: You haven't been aggravating me as much.

*Therapist* [being persistent]: If he's not aggravating you, what is he doing instead?

Wife: *He's talking to me like an adult.* He's trying harder . . . .

By being persistent in his questioning, the therapist enables the wife to state what she wants to see more of, namely, to have her husband "talking to me like an adult." Establishing this allows the therapist to find out what the husband does when he talks to his wife "like an adult." In so doing, the therapist can work toward a clearly articulated goal.

Following is an excerpt from another initial interview. I encourage you to consider the criteria for a well-formed request, mentioned earlier, as you follow the process of the interview. Notice the ways the therapist helps the client zero in on her goals. The "miracle question" (de Shazer, 1985) is used as a way to get the client (Nora) to give me a picture of the changes she is looking for. We come into the interview after about 5 minutes of social conversation.

*Therapist:* Tell me what you were hoping to accomplish coming here today?

*Nora:* I don't know. I came for counseling when my parents were going through the divorce. I came with my mother. I was having trouble adjusting. I don't know. I'm stressed all the time. I think a lot of it has to do with family situations. I thought maybe I could find some way to relieve my stress, so it doesn't affect my current relationship.

*Therapist:* What would things look like ideally for you? Let's say a miracle happened during the night and you woke up the next morning . . . . How would you know and how would other people know that things were different?

*Nora:* Ideally, my parents would be speaking. Ideally.

*Therapist:* And they're not now?

*Nora:* No. That's a tough one.

*Therapist:* So your parents would be speaking, having civil communications.

*Nora:* Civil. They can communicate enough to deal with the children but essentially that's it. I think that would be a big one.

*Therapist:* So, when this miracle happens, they would be talking together, doing things together or just talking?

*Nora:* They're both remarried.

*Therapist:* Okay.

*Nora:* Not necessarily doing things together, but to the point that when the kids in the family had stress they could be talking.

[This focus on change in her parents' relationship is somewhat outside of her control and therefore not a goal that can be effectively dealt with in therapy. I therefore refocus on changes in herself that she might hope to experience "after the miracle" happens.]

*Therapist:* What else would you notice about *yourself* after the miracle happens?

*Nora:* I'd be more relaxed. I think I'd have a better relationship with my father. My relationship with my dad has gone downhill.

*Therapist* [looking for specificity]: So how would somebody tell that you were more relaxed? How would I know?

*Nora:* It doesn't affect me in everyday life. I try to keep it separate because I don't live with them. So the everyday things don't affect me so much. But there's always something going on with this family thing or that family thing, that my mother tells me.

*Therapist:* That she tells you about. You have close contact with your mother?

*Nora:* Very close contact with my mother. My mother and I lived alone for 4 years when I was in high school. It was just the two of us.

*Therapist:* So, you'd be more relaxed. Would you be doing anything different being relaxed?

*Nora:* I would spend more time with my father. Being in contact with him and his wife a little bit more.

*Therapist:* Anything else that would be different after this miracle happens? Anything with you and your boyfriend?

*Nora* [laughing]: I may not be so neurotic about cleaning. I'm absolutely neurotic about cleaning. That relieves stress, because I'm constantly cleaning. And he'll [boyfriend] say, "Would you just sit down." That would be good.

*Therapist:* So, when this miracle happens, you might be cleaning less.

*Nora* [laughing]: I hope so.

*Therapist:* So, that would be a good sign?

*Nora:* Oh, yeah.

*Therapist:* Okay. Anything else that would indicate that your stress level was reduced?

*Nora:* I'd be a little more self-confident, knowing that I could go to either side of my family for support.

[Later in the session]

*Therapist:* So he [father] doesn't really know you as an adult. What would be important to you about him knowing you better?

*Nora:* To understand that I'm an individual. I am like my mother, but that's not bad.

*Therapist* [trying to understand what Nora's priority is in coming for therapy]: Would you say that's the most important thing that you're concerned about now?

*Nora:* Yes. For right now, separating myself from my mother in my father's eyes and becoming an individual where's he's interested in my life. [Nora now presents a clear picture of where she would like to go in therapy. In light of this goal, I encourage her to draft some letters to her father that we review in the next session (one month later). I also encourage short visits with her father between now and our next session. Her letters evolve from initially angry to more loving and supportive as a function of her visits with him. She begins to see her father in a new, more positive light, and by opening herself up to him allows him to be supportive of her in new ways. We agree to meet a third time (one month later), which ends up being our final session.]

At this third session she tells me she has seen improvement in her relationship with her father and feels more supported by him in very concrete ways (e.g., in regard to her upcoming wedding plans). The following excerpt is from the end of this third and final session:

*Therapist:* So, have you accomplished what you came for?

*Nora:* I think so. Yeah. It made me think a little more.

*Therapist:* You've taken some big steps with your dad, which was the thing you were most concerned about—would he treat you like an adult.

*Nora:* I think he is. He's offering help.

*Therapist:* He's there for you.

*Nora:* He is.

*Therapist* [curious about how this change has affected her stress level]: How about your cleaning now?

*Nora* [laughing]: The house has been dirty for 2 weeks. David [her boyfriend] did it this week.

*Therapist:* Really?

*Nora:* So this week I just put my feet up and just took it easy . . . and watched TV.

*Therapist:* Do you remember in the first meeting we had I asked you if a miracle happened, what would be going on, and you were saying spending more time with your father in a more relaxed way . . . .

*Nora:* Which I have.

*Therapist:* And that you'd be cleaning less . . . .

*Nora:* That's true. I forgot about that.

*Therapist:* And that you'd feel more self-confident to go to either side of the family for support.

*Nora:* Which I have.

*Therapist:* I think you've done very well dealing with some difficult stuff.

*Nora:* My goodness. I can't believe it.

*Therapist:* So, should we stop? And if there's a need to call at some point, you can just call me.

*Nora:* Well, thank you. You helped me a lot.

Obviously, not all therapies go this smoothly. However, the steps illustrated here are ones that can be useful in enabling clients to generate well-constructed requests. Having the goals outlined in this way makes achieving them much easier.

## *Engendering Hope*

Therapy can easily become preoccupied with dysfunction, pathology, and incapacity—what went wrong, rather than what is going right. With this in mind, the possibility therapist looks for ways to view limitations or "defects" as opportunities. By maintaining a focus on capacity and resourcefulness, hope is engendered.

> *Think in terms of solutions, resources, and competencies rather than problems, deficits, and limitations.*

Milton Erickson was a master at turning perceived deficits into resources. Take, for example, the woman who had a gap between her front teeth and came to see Erickson because she felt unattractive to men (Haley, 1973). Erickson encouraged this woman to spend some time at the water cooler at work, and when the man toward whom she felt some attraction appeared, she was to take a mouthful of water and squirt him through the gap in her teeth. As in all good Erickson stories, she complied with the instruction, and lo and behold ended up marrying the man! As always, Erickson was looking for ways to turn a perceived deficit or liability into an asset.

Steve de Shazer (1985) worked with a young woman who had isolated herself from social contact because she was ashamed of her disability and her need to use a cane to walk. de Shazer proposed that instead of trying to hide the cane (and her disability) she might get better results if she "advertised" her disability (Fisch, Weakland, & Segal, 1982) by purchasing a very unusual and attractive cane. What do you suppose the effect of doing this would be? How would her social contacts increase using this more interesting cane? Again, de Shazer was taking what could be viewed as this woman's handicap and turning it into a resource. The therapeutic process was transformed into a laboratory for creating new opportunities.

In addition to the use of tasks to create change, the conversations we have in therapy can also have powerful effects on the sense of hope and the abilities to take action. At any moment in a therapy session we are faced with a choice about the direction of the interview. Engaging in conversations that focus on deficits immerses both client and therapist in a whirlpool of pessimism and passivity (Miller, 1992). On the other hand, amplifying what is already working, looking for past successes and coping skills, and searching for evidence of behavior that the client has engaged in that is contrary to the problem (i.e., "exceptions") creates for both client and therapist a more hopeful and hope-generating therapeutic conversation.

For example, Louise and Joanne had a 16-year relationship that had gone through many ups and downs. They came to see me in the hopes of achieving a better understanding of their relationship and improving their "communication." The following conversation took place about 5 minutes into the interview (from Friedman, 1996). Notice the way I use hope-generating questions (Epston & White, 1992) to build on the partners' connection to one another.

*Consultant:* How is it that through the difficulties that you may have experienced in your lives and relationship over time, that you have stayed together and maintained the relationship, which is not easy to do with any relationship these days over an extended period of time? What has allowed you to maintain this relationship in spite of the difficulties you've faced?

*Joanne:* That is a great question! I need to write that question down so that I can remember to ask myself that again and again. I realize there must be something that has allowed us to get this far.

*Louise:* There was always that constancy of being there . . . even when we were apart for periods of time. We could always reconnect on vacations.

*Consultant:* What kept that going? Why didn't that connection wane after a period of time?

*Joanne:* I couldn't imagine not having that connection.

*Consultant:* So it was a given that this is your partner.

*Louise:* Yes.

*Joanne:* Louise has always been such an emotional support to me. I can say anything and together we could work out what is good for my life and for us. We were concentrating on each other. Even with interruptions our main intent was to spend time together. So even with the interruptions I didn't become frustrated because she was always there.

*Consultant:* So you were able to get past those obstacles and keep the relationship alive . . . . Who would be least surprised that your relationship has been able to survive these obstacles?

*Joanne:* Besides us?

*Consultant:* Yes

*Joanne:* No one.

*Consultant:* So there has not been a lot of support from outside, friends or a family member?

*Joanne:* Right.

*Consultant:* So, even in spite of not having support, this relationship has been able to survive.

[Later in the interview]

*Consultant:* What is it that you know about yourself that would have allowed you to predict that this relationship would last as long as it has and your connection would continue to be there?

*Joanne:* For me it's connections. I'm a strong connector. In the face of all odds I keep my connections. I'm talented at it, I guess . . . .

*Consultant:* You're dedicated. Once you make a commitment, you follow through. And that's been something constant for you.

*Joanne:* Since forever.

*Consultant* [to Louise]: And that's been something you've been aware of, Joanne's loyalty and commitment.

*Louise:* Yes, yes.

*Consultant* [to Louise]: And what is it about you, that you know about yourself, that would have helped you understand how this relationship would have lasted as it has?

*Louise:* I think I've been able to listen well . . . . Although there was a period that this wasn't happening, it's been getting better lately. [Joanne agrees.]

Beginning this interview by engendering hope set a positive tone for the remainder of the meeting. A focus on the couple's connection and loyalty to one another formed a basis for attending to other issues in their relationship. Engaging in a set of hope-generating questions establishes a foundation from which other more problematic areas can then be explored in an atmosphere of openness and caring.

> *Generate optimism; Take a hopeful, future-oriented stance. The language of possibility serves as a key to therapeutic change.*

A nursing home may seem like a strange place to begin a discussion about hope, autonomy, and the future. As a consultant to several nursing homes (Friedman & Ryan, 1986), I was distressed by the effect of this setting in diminishing the residents' sense of hope and control over their lives. As human beings, we are characterized by our exploratory natures and curiosity about the world around us (R. White, 1959). In many nursing homes, residents no longer experience a sense of control and autonomy but find their lives directed and regimented by the rules of the institution. As the residents' expectations diminish, a sense of despair, helplessness, and hopelessness develops.

In the face of these institutional forces I was continually impressed by the residents' active attempts to regain control and maintain a sense of hope. A feeling of hope and an orientation to the future is so much part of our human nature that even in situations where one would think it would not exist, it does.

For example, an elderly resident who was described as "delusional" was found to pack her belongings each day in anticipation of being discharged from the nursing home (Friedman & Ryan, 1986). The staff, knowing that she was never going home, confronted her about her behavior in hopes she would give up this ritual. However, these attempts were unsuccessful. When I asked her about this behavior, she said, "After all, where would I have gone? I packed my bags so that I could keep track of my belongings. But I'd still like to see my home town some day, you know." This woman was obviously not planning to leave the nursing home; the packing behavior simply allowed her to experience some sense of control and hope about the future. In fact, research studies have shown that when nursing homes allow residents to make choices that increase their sense of control and autonomy, even their physical well-being is improved (Langer & Rodin, 1976; Rodin & Langer, 1977: Schulz, 1976).

## Self-Fulfilling Prophecies

We are all susceptible to "self-fulfilling prophecies" (Watzlawick, 1984) such that our very expectations and predictions about the future influence the outcome of those very same events. A person's expectations about the future can even affect one's survival. In one recent study reported in the *New York Times* (Blakeslee, 1993), researchers found that Chinese Americans who maintained traditional and fatalistic beliefs about their birth year and its associated disease entity died 1 to 5 years sooner than those who didn't harbor those beliefs. The reader is referred to the classic study by Rosenhan (1973), who employed "confederates" to play "mentally ill" people, to appreciate the power of expectations in determining people's behavior. In regard to the process of psychotherapy, recent research (see Herron et al., 1994 for review) has supported Frank's (1974) contention that "patients will comply with the therapists' expectations of how long therapy should take . . ." (p. 158). In working from a time-effective frame that emphasizes hope, possibilities, and a future vision for change, the therapist is incorporating a set of assumptions that will, in the same way, influence the outcome of the process.

In addition to the psychological effects of employing a language of possibility, hope, autonomy, and choice, this stance also has a significant and positive physiological impact. As Cousins (1989) pointed out: "Hope, purpose and determination are not merely mental states. They have electrochemical connections that play a large part in the workings of the immune system . . . . Hope, faith, love, will to live, festivity, playfulness, purpose and determination are powerful biochemical prescriptions" (p. 73). Because language is a mediator of mind-body connection,

> the words we use in conversation compel experience in the listener . . . . We blush when we hear a compliment; our heart rate increases and mood changes upon hearing threats and insults; we may laugh or cry while reading a book. Since words evoke both physiological and psychological states, we need to choose our words with care . . . . Through the language that we use we can create optimistic moods that foster [hope and possibilities]. (Friedman & Fanger, 1991, p. 29).

Adding further evidence to the connection between life events and physiology, a recent study reported in the *New York Times* (Goleman, 1994) found that pleasant events (e.g., fishing, jogging, contact with friends) positively impacted on immune system functioning, while stressful events (e.g., criticism by the boss) lowered immune functioning.

By engaging solely in "problem talk," we end up immersing both ourselves and our clients in a morass of diminished expectations and despair. When we talk the language of deficit and despair, a person's mood rapidly becomes synchronous with the language process. If you doubt this effect, you can try a little experiment. Next time you are with a client, notice the differences in the client's nonverbal behavior when he or she is talking about the problem in contrast to when he or she is talking about his or her hopes, dreams, wishes, and expectations for the future. And if you think this phenomenon is evident only with the client, you might try videotaping a session and notice your own posture, mood, and state when working from a problem frame in contrast to a possibility frame. Write to me with the results!

The language of possibility offers opportunities for both client and therapist to feel more hopeful and resourceful. A sense of hope and a positive set of expectations for the future are indissolubly interwoven. The value of hope in creating effective outcomes should not be overestimated. The possibility paradigm, rather than focusing on fixing or excising pathology, emphasizes hope and focuses on a future based on the client's goals and wishes.

## A Practical Exercise[2]

Think about some of the ways you generate hope in therapy. What questions do you find most helpful in engendering a sense of hope and optimism in your clients?

I find it useful to ask clients to tell me about how they have overcome some adversity or difficulty in their lives, ways they have drawn on their own resources to solve problems in the past, examples of how they have acted that has enabled them to make a better life for themselves, and so on. Look for other examples in the transcripts presented.

## Developing a Future Vision

There are many ways to engage clients in developing a future vision. We have already seen the miracle question in operation, a method that Insoo Berg and Steve de Shazer (1985, 1988, 1991) developed (based on Milton Erickson's [1954] hypnotic technique) that enables clients to both clearly articulate their goals in therapy and generate hopeful and future-oriented pictures of life without the problem. One can also ask clients to present a "video description" of life without the problem (O'Hanlon & Wilk, 1987), a detailed view of an ideal future state. When you help the client articulate the details of this picture, the ideal becomes clearer, more prominent, and more possible. With couples, therapists can prompt the partners to enact scenes of a more satisfying future (Chasin, Roth, & Bograd, 1989; Mittelmeier & Friedman, 1993), demonstrating the ways they would like to be with each other. Although this is done in a "pretend" frame, the effects on the couple's relationship can be very powerful and meaningful. These techniques, and others, will be discussed in more detail in Chapters 2 and 3.

*Respect the complexity of a situation while trying to act simply. Look for points of maximum leverage for change. Keep assumptions simple and avoid elaborate explanatory thinking and hypothesis generation.*

Recently a woman presented for therapy saying, "My doctor thinks I'm depressed." When I asked what her concerns were, she said, "My drinking and my weight," and then added, "I'm also not sleeping well at night." From her conversation with the doctor she had come to believe that her difficulties sleeping, her overuse of alcohol, and her overeating were related to her "depression."

This is an example of how psychiatric terminology can muddy the waters of therapy. The internist applied the term "depression" to this woman's behavior, leading her to think that, rather than a sleeping, drinking, or eating problem, she now had a bigger problem called "depression." "Depression," in this case, reflects what Gilbert Ryle (1949) referred to as "the myth of the ghost in the machine," a term without existence. When I asked her to tell me where she wants to put her energies in the therapy, she said, "My drinking." We then talked about what steps she had been taking and what steps might be useful in reducing her alcohol consumption.

We scheduled a meeting 2 weeks later. She reported making good progress in reducing her drinking, that she had developed several strategies for changing her behavior and was feeling better about herself. She also reported her sleep had improved and that maybe she wasn't in fact depressed after all. We met several more times over a 3-month period, during which she not only stopped her drinking, but lost weight. Although we never discussed her concerns about her weight or her sleep problem in therapy, both improved as a function of her abstinence from alcohol. Attention to one pivotal area in her life, her drinking, transferred to other areas. Although she came in initially about a problem of "depression," a focus on her drinking behavior opened the door to changes in an array of other domains.

Staying simple, and finding a gentle leverage point for change, becomes the focus in this approach. By so doing, the clinician opens the door to a more hopeful and time-effective therapy, one that does not pathologize or stigmatize the client.

Here is another example to illustrate this mode of thinking. An 8-year-old boy was referred by his pediatrician for fears. He was having trouble sleeping in his own room, talked a great deal about ghosts and monsters, and was having nightmares. The parents had taken him to see a therapist who saw Matthew individually and engaged in "play therapy" in which the boy would draw pictures of the monsters and talk about them. As he talked about these fantasies, he sounded crazier and crazier. The therapist believed that Matthew was significantly depressed and might benefit from medication. The parents, hearing this diagnosis, became very worried about their son but did not like the idea of using medicine and sought out another therapist.

I met with the mother, father, and Matthew and asked the miracle question. The parents responded that they were hoping to see Matthew "tell a straight story that didn't include ghosts and demons [and] . . . be able to sleep in his own room . . . ." I realized that the more I talked with Matthew about these ghosts and monsters, the more he sounded out of touch with reality.

I approached this situation using a narrative or "externalizing" frame (White & Epston, 1990), defining these "fears" as an external force that was wrecking havoc on the lives of Matthew and his parents. Matthew agreed that he wanted to free his life from the monsters. The parents' lives were also affected as the fears increased their worry about their son. While the details of this clinical situation are available elsewhere (Friedman, 1994), the upshot of this work was that the parents, Matthew, and I teamed up to develop strategies to free their lives from the influence of these fears.

As the story turns out, Matthew earned a "fear-buster" certificate (see White & Epston, 1990) and was successful in freeing himself from the domination of the monsters. He was sleeping in his own bed, was not having nightmares, and was not spending so much time in "monster talk." At the session in which the parents reported these positive outcomes, they surprised me by asking if we could now work on the "depression." Having forgotten all about the previous therapist's diagnosis, I blurted out, "What depression? . . . I don't see any depression." The parents seemed to relax into their seats with relief. They had accepted the earlier diagnosis as a description of their son. My therapy put aside this description and worked on a pragmatic level to team up with that part of Matthew that wanted to be free of these fears, to grow up, to become more independent and self-sufficient.

What this experience reinforced was how the labels and descriptions we apply are often taken quite literally by the people we see, and therefore, as therapists, we need to be careful about our words. By staying away from pathological labels and helping people escape the forces that hold them captive we can more gently and positively achieve positive outcomes.

## Using Creativity/Introducing Novelty

As we know, brief therapy, or any form of psychotherapy for that matter, is not a panacea for all life's ills. People's lives are complicated, and it is simplistic and demeaning of the client's experience to think otherwise. In Chapter 5 we shall look more closely at an example of these complications. However, it is possible to find gentle leverage points that can dislodge clients from a stuck position on the bank of the river and back into the ongoing flow of life. Becoming a possibility therapist requires that the clinician appreciate the complexity of people's lives but also understand that getting a small change going can snowball, creating reverberations in other aspects of a client's life. By thinking small, the clinician can prevent him- or herself from feeling overwhelmed and can begin to structure the therapeutic conversation in ways that catalyze and support opportunities for change. The process requires an ability to shift gears in light of new information and to continually modify and vary one's approach in light of the unique demands of the clinical situation.

> *Use humor, play, and metaphor. Explore alternative perspectives and ideas. Introduce novel action steps.*

One of the great opportunities in doing psychotherapy is bringing to bear your imagination and creativity. Therapy will not be effective by the simple, mechanistic application of a set of techniques or strategies. The therapist must learn to use him- or herself in the process; to improvise (Keeney, 1993); to draw on his or her special talents and style (Selekman, 1993); to introduce humor; and to develop the flexibility to "think on one's feet," modifying the steps as you go along.

While comfort and experience in the therapeutic arena play a large role, the therapist can maximize his or her effectiveness by utilizing his or her own personal style and ways of connecting and relating. In one very interesting study (see Binder, 1993 for review), therapists who were given special training in a certain way of doing therapy (in this case, time-limited psychodynamic therapy) ended up with poorer outcomes than those who didn't get the training! What can we make of this finding? Clearly, training in a particular treatment approach will not, in and of itself, enhance one's clinical effectiveness. In fact, it is possible to become too much the technician who is not sensitive to the nuances of the therapy context and thereby to fail miserably.

Paying close attention to the client is one way to generate novel perspectives and ideas (Budman, Friedman, & Hoyt, 1992). Rather than becoming so internally attuned to what you are going to do next, stay open in the conversation, and you will more likely find a useful focus. Often, in the clinical conversation, clients will come up with metaphors or descriptions that can become the basis for thinking about, and acting on, their predicament in new ways.

In one situation (Brecher & Friedman, 1993), for example, the therapist utilized the mother's description of trying "to make a better life for the family" as a basis from which to help the children appreciate their mother's efforts. Paradoxically, having faith in the power of the clinical conversation to lead to productive and useful avenues, without forcing the process, is something that can make therapy more time-effective (Anderson, 1993; Anderson & Goolishian, 1988).

## Engaging the Client Outside the Therapy Room

Just as the therapist needs to act in the therapy context in offering ideas and generating questions, the client must also be actively engaged outside the therapy room. Although changes in how the client "views" a situation can have significant impact (O'Hanlon & Wilk, 1987), acting in the real world is usually a necessary part of establishing and maintaining change in the client's life (Frank, 1974; Kreilkamp, 1989). As Heinz von Foerster (1984) has said, "If you desire to see, learn how to act" (p. 61). By actively engaging with our environments, we alter feedback processes in ways that open the door to change.

Over 30 years ago the research team of Held and Hein (1963) did a fascinating study on the effects of activity on learning and perception in kittens that has implications for therapy. They rigged up an apparatus that allowed one kitten to navigate through a specially patterned environment while yoked to another kitten who sat passively in a gondola and was exposed to the same environment as the "active" kitten. Each pair of kittens had been reared in darkness prior to this experiment. As the active kitten rotated around the cylindrical environment, the passive kitten followed in its gondola. After spending about 3 hours a day in this apparatus for several days, the researchers then tested each kitten on a series of tasks requiring visual discrimination. The results showed that the kittens who had been active in moving through the patterned environment, who had been in control of the movement, were more successful in the visual discrimination tasks than were the more passive kittens. This finding supports the idea that active movement and engagement with the environment are necessary to facilitate learning.

The passive kittens in the study were in a helpless position, without control over their movements. In the same way, people can be in a state of "learned helplessness" (Seligman, 1975) or "demoralization" (Frank, 1974) when they find themselves repeatedly ineffectual in impacting on the events in their lives. On the other hand, acting on the world in ways that produce effects can lead to "feelings of efficacy" (R. White, 1959), or agency, and a sense of optimism. The therapy process can set the stage for people to take steps in their lives that increase their sense of control, autonomy, and hopefulness. However, it is steps taken by clients in their own life contexts that ultimately establish new patterns. In doing time-effective therapy, it is the client who must ultimately do the work (see Figure 1-3).

## Parsimonious Therapy

Therapy is costly, both financially and psychologically (Budman & Gurman, 1988) and therefore requires the application of the "principle of parsimony" (Hobbs, 1966): Use the least costly, restrictive, and stigmatizing alternatives first. Placement in a psychiatric hospital has more costs than simple financial ones to the MCC responsible for the bill. As ethical therapists, it is our job to seek alternatives that are (1) least disruptive to the client's life; (2) least stigmatizing; (3) least likely to encourage regressive, dependent behavior; and (4) least demoralizing.

*"The work being done on your marriage—are you having it done, or are you doing it yourselves?"*

**FIGURE 1-3  The Work Being Done on Your Marriage**

To put this another way, we need to look for alternatives that allow clients to function in their natural social systems, that foster independence and autonomy, and that engender a sense of hope, dignity and a positive outlook for the future. In addition, when working from a population-based practice model, therapists must allocate resources in the most judicious ways possible. What this means is that an evening treatment program around an issue of drug or alcohol dependence, for example, may be a preferred first alternative rather than a 2-week inpatient stay on a detox/rehab unit. Or, an adolescent shelter program may be a better choice than an inpatient psychiatry unit at a hospital for a teenager who is caught up in conflict with a parent at home. Better yet, could the adolescent stay with a relative temporarily while attending outpatient family meetings? Paying attention to the client's social system opens doors to possible noninstitutional sources of support.

*Appreciate the idea that helping people reach their goals as rapidly as possible is both practical and ethical. Favor treatment alternatives that provide the greatest level of client independence and least cost, both financially and psychologically.*

Many people come for an initial appointment and then never come back. At one time this was seen as "client dropout," representing treatment failure due to client resistance or lack of motivation for therapy.[3] However, in many cases, something useful does come out of this one and only contact (Bloom, 1981; Talmon, 1990; Hoyt, Rosenbaum, & Talmon, 1992). For some people simply having an appointment mobilizes them to take the action they need to take.

Some people seek therapy when in crisis (e.g., around the loss of a job) or when trying to sort out and deal with some complex situation (facing the reality of a recently diagnosed illness) or when engaged in decision making about something of importance (whether or not to have an abortion, to end a relationship, etc.). Often therapeutic contact around these issues can be brief (one or two sessions). In fact, the modal (most frequently occurring) number of therapy sessions that people attend is one! As a provider in an HMO, I did my own small study, based on a panel of over 300 clients seen over a 3-year period. The most frequent number of sessions was a tie between one and two![4] What do these results tell us? For one thing, therapists need to maximize the time they have with clients, understanding that our efforts are only one small part of the change process; secondly, attempts to develop elaborate treatment plans that anticipate 6 months or a year of contact are a setup for failure and frustration.

Many people who do come back for a series of sessions can do so very effectively on an intermittent basis (Bennett, 1984; Cummings, 1986), scheduling appointments at various intervals of time (for example, every 3 weeks, every month, etc.). This model respects the clients' abilities to regulate contact rather than imposing a weekly regimen on them.

Two questions that I usually ask at the end of the first session are: (1) "Do you want to set up another appointment?" And if "yes," (2) "In how many weeks would you like to set an appointment?" Many times the client's choice of when to meet again and my expectations do not match. Usually I'm thinking we should meet sooner, while the client is thinking about a later date. Obviously, in situations where a client is at risk (e.g., for suicide) I would more clearly advise a rapid followup appointment with me or a colleague. Part of the HMO framework depends on teamwork or collaboration with colleagues to manage difficult situations. Clients often develop a relationship with several clinicians whom they may see in crisis, or in a group, or on a more regular basis for therapy.

In an HMO practice there is no such thing as "termination" (Budman, 1990). As Freud (1937) pointed out, treatment (or analysis) does not necessarily immunize us against future stresses. Understanding that people will come back as needed and that this doesn't represent "treatment failure" is an important part of the HMO philosophy. It is similar to going to see a dentist—just because the dentist filled a cavity in one tooth doesn't mean you won't develop a cavity in another tooth (Cummings, 1979).

In summary, it is useful for the therapist to assume that (1) it is possible for clients to achieve their desired goals, (2) it is possible that these goals can be reached in the course of a small number of meetings, and (3) it is possible for these goals to be attained in an atmosphere that is both playful and focused (Friedman & Fanger, 1991).

## Therapy as a Two-Way Street

Because our interventions can have "iatrogenic" effects,[5] we must be vigilant about the impact of our methods and processes (Tomm, 1990). The goal of a useful therapeutic consultation is to increase options or open space for the generation of new ideas, new alternatives, new descriptions, and new meanings. As we discussed earlier in the book, the approaches we take are ultimately dependent on the views we have of the people we see. Our assumptions affect our actions. It makes a big difference, for example, if we see people as misguided, mistaken, wrong, abnormal, resistant, uncooperative, obstinant, and the like or as resourceful and resilient, but oppressed and subjugated (Tomm, 1990).

> *Maintain a sensitivity to our methods and processes as a way to avoid a "colonial mentality" in therapy.*

As Rachel Hare-Mustin pointed out (1994): "The therapy room is like a room lined with mirrors. It reflects back only what is voiced within it" (p. 22). As therapists, we are susceptible to perpetuating "discourses" or conversations that mirror the prevailing or dominant cultural norms (e.g., around sex roles, cultural and racial stereotypes, etc.). In the therapy context we need to be aware of these cultural norms and dominant societal discourses so that we do not perpetuate these values in our work.

The therapeutic system includes the therapist as an active and influential element. Because influence goes two ways, the therapist is also in a vulnerable position to change as a function of the clinical encounter. As we have discussed, the stories we tell about ourselves shape our ways of viewing the world. As therapists, we need to widen our lenses by providing ways for clients to have access to our thinking. We are less likely to become a "colonial" presence (Hoffman, 1991), if we open ourselves to scrutiny by the people we serve. By so doing we become, not only more human, but also more accountable for our ideas and assumptions. Taking a "transparent" position (Freeman & Lobovits, 1993; Hargens & Grau, 1994a, b; Madigan & Epston, 1995) requires situating our comments in a personal context instead of hiding behind formulaic prescriptions.

In practical terms, what this means is that the possibility therapist needs to be constantly vigilant about imposing his or her ideas and assumptions on clients. The goal of the therapy process is not to dominate or control people but to facilitate a dialogue that opens space for new options and ideas to emerge. "The goal is *not* one of imposition of one idea over another, but of respect for the client's systems of meaning, introducing ideas into the dialogic field such that the client's lens or framework expands" (Friedman, 1995, p. 355).

## Practical Exercise

The following exercise is an opportunity to think through a clinical situation from two distinct perspectives and then develop treatment plans based on these ideas. The goal is to see how our assumptions influence the treatment process.

You receive a call from the Department of Social Services (DSS) regarding the Rogers family. Mrs. Rogers is a 28-year-old woman, recently separated from her husband. For the past several months she has been on welfare. There are three children in the family, ages 10, 7, and 5, who are living with the mother. The father lives an hour away and visits the children about once a week.

You learn from the DSS worker that Mrs. Rogers has a high school diploma and prior to the birth of the children worked outside the home. The DSS is involved because of an anonymous report that the mother has been hitting the oldest child, Jose. Jose has also been caught stealing and has been involved in some incidents in which he and some other children broke windows at the school.

The DSS worker has learned from Mrs. Rogers that when the husband visits, there is occasional conflict, which sometimes ends up with the husband physically abusing Mrs. Rogers. The children have observed these episodes. Jose seems to be the one to try to protect his mother. He also has some child care responsibilities for his younger siblings. The siblings seem to be doing okay, although the 5-year-old occasionally wets the bed. The children look forward to seeing their father, who treats them well on his weekly visits, which usually last about 3 or 4 hours. The school sees Jose as bright but sometimes aggressive. He is doing "okay" academically, although he is seen as capable of doing better. He has friends and is relatively well liked by both students and teachers. In one incident he stood up for a smaller boy who was being picked on by a bully.

Mrs. Rogers has a sister who lives nearby and who is a source of support. A brother is currently in a drug rehab program. The maternal grandmother lives close by and is considered a support both financially and emotionally in times of need. The DSS worker has found evidence for physical abuse of Jose by his mother and is referring the family to you for therapy.

- *First:* What are your concerns about this family? What factors make you least hopeful about change? Outline the problems in this family. Then answer these four questions:

  *Questions to Consider:*
  1. Who would you see in therapy? Why?
  2. How would the goals for therapy be decided?
  3. How would you frame your feedback to this family?
  4. How long do you expect therapy to last?

- *Second:* Rethink this situation in ways that support a picture of this family as having significant resources and strengths. What factors make you most hopeful about change? How would you apply competency-based thinking in working with this family in a time-effective manner? Then again consider the four questions.

## KEY IDEAS IN THIS CHAPTER

- It is no longer simply the therapist and the client in the room. The managed care company (MCC) is a third party in the therapeutic system, requiring the therapist to engage in a delicate balancing operation in meeting the client's needs as well as the expectations of the MCC.

- Therapists in a managed care setting must juggle resources in meeting the needs of a large population of people seeking service rather than providing intensive services to a select number of people. This requires a shift in attitude from seeing oneself as the person who will "be there" as the client takes each step, to a view of oneself as a consultant or catalyst for change, offering ideas that mobilize clients to take action in their own inimitable ways.
- Managed care poses special challenges to clinicians who have grown accustomed to being autonomous in clinical decision making. In effect, the managed care provider no longer has the "luxury" of seeing someone week after week without clinical oversight. Such oversight, while being experienced as intrusive, provides a much needed level of accountability that serves the needs of the MCC to conserve resources and the needs of the client, who is less likely to become immersed in an interminable, and at times, iatrogenic therapy.
- Doing time-effective therapy is not a simple endeavor, and it requires the development of significant self-discipline. A shift in attitude is needed in giving up traditional assumptions about what works in the therapy process and opening yourself to a revised set of assumptions.
- A set of principles and assumptions have been outlined that emphasize client resources, strengths, and competencies. Rather than using the dominant medical model of pathology and illness, the competency-based therapist employs nonpejorative language to engender hope and enable clients to meet their goals in a time-effective manner.
- Integrating ideas from solution-focused therapy and the narrative frame allows the therapist a range of flexible clinical options that can be effectively applied to a diverse range of client issues and problems.
- By maintaining a naive, curious, open, and inquisitive mind, the clinician will be able to (1) effectively connect with the client and his or her dilemma, and (2) find openings that can effectively build on client resources and successes. Naiveté favors optimism.
- The therapist needs to take seriously the client's request and develop a cooperative and collaborative relationship based on the pursuit of a mutually agreed upon set of goals. This is a request-based therapy in which goals are negotiated and formulated in such a way that success is a possible outcome.
- The language of possibility enables the therapist to engage in a structured conversation with the client such that new ideas or perspectives are generated that can be applied in the real-life situation of the client.
- Expectation and hope are two fundamental factors in generating effective treatment outcomes.

- Action by the client is usually a necessary part of establishing and maintaining change.
- Helping people reach their goals quickly and efficiently saves costs both financially and psychologically.

## NOTES

1. Fifty years ago Alexander and French (1946), radical therapists of their time, began to doubt the validity of many traditional views about the process of therapy. For example, they questioned whether (1) "the depth of therapy is necessarily proportionate to the length of treatment and the frequency of the interviews; (2) therapeutic results achieved by a relatively small number of interviews are necessarily superficial and temporary, while therapeutic results achieved by prolonged treatment are necessarily more stable and more profound; and (3) the prolongation of an analysis is justified on the grounds that the patient's resistance will eventually be overcome and the desired therapeutic results achieved" (p. vi).

2. I wish to thank Ben Furman, M.D. for originally introducing me to this exercise.

3. Obviously, client dropout can also be accounted for by ineffective engagement of the client by the therapist (e.g., see hypothetical "problem-focused" interview described on page 9 of this chapter).

4. The median number of sessions was 3.3, with a range from 1 to 20. Ninety percent of clients were seen for 10 or fewer sessions.

5. The word "iatrogenic" is a medical term that refers to any adverse effect introduced by the treatment procedure itself.

# ▶ 2

## Starting Off: Honoring the Story and Moving Forward

*People do not present pathologies that need to be removed through some scientific process. They share stories that need to be honoured . . . .*
—*CHARLES WALDEGRAVE*

The first contact with the client is crucial in setting the stage for time-effective therapy (Budman, Hoyt, & Friedman, 1992; Friedman & Fanger, 1991). As Friedman and Fanger (1991) point out:

> It is here [the first session] that the process of mutual discovery begins. Never again will so much fresh information about the client be available. Selection, which will make some of it marginal, has not yet begun. All is new, undimmed by familiarity. You are doing much more than simply forming an impression of the client. You are beginning to learn the client's reality. To enter the client's world, you must observe and respond to the client's assumptions . . . . for these will be negotiated in the therapy to achieve the client's goals. (p. 67)

The initial interview plays a major role in influencing expectations. It is also a unique opportunity to rapidly enter the client system and to both seed novel ideas and explore options that can alter the problem pattern. As we shall see, approaching the client from an inquisitive and curious perspective engenders a sense of hope and supports the achievement of a positive out-come in therapy. By assuming a competency-based perspective, the therapist can quickly tune in to client strengths and resources and use these as build-ing blocks for change.

Stephen Lankton (1990) tells a wonderfully instructive story about his interaction with his son Shawn:

> Shawn when he was 15 months . . . . could say very little. In fact, the only thing he said at that age was "want this!" He came into the kitchen one day as I was putting the groceries away and pointed to the laundry detergent box and said, "want this." I offered the box but he repeated his singular verbalization . . . . I offered everything on the countertop to him and he continued to request something else. As a good mental health professional would do, I picked him up and asked him to put his finger on what he wanted because I couldn't understand him. He placed his finger on the box of laundry deter-gent! The box displayed a picture of a magnifying glass and beneath that, a magnified view of some brown fabric fibers. I thought he must be making a request for a magnifying glass and I made an offer to get him one. He refused it. I even went and got one for him thinking he merely did not know the word for it. He refused it and pointed and said, "want this."
>
> Now any reasonable parent would have been inclined to set him down and tell him to go play elsewhere with the instruction "there is nothing here you need." Had I done this, he would have thrown a fit: He was so determined and he would have been frustrated. And if he had thrown a fit, I would have been tempted to say to myself, "he's been a brat." I might have even told my wife Carol about the incident when she came home and we would have both "remem-bered" several other times when he seemed to "have a mind of his own" and thus concluded, that, in fact, he was a brat. (p. 65)

Lankton goes on to describe what happened next:

> What did transpire, however, was quite different. [Shawn] put his hand on the magnifying glass in the picture. I looked at the "fabric" below it and wondered, "what in the world could this look like to him?" I said, "do you want a pretzel?" And he replied, "Yes Daddy, a prentzel"—saying it incorrectly and thus indicating that he did not know the word. Then he hugged my neck tightly and said, "I love you, daddy." This was not a manipulation to get a pretzel—it was clear he was getting one. This was a way of saying, "I know you respected my observation enough to stick with me and figure this

out and thank you for believing in me." I concluded he was smart and persistent. (p. 66)

What characteristics of Lankton's interaction with his son are similar to doing a first interview with a client? What does this example have to teach us about how we construct realities with our clients? What does this story tell us about the art of doing therapy?

In this chapter we'll focus our attention on ways to do a time-effective clinical interview. The main elements that will be emphasized here are:

- Listening to the client's story
- Collaborating with the client in developing clear measures of outcome (goal setting)
- Persistence in moving with the client along his or her desired path
- Generating a hopeful, optimistic stance
- Introducing novel ideas or perspectives

Again, each clinical situation is unique and requires the therapist to flexibly adapt techniques and practices to the realities of the clinical situation.

At times, clients come into therapy needing to tell their stories and have someone understand and validate what they experienced and how they managed to cope and survive under difficult circumstances. At other times the therapist must not only validate, respect, and acknowledge the client's struggle but also provide avenues for a productive conversation that leads toward a desired future state. While this may require a series of meetings over time, therapy can lead to a successful outcome in a single interview (Bloom, 1981; Talmon, 1990). When I meet with a client initially, I do not know how long treatment will last. I simply consider how I can make the time we have together today most productive; that is also the reason I generally do not make more than one appointment at a time. To do so assumes that more appointments will be necessary.

## SETTING THE TONE FOR THE INITIAL INTERVIEW

Recent studies have looked at communication processes between physicians and patients (Frankel et al., 1991; Kaplan & Greenfield, 1993; Levinson, 1994; Novak, Goldstein, & Dubes, 1993), with significant implications for how we do therapy. These studies found that problems arise between doctors and patients, usually in the form of patient complaints, when doctors "devalue patients' views . . . [and] fail to understand and respect patients' perspectives (Levinson, 1994, p.1619). As Levinson (1994) states, "Patients want to be active partners discussing treatment options" (p.1620). In fact, "patient control in the form of questions, interruptions and statements expressed during office visits was associated with improvements in physiologic and functional control of the disease" (Kaplan & Greenfield, 1993, p. 11).

When physicians, at the initial visit, were "less controlling, [the patients] . . . gave more information . . . [and] reported fewer functional limitations at follow-up" (Kaplan & Greenfield, 1993, p.10). What was positively associated with patient satisfaction was "physician warmth, friendliness, expressed concern and empathy . . . [plus] allowing patients an opportunity to express problems and concerns in their own words" (Novak, Goldstein, & Dube, 1993, p. 3). In the psychotherapy process, per se, research (summarized by Duncan & Moynihan, 1994) demonstrates that the best predictor of outcome is the therapeutic alliance. And the factors that enhance this alliance are *empathy* for the client's dilemma; *respect* for the client's dignity and resources; and *genuineness*, reflected in the therapist's emphasis on clients as experts on their own lives (Duncan & Moynihan, 1994). What are the implications of these findings for doing an initial psychotherapy interview?

The initial interview is an opportunity to engage the client in a productive and useful conversation. Since our views of ourselves are based on our interactions with others, the therapist is in a privileged position to engage in conversations that begin to shift those views and self-perceptions. In order to do so, however, the therapist must set the tone by listening carefully to the client's story and immersing him- or herself in the client's frame. While listening to the client's story, the therapist needs to be vigilant for "openings" or descriptions that are hopeful and that reflect the client's strengths, resources, and coping abilities.

A question I like to keep in mind is "How has this client been able to cope, and be resilient in the face of current circumstances?" What impresses me most is not how people can succumb to hardships but how people are able to cope under adverse circumstances (e.g., see Sawatzky & Parry, 1993). Setting a hopeful, optimistic tone; exhibiting warmth, empathy, respect, and acceptance; and being willing to listen to the client's story are ways to set a positive and productive emotional climate for the interview (Duncan, Solovey, & Rusk, 1992; Frank, 1974; Lipchik, 1992).

## An Initial Interview

The following is an initial interview with a 32-year-old Latina woman that illustrates the importance of honoring the client's story, persistence in following the client's lead, an empathic attitude, and a respect for the client's wishes. As you read this transcript, track these elements and their impact on the therapeutic process.

I had expected to see the couple for this initial appointment, but only Renee came to the appointment. Renee's husband has been unemployed for a long period and that has been a source of worry for her.

*Therapist:* Tell me what you were hoping to accomplish coming here . . . considering you are coming here by yourself now . . . .

*Renee:* To put myself in balance again . . . . I'm pulled in all different directions. I come home he's [husband] depressed. I go to work there are stresses there. So it's like . . . I'm not achieving anything positive.

*Therapist:* How is it that you're coming in now rather than 6 months or a year ago, since some of what you've been telling me about has been going on for a while?

*Renee:* I'm tired . . . . I'm very tired . . . . I've reached a point with my job where I just don't want to deal with it . . . . but I can't get out of it [considering the job market] . . . and then there's the situation at home [her husband's unemployment].

*Therapist:* So, it's not a good time to take risks.

*Renee:* Exactly . . . .

*Therapist:* So, it's that feeling of being boxed in . . . .

*Renee:* Yes. Also I was so worried about him [husband] because he was so depressed . . . very depressed.

*Therapist:* Very down . . . .

*Renee:* Really down . . . and this week it's my turn. I think we're taking turns [laughs].

*Therapist:* It's hard to see him be depressed . . . .

*Renee:* Yes. I can't help him . . . .

*Therapist:* It's frustrating to try . . . .

*Renee:* Yeah . . . I don't know what to do.

*Therapist:* You were trying to help?

*Renee:* Yes . . . to open options to him . . . to hear other points of view. I end up telling him to do this and do that . . . . Everyone has been there [depression] and I'm sure his head's spinning from all that . . . . On the other hand, I can't just sit back and not tell him anything.

*Therapist:* So, it's a real bind what to do . . . how to be helpful. But all this is taking a toll on you . . . . It's a drain.

*Renee:* Yes. Seeing a person in that situation is very sad [crying]. When we were first married I used to get very mad because I couldn't do anything. Now I'm not mad . . . . I'm just very sad.

*Therapist:* It's more of the frustration and disappointment . . . .

*Renee:* Yeah . . . there's also disappointment in other areas . . . so it all adds up.

*Therapist:* So this has been your turn to let down a little bit and allow yourself to experience the frustration and disappointment . . . .

*Renee:* My husband says, "What's wrong with you" and I tell him, "I'm just depressed."

*Therapist:* And you have every right to be . . . considering what you've been dealing with. It sounds like you've been trying to hold it together . . . to be strong because your husband has been going through so much . . . and there's just so much you can . . . .

*Renee:* . . . be strong. I have to be strong at work also . . . .

*Therapist:* Yes, yes. It seems to me that you need sometimes to let down and not be so strong . . . .

*Renee:* [cries and shakes her head in agreement]

*Therapist:* It's okay . . . . [hands Renee some tissues] I was saying how it is your turn to let down a little bit and be sad . . . . So your husband noticed that?

*Renee* [still crying]: I was trying not to drop my feelings on him . . . .

*Therapist:* . . . to not burden him with anymore . . . .

*Renee:* His burden is big enough.

*Therapist:* How has he responded to your sadness?

*Renee:* He's been very supportive . . . telling me everything is going to be okay.

*Therapist:* So, he was trying to help you . . . .

*Renee:* Yes . . . "don't worry."

*Therapist:* I think it's important that you allow yourself to hear that from him . . . since it's been the other way around for so long . . . . You deserve a turn to hear that . . . and he deserves an opportunity to be able to say that to you . . . "It's okay." From what you've told me about your husband, he sounds pretty strong. My feeling is that he's going to be able to handle this and to understand about your frustration. [Renee is crying while therapist talks]

*Renee:* [wipes her eyes] . . . [long silence] A lot of people have it tough these days.

*Therapist:* A lot of people are struggling . . . and it sounds like you and he are trying to do the best you can . . . but there's a lot of forces out there that are keeping you from moving as quickly as you'd like. But I get the sense that there's a determination there . . . .

*Renee* [smiling]: Yes.

*Therapist:* . . . to make things better.

*Renee:* Yeah . . . yeah. I think so also.

*Therapist:* Because I get the sense you like to move.

*Renee:* Some of my friends say, "Why are you still with him?" because I was always fast . . . .

*Therapist:* Yes . . . so they think he is holding you back . . . .

*Renee:* Yes.

*Therapist:* What do you think about that?

*Renee* [laughing through her tears]: I guess it's love . . . .

*Therapist:* Yes . . . you care about him.

*Renee* [crying]: And I do . . . . It's not easy but that's the way it is.

*Therapist:* Why is it that your friends say that?

*Renee:* Well, they know me as someone always on the go . . . always on my toes. They say, "It's been two years, what's he waiting for? So forget it . . . ."

*Therapist:* Is that hard to hear from them?

*Renee:* Sometimes the rational part of me understands it but . . . he's my husband also and he's not bad . . . he doesn't drink, he doesn't beat me. You hear all these disaster stories . . . he's not all of that.

*Therapist:* So, he's a good man . . . going through some difficult times.

*Renee:* Yes, a good man . . . . But there's part that says maybe he'll never get his act together. Maybe he'd do better on his own . . . . I don't know. Maybe because I'm so strong it's not helping him . . . you know . . . to do his own homework. Sometimes I want to put the newspaper [job ads] in his face but I know that's not my job.

*Therapist:* Yes.

*Renee:* I can talk, tell him, but he doesn't have to do it.

*Therapist:* You can throw out ideas but you don't want to be in a position to push things on him . . . .

*Renee:* He has his mother already doing that.

*Therapist:* So, it's tempting to want to jump in and help that way but you realize you need to give him the space to do it on his own.

*Renee:* All my life I've always done my thing [been independent]. I've always called my own shots. I've done some good things. I've done some bad things . . . but nothing that bad.

*Therapist:* You've been in control of your life and now you're hitting on to some things that put you out of control . . . .

*Renee:* . . . out of control . . . .

*Therapist:* And that's . . .

*Renee:* . . . scary.

*Therapist:* Yes.

*Renee:* Because I've never been at that place before.

*Therapist:* Yes . . . . What do you think is a step you can take to help get a sense of some movement . . . and I realize you're used to moving along . . . determining your own life and now you're in a situation where you don't have total control and your husband is going through some difficult times . . . there are lots of family issues and frustrations and work stresses, too. What is it that can allow you to experience some sense of optimism, a very small step that would help on a day-to-day basis?

*Renee:* I don't know . . . . On the weekends I try to keep active . . . see friends . . . .

*Therapist:* Not to let the situation completely immobilize you.

*Renee:* Yes . . . but I feel like I'm pushing myself . . . .

*Therapist:* I think that's important though, to push but also to allow yourself to experience those feelings of sadness and disappointment and for your husband to have the opportunity to take care of you because you're both going through a difficult time.

*Renee:* It's been tough.

*Therapist:* Yes . . . . Do you want to set another appointment . . . what would you like to do?

*Renee:* I don't know. I can call if I need to?

*Therapist:* Yes, you can call. I can give you my card. Was it helpful to come and talk today?

*Renee:* Yes. At least by talking about it I get it in perspective. And things had gotten out of perspective on all fronts. I think that's what I'm trying to do— so I can focus again.

*Therapist:* Right.

In this interview the therapist, by carefully listening and connecting with the client's story and picking up on the issues of loyalty to her husband and her own growing state of frustration, opened space for the client to gain some perspective and understanding.

## ESTABLISHING CUSTOMERSHIP: THE PRINCIPLE OF COOPERATION

Our relationships with clients, and the part we play in developing those relationships, set the stage for therapeutic movement and change. In fact, Lambert (1992) estimates that only about 15 percent of therapy outcome can be attributed to techniques or the specific model employed by the therapist. Rather than technique, clients view the nontechnical elements of the therapy encounter (the therapeutic relationship) as most memorable, especially the therapist's attitude in generating hope and a positive expectancy for change. Waters and Lawrence (1993) also report that "when we push ourselves to find something we like about a client, a change occurs; a change in us, in our client, and in our relationship" (p. 117).

Too often, poor therapeutic outcomes are attributed to the client without adequately looking at the therapist's style or the client–therapist interaction (Miller & Rollnick, 1991). As mentioned earlier, the therapeutic conversation has the potential to create so-called "resistance" or it can open the door to change. Many times, therapists create "psychological reactance" by their approach to the client.

Working in a nursing home (Friedman & Ryan, 1986), I noticed that the more restrictions that were placed on residents and the more their autonomy was diminished and limited, the more feisty and conflictual they would become. Confrontational and coercive strategies evoke reactance and protest in most people—in effect, a desire to fight against the restrictions (Brehm, 1966). I've seen this repeatedly in the managed care setting in which I work. If clients feel in any way pushed out of treatment or that their concerns are disqualified, they will push even harder to get services. When offered choices, the client can assert his or her autonomy and retain self-respect.

Motivation is dependent on context. It is the therapist's job to facilitate and catalyze possibilities by engaging in conversations that open the client to change. Let's look more closely at three possible relationships that can occur in the therapy context: the visitor, the complainant, and the customer (after Berg, 1989; Berg & Miller, 1992; Fisch, Weakland, & Segal, 1982).[1]

## The Visitor Relationship

The visitor relationship is one in which the client is usually sent to you by someone else (e.g., a court, Department of Social Services, a parent, spouse, etc.). The client presents with no specific complaint or problem. The hope here is that in the conversation something may come up that the client may want to work on. However, it is risky to assume that this person is ready to take action. The most common error is to assume you have a customer relationship when, in effect, you have a visitor.

One way you know this is if you find yourself working too hard trying to convince the client there is a problem. The best you can do is to try to interest the client in coming back and talking. As Berg and Miller (1992) point out, it is important to (1) avoid telling the client what to do, (2) compliment the client on coming in (emphasizing the client's autonomy of decision making), (3) highlight anything the client is doing that is good or useful, (4) give credit for steps taken, and (5) find out what the referring person expects from the client's coming to treatment. Let's look at a dialogue that illustrates these points.

*Therapist:* What do you think the court is looking for in suggesting you come here?

*Client:* For me to stop skipping school and get off drugs.

*Therapist:* If that happens, will the court say you wouldn't need to come here anymore?

*Client:* I guess so.

*Therapist:* What do you think about that?

*Client:* I really don't like school . . . .

*Therapist:* What do you find difficult about it?

*Client:* Getting up in the morning . . . . Well, school's always been hard for me . . . .

*Therapist:* What do you think would be a first step to get back on track with your schoolwork?

*Client:* I'm not sure . . . maybe seeing my math teacher after school to get some extra help . . . . I don't know.

*Therapist:* Talking with your math teacher sounds like a good idea to me. What other ideas do you have for getting back on track at school?

## *The Complainant Relationship*

While seeing a problem that needs to be resolved, the complainant does not see him- or herself as part of what needs to change. This occurs frequently with couples when one partner thinks the other needs to, for example, quit drinking or get help dealing with unresolved childhood trauma. The client in this position needs to begin to see that he or she can make changes also that can help the situation.

Again, it is useful to compliment the client on coming in and looking for help and for any steps he or she is taking to improve the situation. Tasks, in the complainant-type relationship, should not encourage doing anything (taking action) but simply focus on the client observing or thinking about the situation. The following dialogue illustrates this approach:

*Therapist:* It sounds like your husband's state of depression is taking a toll on you.

*Client:* It is. I think he needs help to see that there are other things he can do to get himself straightened out.

*Therapist:* What ideas have you offered him so far?

*Client:* I've certainly suggested he come here and get therapy and I've tried to talk with him about getting out more and being more active . . . but he doesn't seem to listen to me.

*Therapist:* It sounds like you've been working very hard to help him. I admire your persistence.

*Client:* His behavior really is problematic and I hope he does something about it.

*Therapist:* I wonder if you would be willing to try something that might be helpful to him?

*Client:* Of course. What do you have in mind?

*Therapist:* Would you be willing to notice when he is being active and behaving in a less depressed way?

*Client:* Sure, if you think that would help him.

*Therapist:* I do. It would be important to notice when he is more energized and active. Also, I wonder if you would, during this time you are observing, not do anything to alter his regular routine, like make suggestions for things he could do. Do you think that would be possible during this period of observation?

## The Customer Relationship

The client in this situation is coming with a specific concern and wants to do something about it. He or she may have already taken steps to improve the situation and may be feeling at a loss about what to do next to make things better. In this instance, tasks can be given that build on steps already taken or that offer opportunities for gaining new perspectives on the situation. As with the other type relationships, complimenting the client on positive actions already taken is a good first step. A good example of an interaction of the customer type was presented earlier in the interview with "Nora."

## A Practical Exercise

1. Think about a session you've had recently that went very well. How did you match the client's state of readiness in facilitating change? What concrete steps did you take to match the client's position?
2. Think about a client who came to see you recently and with whom you had a "complainant-type relationship." How did you go about creating "customership?" What are your favorite ways to encourage a customer-type relationship?

3. Think about a client with whom you've been struggling and feeling frustrated. How can your understanding of the client's state of readiness to change influence your work? In what ways can you modify your approach to better match the client's position?
4. Notice in your next clinical encounter, the ways you work to match the client's position and jot down your findings. If possible audiotape or videotape a session or two and observe the process.

## THE INITIAL INTERVIEW: GUIDELINES FOR PRACTICE

The following are some general guidelines for conducting an initial interview. This should not be considered a blueprint for conducting an interview, merely a pool of ideas that might be helpful to consider in the interview process (adapted from deShazer, 1985, 1988; Durrant & Kowalski, 1990; Friedman, 1993; Friedman & Fanger, 1991; Lipchik & de Shazer, 1986; O'Hanlon & Weiner-Davis, 1989).

**Setting the Stage.**    Establish rapport. Validate and acknowledge the client's (family members') concerns, feelings, wishes, and hopes. Ask about interests, work, hobbies, and so forth. Do a quick genogram (McGoldrick & Gerson, 1985) to get an overview of the extended family network and to establish potential resources in the client's larger social system.

**Opening Questions.**    Begin with a question like "What were you hoping to have happen by coming here?" or "How can this time (session) be useful to you?" or "Let's imagine our talking together turns out to be helpful, useful to you—how will you know, what will be different?" Determine what the client is a "customer" for.

**Co-Construction of Goals.**    Ask the miracle question (de Shazer, 1985): "Let's imagine that a miracle happened in the night and you woke up in the morning to find the problem no longer was there—what would be different? What will be happening when this miracle happens? What will you be doing more of when this miracle happens?" Or have the client imagine him- or herself at some point in the future when the client will be doing the things he or she wants to be doing. "What will you notice about yourself that will tell you things are better?" "What might your friend, sister, or others notice about you that would tell them things are different?"

"Negotiate" with the client in defining an achievable goal. Get the client to be specific about what he or she means by a certain word. For example, if a client says, "I want more appreciation," find out what the client means by the word "appreciation." Keep expectations low and realistic (e.g., "What would be a signal that things were moving in a positive direction?"). Get the client to provide a concrete (observable) definition of the goal by operationalizing words into behaviors (e.g., "What will you be doing differently when your self-esteem is improved?"). Work for "small accomplishable wins" (Weick, 1984). Since motivation increases when a discrepancy exists between people's desires (goals) and their present state (Miller & Rollnick, 1991), it is important to have clients state their goals in clear and positive terms. Emphasize the clients' control and autonomy in making choices (and don't align with referral sources as an agent of social control).

**Look for What Is Working.**   Or look for what has worked in the past; Search for those behaviors that the client engages in that have been (are) effective; Ask the client how he or she got a successful outcome to happen. Search out and identify any exceptions to the presenting complaint: "What is different at times when the exception happens?" Have the client elaborate on the details of the sequence that led to the exception.

**Challenge Negative/Pathological Self-Assessments. Introduce Uncertainty.** For example, "I wonder if there is another way to look at the situation. Could it be that . . . ?" Look for alternative realities in helping the client view the situation in a more positive, normalizing light; for example, "Other people in your situation would have thrown in the towel a long time ago—how have you been able to stay so level-headed about this situation?" Avoid psychiatric terminology; use plain language.

Externalize the problem. Separate the person from the problem; for example, "How has the problem been influencing your life?" "In what ways has the problem been keeping you from moving ahead?" "How has this problem fooled you into thinking you aren't able to do . . .?" Then look for "exceptions," times when the client did not fall under the influence of the problem and did not let the problem intrude into his or her life or relationships.

**Use the Language of Possibility.**   Include presuppositional statements or questions; for example, "*When* you decide to make this change, how will your father respond?" rather than "*If* you decide . . . ." Notice when the client states the complaint in the past tense; for example: (Mother) "When I called for the appointment, Joe was depressed"; (Therapist) "What changes have you made over this period that enabled Joe to start feeling better?" Be prepared to amplify client comments that point to change.

**Generate Action Steps.**   The therapy encounter can be viewed as a "laboratory" in which to consider options for action. It is useful at the end of the first session to compliment the client on steps taken that are in the direction of change and ask for more of the same. Because a small change can have a ripple effect, encourage a small alteration in the way the difficulty is handled or ask the client to do an experiment that will provide an opportunity to generate new behavior. Consider writing a letter to the family to amplify ideas. The goal is to set the stage for the client to notice exceptions and account for these developments. (The mechanics of letter writing, and ways to construct useful tasks will be discussed in Chapter 3).

**Assess Outcome.**    Assess whether the client's goals have been reached. Conclude therapy if the client is satisfied with the results, or recycle (see Figure 2-1). In Figure 2-1, "contextualizing" means presenting feedback, placing the predicament in a context or frame, or normalizing; "Authenticating" is acknowledging and applauding client steps toward the goal; situating or embedding the changes in the client's life. As we shall see in Chapter 4, the

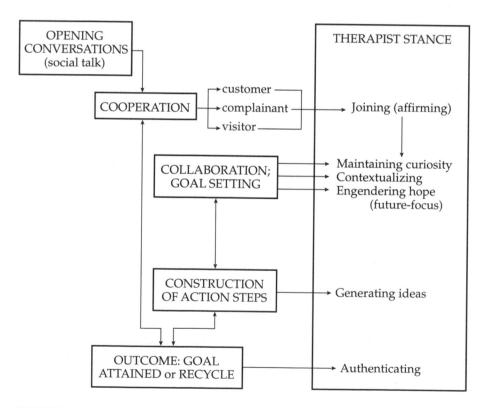

**FIGURE  2-1    Competency-Based Practice: An Overview**

Reflecting Team can also be a useful means of (1) generating ideas, (2) engendering hope, (3) contextualizing the problem, and (4) authenticating change.

## AN INITIAL INTERVIEW WITH A COUPLE

The following are excerpts from an initial session with a couple that demonstrates a number of the ideas already mentioned, including the construction of a well-formed request, negotiation in arriving at a mutually agreed upon goal, and the generation of tasks that facilitate movement toward that goal.

The wife, Rose, called an for appointment because she believed her husband, Tony, "has a split personality," one minute being pleasant, the next angry and irritable. Rose felt she could no longer live this "dual life" and wanted to come in with her husband for therapy. As you read this interview, consider the following questions:

1. What clinical assumptions might lead a therapist to view this situation as one needing longer-term treatment?
2. How is the therapist "staying simple and staying focused" in his approach?
3. What ideas do you have for working with this couple that might have worked equally well?

After several minutes of making social conversation I set the stage for the interview in a goal-directed manner and establish a structure that holds them responsible for guiding the process.

*Therapist:* Why don't you tell me what you were hoping to accomplish by coming here? What would you like to accomplish today?

*Rose:* I don't know if there's anything going to be accomplished . . . but I just told him the other day that I'm tired of living a dual kind of life. It's just like it was before [2 years earlier when I saw the family around an issue with their son] . . . problems with Mark [her son], problems with Tony [her husband].

*Therapist:* How old is Mark?

*Rose:* He's 15 and he's very difficult to live with.

*Therapist:* Which one, Mark or Tony? [I want Rose to be specific about her agenda.]

*Rose:* Both.

*Therapist:* Who's more difficult to live with, Mark or Tony?

*Rose:* It's a toss up. Tony has a very definite split personality. I never know what to expect. One minute he's enthusiastic or calm and the next he flies off the handle.

*Therapist:* When we met before, we talked about the two of you taking time by yourselves, away from the kids, going off on a weekend or something like that. Have you continued to do that?

*Rose:* We've done it. When he's away from "life," he's fine, but when the day-to-day little routines happen, he can't handle it.

*Therapist:* What works so well when you're away from the house, when the two of you go off somewhere? [I inquire about "what works."]

*Rose:* He doesn't have to think about dealing with Mark.

*Therapist:* How is your behavior different when you go away from the house?

*Rose:* Mine isn't different. I don't change.

*Therapist:* You don't see any differences?

*Rose:* No.

*Therapist:* Do you [Tony] see a difference when Rose is away from the house . . . when you have that time separately?

*Tony:* No, nothing significant.

*Therapist:* Do you see a difference in your behavior in the way Rose is describing it?

*Tony:* Sure. I may be more relaxed . . . but Mark, in my opinion, creates this tenseness at home, on my part. He continues to be impulsive . . . .

*Therapist:* So, it [Mark's behavior] still gets to you?

*Tony:* Yes.

[Tony and Rose are in agreement that although Rose's behavior doesn't change when they are away from the house, Tony's behavior is different. In addition, they agree that Tony is not as relaxed at home as he is when away from home. I now return to my original focus on the goals for the meeting.]

*Therapist:* You said you didn't know what we could accomplish today. What were you hoping for?

*Rose:* Basically, what I'm hoping to accomplish is for him to change some of his ways.

[Rose "goes public" with her agenda—for her husband to change, not her. *Question:* Should I accept this agenda or try to expand the problem to include her? Would it be more time-effective to expand the problem or contain it? How might you approach this situation if you consider Tony as a "customer" for change and Rose as a "complainant?"]

*Therapist:* And what do you [Tony] think about that? Do you think that's reasonable? She wants you to change.

*Tony:* In my opinion, I have changed. I don't like when Mark abuses her and yells at her and I say, "Why do you let him do that?" She just lets it happen and I don't like that.

*Rose:* But that's really not the way it happens. You get involved in a confrontation that I might be having with Mark and then a whole different thing is happening. You have the same inability that Mark has—self-control. You don't know when to pull back and not say something.

*Therapist:* So, what do you imagine when Mark, 3 or 4 years from now, is moving out. Sharon [Mark's older sister] would probably be out by then too. You're not that far from the point when both of them will be off . . . a few years from now . . . 3 or 4 years. What do you imagine that time will be like? [I move the discussion to the future as a way to focus on their relationship as separate from the children.]

*Tony:* It will mean that we will have a real harmonious life, I would think. There's going to be some emptiness and loneliness but . . . I don't think we will have any problems letting the reins go. I'll miss Sharon a hell of a lot more than I'll miss Mark. I have to be truthful about that. He gives me hell all the time. It's not pleasant . . . it's just not pleasant.

*Therapist:* We're talking about this point when neither of the kids will be at home and you're [Tony] saying that it will be harmonious . . . nirvana.

*Tony:* When it's just the two of us we get along fairly nice.

*Therapist:* So what's your [Rose's] sense about that time, which is not that far away?

*Rose:* I don't agree with what he says at all, that when it's just the two of us things go fairly nice.

*Therapist:* What would get in the way of things going nicely, at that point? You'd have Mark, who seems to be a source of a lot of aggravation, out of the house . . . .

*Rose:* That is a big source of aggravation, but when Mark is not around, there's always something that he [Tony] finds to get upset about. Whether he disapproves of something I say or do.

*Therapist:* So that it might be that he would focus on you [rather than on Mark] a little more.

*Rose:* Yeah. This is what I said when we first came in. I'm tired of living this dual life.

*Therapist:* What's the dual life for you?

*Rose:* He's either nice or he's nasty.

*Therapist:* So, you don't get the middle ground?

*Rose:* No.

*Therapist:* But you can see that very nice side of him . . . .

*Rose:* Oh, yeah.

*Therapist:* And you see it more when you're away from the home.

*Rose:* Yeah.

[Later in the interview: An incident is described in which Tony walked away from a potential confrontation with Mark. He avoided being provoked. I pick up and expand on this "exception."]

*Therapist:* He's [Tony] definitely capable of resisting that urge to get involved. But every so often, you are at a more vulnerable place and he [Mark] seems to be able to get to you. How could you [Rose] tell that Tony was changing? Because there are these times [when Tony does walk away]. You weren't there to see it [this recent episode] happen. What would be an indication to you that Tony was making some progress with Mark? [Here I focus on developing evidence for change. What concrete behaviors would represent change, progress, a well-defined outcome?]

*Rose:* Generally?

*Therapist:* Around this issue—how could you tell, how would you know that Tony was making progress?

*Rose:* I don't follow. You mean the incident just mentioned or the whole issue of Tony?

*Therapist:* The whole issue. How would you know that Tony is doing better in dealing with Mark?

*Rose:* By him being able to walk away and not getting encompassed in things that he doesn't need to.

*Rose:* For you to see that yourself? Do these things happen when the two of you are at home?

*Rose:* Yeah.

*Therapist:* So if you saw Tony walking away from some of these situations, you'd say Tony is doing better?

*Rose* [tentatively]: I guess.

*Therapist:* Well, yes or no? Would you think so or not?

*Rose:* I would think so, yes [laughing at my persistence].

*Therapist:* It seems to me that would be a good sign.

*Rose:* Yes [laughing].

*Therapist:* How often is there an episode with you and Mark—every day? Let me put it this way: How many opportunities are there?

*Tony:* The opportunities are daily, because any time he talks to me he yells at me.

*Therapist:* So, the opportunities [to be provoked] are every day. So, if you [Rose] saw Tony walking away more, and there are opportunities every day to get into some struggle with Mark . . . .

*Rose:* Of course.

*Therapist:* You would say Tony is making progress.

*Rose:* Yes.

*Therapist:* Do you [Tony] think that would be a good sign?

*Tony:* Yeah.

*Therapist:* It doesn't mean every time but . . . .

*Tony:* I know deep inside that I'm trying . . . .

[Later in the session]

*Tony:* For 6 months she [Rose] was working her butt off.

*Therapist:* I can see she sets goals for herself. She's ambitious. But it takes a toll on her and you don't want to see her so fatigued. [I refocus on times when the couple are away from home and things go relatively well.]

*Tony:* She was straight out there for 5 or 6 months.

*Therapist:* You were telling me you went to New Hampshire and it was a nice weekend.

*Tony:* It was wonderful.

*Rose:* [shakes head in agreement]

*Therapist:* How did you do that? I admire that the two of you are able to get away from a situation that's very frustrating and separate yourselves from it and have a wonderful time together. It's incredible.

*Rose:* He separates it more than me. That's what I mean by his dual personality.

*Therapist:* For you [Rose] it's harder to let go . . . but when you're [Tony] away, you're just away and you're gone.

*Tony:* Yes.

[I frame Tony's ability to change when away from home as positive, while tuning into Rose's upset with her husband's "dual personality."]

*Therapist:* It's a wonderful ability to be able to switch off that way . . . but you [Rose] can't switch off so quickly.

*Rose:* And that's a good part of the problem as well. When he's in Spain, he'll be a totally different person . . . completely different. He'll be smiling, he'll be happy. At home he's never smiling and happy, he's miserable. I'm putting in a stressful day just like him. He's got to come home and be miserable . . . to me.

*Therapist:* That's the hard part.

*Rose:* Yeah. Because . . . . [Rose begins to tell me how awful her husband can be, and I interrupt and shift back to the picture of him she wants to see more of.]

*Therapist:* Because you know there's that side of him that can be happy, calm, and relaxed and you don't get to see that side as much as you'd like.

*Rose:* And I told him, I'm not going to play this dual game anymore.

*Therapist:* And just as you [Tony] were saying earlier that you want your wife to be relaxed and not so overwhelmed, she wants to see that side of you, that she wants to see more of, that can be relaxed and happy and more carefree and not so tuned in to everything going on around you . . . sort of going with the breeze a little more. And you're clearly capable of doing it. Some people can't shift gears the way you're able to shift into a nice, relaxed state.

*Rose:* But the verbal damage that he does along the way, shifting gears back and forth, is the thing that I can't stand anymore.

*Tony:* I'll give you an example . . . and I know I'm wrong . . . okay? But I don't know how to say it any other way. I was in the cellar and I noticed one of the shades was up on one of the windows. Mark. Mark must have forgotten his key and came in through the window. So I said to him the next day, "You came in through the cellar window, didn't you?" And he said: "Yeah, I couldn't find my key." So I'll say, for example, if the front door was left open in the house, things to her like "Why was this door left open?" and she'll say, "How do I know?" And I'll say, "Don't you live here too . . . don't you know what's going on in your own house?"

*Therapist:* That's the kind of thing you're [Rose] talking about that feels like a criticism, that you should do something about it before it happens . . . . You've [Tony] got to be nicer to her, and you're capable of doing it.

[I directly confront Tony about his behavior by letting him know I think he's capable of acting differently. I can do this because Tony has accepted the role of "customer."]

*Rose:* [shakes head in agreement]

*Tony:* Yes, I know I am.

*Therapist:* If you [Tony] have a concern about the window, you can deal with it . . . .

*Tony:* Well, what about Mark breaking in [through the window] and doing stuff like that?

*Therapist:* Well, you're his father. You've got a responsibility. You can't be looking to Rose to take care of that.

*Tony:* You're absolutely right.

*Therapist:* He's got to be nicer to you—because you deserve it.

[I validate Rose's concerns by pushing Tony to show his calm, caring, and considerate side.]

*Rose:* [shakes head in agreement, with tears in her eyes]

*Therapist:* And I know you [Tony] care about her a great deal. I can see.

*Tony:* If I didn't, I wouldn't be here. I would've walked out of this whole situation a long time ago. I would've, but I love you so much. I do.

*Rose:* You have a very strange way of showing it [crying].

*Therapist:* And Rose has stuck in there with you, as frustrated as she's gotten.

*Tony:* You say, how have we all survived it. We've survived it because of the love we have for each other.

*Therapist:* I think it's very strong. I think it's strong.

*Rose:* Either that or I just have this sadistical desire to be abused all the time.

*Tony:* No..

*Therapist:* I don't think that's it. I don't know if you're interested in getting together again.

*Rose* [quickly responds]: Yes!

*Tony:* Sure.

[Before reading any further, take 5 minutes or so to develop a task that takes into consideration Tony's capacity to be caring to his wife and information about what they both agreed would represent a step toward a positive outcome. Also base your suggestion on knowing that Tony is a "customer" while Rose is a "complainant."]

*Therapist:* What I'm thinking about is, between now and the next time we meet, you [Tony] work at being nice to Rose, okay? Other than when you're away. When you're away you do it well. So you need to transfer that to when you're at home.

*Tony* [laughing and clearly connecting with the idea discussed]: I'm going to make believe I'm away all the time!

*Therapist:* What I'd like to ask you [Rose] to do is to notice, when you're at home, when you see Tony walking away from situations [with Mark], okay? And for you to notice how he did it. Because it'll be easier for you [Rose] to notice . . . how he managed it. It'll be harder for you [Tony] to notice what you're doing. Okay, let's set something up then.

At the next session, 2 weeks later, Rose noticed Tony resisting the urge to get into arguments with their son; at the third session, 3 weeks later, Rose reported improvement in Tony's ability to back off from Mark's provocations; Mark was seen as "yelling less" and showing more respect for Tony. Tony saw his internist during this period, who told him that his blood pressure and cholesterol levels were too high and encouraged him to "reduce stress." This contact with the internist scared him, and he was beginning to see things in a new light.[2] By the fourth session, 2 weeks later, both Tony and Rose reported a significant decrease in arguments between Tony and Mark. Mark got his best report card in a long time and was spending more time with the family. Rose described herself as feeling closer to her husband now. At a meeting 1 month later (fifth session), the couple continued to report good progress and decided they didn't need to schedule another appointment.

One year later Tony and Rose came in to see me about their daughter, who was dating someone they didn't like. We met only this one time. When I asked for some followup on our previous contacts, they both agreed that their relationship had improved, and, in fact, they demonstrated this in their playful interaction.

## A Practical Exercise: Shirley

Let's look at the following clinical vignette as a way to experiment with some of the ideas outlined in this chapter. Assume you are the therapist and consider the following questions:

1. What assumptions might lead you to become pessimistic and overwhelmed with this client? What is required in order to avoid these assumptions?
2. How would you frame or contextualize Shirley's predicament in a way that is hopeful and future-oriented?
3. What are some metaphors that might be useful in talking to Shirley about her situation?
4. What suggestions would you make to Shirley based on her presentation?

At the outset of her initial interview, Shirley said, "My life is a mess. I wish I could just start over again." Shirley is a 42-year-old married mother of three who has been at home with her children during most of the 20-year period of her marriage. She reports waking up in the middle of the night "worrying about things." She has gained some weight recently and reports being angry and "irritable" with family members. She wondered where this "deep-seated anger" comes from. Shirley sees herself as a "failure" with no goals or purpose and believes that she always puts other people's needs ahead of her own.

Growing up with an alcoholic mother, Shirley learned to keep the peace and "to go along with things" even though she currently feels resentful about this at times. She tells you that this coming weekend a trip is planned with the whole family, even though she would prefer to have her husband go with the children and leave her at home. In the session, Shirley is tearful and wonders if she will turn out like her mother, who was depressed and unhappy all her life. In talking with Shirley, you learn that she completed an associate's degree program many years ago, has interests in music and dance, and has thought about joining a weight-loss group. When asked the miracle question, Shirley says, "Time for myself . . . maybe exercising . . . reading a book . . . having more of a sense of purpose in my life." She adds, "I know changes are hard to make."

Before reading further, take 10 minutes or so to respond to the questions outlined earlier.

Because this is a situation that I recently encountered, I'll tell you how I approached this client. I framed my comments in the context that this was a period of self-examination for Shirley; that she had incorporated and accepted a story about her life that didn't quite fit anymore. This story about her life had her in the position of putting others' needs ahead of her own and not giving much credence to what she wanted or needed in her life. Family members had accepted this story about her and now expected her to behave in a certain way. Her resentment told her that this story was no longer working for her and that she needed to construct a new story about her life, one that offered more options and was less constraining and limiting.

I talked about her "anger," not as something negative inside of her but rather as a form of valid protest against what was not working in her life. I agreed with her that change was hard and, considering the degree to which she had accepted the old story for so many years, it would make sense not to move too fast in making changes. I wondered out loud about some "small steps" that Shirley might take that would allow her to feel some sense of purpose in her life.

We discussed the possibility of her checking out music schools to see if they offered a course she might be interested in. I reiterated my sense that this would only be a "checking out" process, not anything more. Shirley then brought up the idea of joining a weight-loss group, which I supported. Finally, in regard to the weekend trip planned that Shirley really didn't want to go on, I asked if she would be willing to give her family a little surprise. She seemed curious about what I would say. What I suggested was that during the weekend she do something that was good for her and unexpected (different from the old story her family had come to anticipate). She smiled broadly and agreed to try this. We then scheduled an appointment in 3 weeks.

Shirley entered my office for the second appointment with a big smile on her face. She then reported, with delight, how she surprised her husband on the weekend trip by doing something "out of character," namely, entering a ski race! Although her husband was not having a good time at several points in the weekend, she managed to "have a ball." She also had begun an exercise regimen of walking three mornings a week with a friend and had started on a low-fat diet. With regard to doing research on music programs, which we discussed in the previous session, she had taken steps to investigate some school programs and had plans to go back to do more research. I complimented her on the positive steps she had taken. We spent the remainder of the session discussing ways she could build on these steps while "not moving so fast that it will totally upset your husband and children." Interestingly enough, one of her children, while on the weekend trip, commented to his father about how "what Mom wants to do never gets listened to," which I framed as a reflection of her son noticing increased assertiveness on his mother's part in stating her needs.

As this clinical situation demonstrates, it is possible to utilize and build on what the client brings in, rather than imposing from left field a task that doesn't connect with the client's frame. One of the guidelines I use in generating tasks is not to be so provocative in presenting an idea that the client won't connect to it. On the other hand, the task needs to be enough of a challenge that it creates movement and generates optimism for further change. At times I will ask clients what ideas they have for steps to take; or throw out multiple options and let the clients chose one; or ask clients to write a letter to me specifying what they got from the session and what steps they might take to improve their situation. Most of the time, however, my suggestions emerge from the clinical conversation. In effect, the suggestions are "co-constructed" and tailored to fit each unique clinical situation. The next chapter focuses on ways to tailor suggestions and tasks to specific clinical situations and highlights the usefulness of letter writing in the therapy process.

## KEY IDEAS IN THIS CHAPTER

- In this era of managed care the first session is especially crucial in generating a clear set of expectations that will lead to a well-defined outcome. In this way, therapy becomes a goal-oriented process rather than an interminable exploration without direction.
- Assume a competency based perspective. Maximize the potential for achieving a positive result by building on and amplifying the client's own solutions, ideas, and successes.
- Develop a collaborative relationship by listening to the client's story and acknowledging the client's concerns.
- Maintain a position of naive curiosity, optimism, and respect for the client.

- Learn to be distracted by important information, especially evidence of change or success. Look for resources in the client and in the client's social network.
- Stay tuned to the client's goal. Find out what he or she is a "customer" for and take this focus seriously.
- Stay simple and focused and avoid unnecessary hypothesis generation.
- Help frame the outcome in clear, observable terms.
- Provide feedback by placing the client's concerns or issues in a hopeful, change-activating frame.
- When progress toward the goal is not forthcoming, examine your own attitude and approach and make adjustments to better match the client's position.

## NOTES

1. Prochaska, DiClemente, and Norcross (1992) have independently developed a model that is comparable to the one discussed here. Clients are viewed as falling along a continuum of readiness for change, from "pre-contemplation" to "contemplation" to "preparation for action" to "action."

2. Forces outside therapy affect people's lives in mysterious and often helpful ways. As a time-effective therapist, it is useful to acknowledge and build on the occurrence of fortuitous events in the client's life (see Miller, Hubble, & Duncan, 1995 for examples).

# ▶ 3

## Taking Action: Therapy as a Laboratory for Change

*The therapist's job is . . . to create a context within which the client can generate his own possibilities . . . taking the action he needs . . . in his own inimitable way.*
—JOHN WEAKLAND

The managed care revolution has been instrumental in moving therapy in an action-oriented direction. No longer do therapist and client have the luxury to sit and explore psychological issues over an interminable period. The therapist must set the stage for action both in the session and, more importantly, outside the therapy room. Managed care companies, like most people coming for therapy, expect the therapy process to result in concrete changes in the person's life.

As Alexander and French (1946) pointed out many years ago, "This assumption that the interviews will solve everything as if by magic has prolonged many treatments unduly" (p. 39). Action by the client in the real world is usually required at some point in the therapy. Freud himself realized, in the case of people experiencing phobias, for example, that it was necessary at times to encourage clients to approach and face the feared situation in vivo rather than merely talking about it (see Alexander & French, 1946). The time-effective therapist generates suggestions or possible action steps, utilizing the client's motivation for change. The first step in this process is for the client to develop a future vision that includes the goal. The next step is to co-construct with the client a pathway that leads in the direction of the goal and that leaves room, in its implementation, for client creativity.

Although action steps are an important part of the therapy process, people generally don't do what you ask them to do—at least my clients don't. If it was that easy, you could simply lay out a series of steps that might solve the problem and tell the client to do them. Why doesn't this work? For starters, people generally do not like to be told what to do. They like to have a say in what they do and how they do it.

To put this in another way, "knowledge is participatory not instructive" (Efran, Lukens, & Lukens, 1990). We learn by incorporating information into our already established structures or schemas (Maturana & Varela, 1987). It is important, therefore, for the therapist to provide space for clients to come up with their own solutions and ideas and for the therapist to build on or augment these ideas. People tend to do what they verbalize and publicly articulate as important for them. As we have already seen, ideas will emerge from the interview that can be developed and amplified.

What follows next is an example of tailoring a homework assignment to the specific clinical context. In meeting with a couple, the following pattern emerged: Whenever the husband approached his wife in what she viewed as a "needy, dependent way" looking for affection, she would become anxious and withdraw; the husband would feel hurt and unattended to. The wife acknowledged her discomfort with closeness and affection, having not experienced much of this growing up. The husband acknowledged his needs for affection and attention and his history of moving closer when under stress. This pattern or cycle was "externalized" as a force that was intruding on their mutual satisfaction and happiness. They both agreed the pattern was affecting their relationship negatively and that they wanted something more satisfying. The benefit of externalizing the pattern in this situation is that neither partner feels blamed because "the pattern" is seen as the culprit.

I told the couple I thought progress was possible if they could work together to prevent this pattern from intruding into their mutual wish for happiness. I then suggested the following "experiment": The wife, on one or two occasions of her own choosing, was to approach her husband affectionately (e.g., giving him a hug). This was to be done when the husband was distracted by other things. The husband was to "sit back and relax into it" but to do so without further pursuing his wife in an affectionate manner. In addition, the husband was asked to initiate affectionate contact with his wife on several occasions, and the wife was to choose, in one or two instances, to allow herself to "sit back and relax into it" rather than withdraw.

Both agreed to experiment with this over a 2-week period and report back on their progress. Instead of spending much time discussing how these styles developed in each partner, I designed the therapy as a laboratory to experiment with new patterns and new possibilities and encourage the couple to take action to break free of old, constraining patterns of behavior that are intruding into their relationship. In this particular situation the experiment enabled the couple to take some small steps toward one another.

## THERAPY AS A LABORATORY FOR CHANGE

Therapy can provide a forum for clients to practice or rehearse new ways of behaving that can then be transferred to their lives outside of therapy. As Milton Erickson (in Haley, 1967) noted, "Practice leads to perfection . . . . Action once initiated tends to continue" (p. 369). This notion of practice or rehearsal is especially effective when working with couples. One way to do this is to ask each partner to articulate (1) their strengths and competencies; (2) their wishes and desires; and (3) a concrete example of their "ideal picture," which is then "enacted" in a scene developed "in vivo" in the office (see Chasin, Roth & Bograd, 1989; Chasin & Roth, 1990; Roth & Chasin, 1994 for details). The following are excerpts from sessions with two couples demonstrating variations on this process.

### *Couple 1: Enacting Positive Futures*

*Therapist:* Let me tell you how I'd like to proceed, which may be different from what you've experienced before in therapy . . . . What I'd like to do is not start by talking about the problem immediately, but rather talk about some other things that I think will make it easier and more useful to talk about the problem. Is that okay? [They each agree.] What I'd like to start off with is something that is often overlooked, which is people's strengths. I'm interested in hearing from each of you what you consider to be your strengths. What are those strengths, or skills or things about yourself that you like and have been successful at? Either of you can start.

*Husband:* Well, I'm fairly strong and healthy. I have a high tolerance for understanding. I'm a good listener. I'm not a complainer. I kind of roll along and not too much bothers me. I have a strong dedication to my work . . . consistent, doing the job. I'm disciplined. Those are the foremost.

*Therapist:* What would you [wife] add to your husband's list?

*Wife:* He's a wonderful father. He has an ability to be compassionate. Those are two off the top of my head.

*Therapist:* Maybe you [wife] can tell me about some of your strengths.

*Wife:* I also think I'm a good listener and that I'm sensitive to others around me. At work I supervise six people and I think I can easily tune in to what needs to be talked about. I'm extremely well organized . . . . I think I get quite a lot done in the course of a day . . . including nurturing and caregiving [with my children]. I'm able to do that I guess because I'm very organized. I'm also very social and gregarious. I have a few very close friends that I feel a great deal of love for. I have a capacity to learn and to change and to be very flexible. I like to discuss things. I like to solve problems rather than allow them to continue.

*Therapist* [to husband]:  Anything you wanted to add?

*Husband:*  Strengths that she hadn't mentioned about herself?

*Therapist:*  Yes.

*Husband:*  She did mention that she is a good mother. She has done a good job with the children.

*Therapist:*  What I would like to hear about now are the goals that each of you has for the relationship. What I would like is for you to put those goals in the positive, not what you don't like but rather what you do want the relationship to look like. How do you envision things being in an improved state?

*Wife:*  I think the most comfortable way for me to do this would be to say what a normal day would be like, what a nice day would be like. I would like to see me get up with Jim in the morning, and spend a few minutes in the morning chatting about what's coming up for the day, give him a hug good-bye, and then I could go about my business. As it relates to Jim, I would see him doing the things he likes at the end of the day and then we'd sit down to dinner and talk about our day. I would like Jim and I to share the responsibilities of the remainder of the day, of things to be done so we can spend time together after the kids have gone to bed. Perhaps have a glass of wine and sit and talk. And also spend time together outside the house, like once a week . . . . A partnership with a lot of sharing and support for each other. And I also enjoy a good sexual relationship and would like that on a basis that would be comfortable for both of us. And I like a lot of affection, hugging, touching . . . .

*Therapist:*  How about your goals? [to husband].

*Husband:*  I would want things to be more spontaneous. Most of all to be happy . . . . I'd like to spend more time with the kids . . . but my work schedule doesn't permit it. Cooperating in our work and play together. I would like things to be more spontaneous rather than being so planned. At one time it was very spontaneous—I didn't have to think of what I have to do to make her happy . . . it just happened. There was a lot more spontaneity before having children and other responsibilities. Now we have to plan everything, there isn't that freedom.

*Therapist:*  What I would like, at this point, is for each of you to show me one way that things could be better in your relationship. [To wife] You mentioned several things that you said would make for a positive day, and what

I'd like you to do is pick one specific thing and play it out together; develop the scene the way you'd like to go and then enact it right here in the office.

*Wife:* Can I use something that turned out negative but which I would like to go a different way?

*Therapist:* Sure. The way you would like it to turn out.

*Wife:* The conversation I'm thinking about is about my going to the PTA meeting. We actually sat down at the kitchen table. And I said, "I know your night out is Wednesday evening but I wonder if you could make an adjustment in your schedule once a month so I can go to the PTA meeting." What I would have liked him to say is, "The PTA is important to you and tell me when it is . . . which Wednesday of the month . . . and I would be happy to change my night to make it possible for you to go." And I would say, "Gee, thanks, Jim, I appreciate that."

*Therapist:* Okay, let's try this. Now Jim, you're going to be the person Marge wants you to be for the purposes of what we're doing here. You're not committing yourself to anything. [laughter] I want to get a picture of how this scenario can play out in the way Marge wants it to. [To wife] And if he's not doing it the way you want him to, we will need to stop and start this over again. So you're [wife] the director of this.

[The couple then enacts the scene: The wife is not satisfied with the result and the scene is repeated several times until she is satisfied. The roles are then reversed and the husband asks his wife to enact a scene that he chooses to direct. Following this, I ask about what brought them in to therapy. The husband describes a growing distance between him and his wife and wanting to be closer; the wife talks about needing a better way to talk to one another with mutual respect and to let go of "baggage" that has accumulated. I use the material that each partner presented in the early part of the session to instill hope for the possibility for change and to focus in on one goal that both partners agree is important.]

*Therapist:* From what I've been hearing I think the two of you have a lot of strengths and resources to bring to bear in improving your relationship. You [husband] were talking about your tolerance, your understanding, your ability to listen and to keep your cool under pressure. You [wife] were describing your capacity to listen, to be nurturing and understanding, and to get things accomplished. And your ability to learn, change, and be flexible is also important in turning this situation around. Both of you agree that you would like to see changes in your relationship to get back a certain spontaneity and closeness and communication that you both experienced at an earlier point in your relationship. Unfortunately, sometimes to get that spontaneity back it is necessary to do the reverse, that is, to do more planning, to look at things more closely.

If you do want to come back, I have a suggestion. [They agree they do want to come back for another session.] I wonder if you could do some thinking about things you did before you had kids and all the responsibilities . . . and see if there is one thing that you used to enjoy doing together that you're not currently doing now, but would both enjoy, something you can reclaim from those times you remember being happier and more content. It could be something simple like going out to the movies or dancing. Are you willing to do this?

*Husband:* We could look back at some of our old photos.

*Therapist:* Yes, that might be very helpful.

We met another five times over a period of 2 months. Although experiencing some "ups and downs" over this time frame, the couple was able to increase their closeness and intimacy with one another and reclaim some spontaneity that had been missing for a while. They attended a couples workshop together and began doing the exercises suggested there. At the final session they were working together more harmoniously and were both pleased with the progress made. Starting the session off with strengths helped set the stage for their resourcefulness in reclaiming the intimacy and closeness they both were seeking. Most importantly, their having taken action steps outside of the therapy context was a major factor in their achieving a successful outcome.

## Couple 2: Creating Change Through Reflective Listening

This couple came to therapy because the wife felt she gets no emotional support from her husband when she becomes frustrated and overwhelmed in dealing with their three young children. According to the wife, "I need support . . . I want him to acknowledge my feelings." They both took a parenting course on techniques of "reflective listening," and the wife was hoping her husband could put those skills to use in listening to her. With this couple I ask them to enact a scene that meets the wife's expectations for support. We run through this scene multiple times before the wife feels satisfied with her husband's response. The wife stated her goals as "I need to learn how to stay cool—but also want him to support me more."

*Therapist:* Let's stay with that for a minute [wanting her husband's support]. You know what you'd like him to say to support you more. Okay. What I'd like you to do is role play this scene in the way you'd like it to be. Let's assume you're frustrated after having a tough day with the kids and you're going to let your husband know. Your job [to husband] is to provide support in the ways your wife wants it. You have to do it in a way that's believable or we'll have to run through this again.

*Wife:* So, I should tell the circumstance of what just bugged me, right?

*Therapist:* Yes. Let him know you're frustrated in the ways you usually do.

[The wife begins to express her frustration and upset in dealing with the children.]

*Husband:* You did the right thing in putting the kids upstairs.

*Wife:* But they're relentless. They call me on the intercom and then I can't control my screaming. All I do is scream at them.

*Husband:* It's hard. You just need to try not to scream.

*Wife:* I know.

*Husband:* Keep your voice low . . . keep it low.

*Therapist:* Hold on a minute. He's trying to give you solutions. Is that what you're wanting? What do you want?

*Wife:* It's funny you brought that up, because a lot of times I get mad when he tries to tell me what to do, but I know he's trying to help me in his way. I do want solutions when I talk with my girlfriends, but from him I want understanding and support.

*Therapist:* Okay, let's get back to business.

*Wife:* I just want you to say, "I know you're frustrated . . . . "

*Husband* [mimicking wife]: "I know you're frustrated . . . you're doing a great job."

*Wife:* "You're trying hard . . . you feel overwhelmed." You can say to me, "I see you're overwhelmed. What can I do to help?"

*Therapist* [getting frustrated, too]: So, that would be good, just that piece. "I can see you're frustrated, you're feeling overwhelmed . . . ."

*Husband:* I can see you're frustrated. What can I do to help?

[Toward the end of the session]

*Therapist:* I'd suggest you take every opportunity to practice this [giving support] at home. Okay? And keep a coin available. It seems like a small thing, but it can help break the cycle . . . because there's a critical point whether to respond and get pulled in or make the decision not to. Depending on what you choose, the outcome will be different. With the coin, if it comes up "heads," feel free to respond to the kids in the usual way. You don't have to but you can. If it comes up "tails," do something different.

*Husband:* I think the coin flip thing is good.

*Therapist* [to husband]: And you need to practice expressing your under-standing. Let's start simple and see where we go, okay?

[Followup session, 2 weeks later]

*Wife:* You know what I've been doing? I tell them [the kids] to go to their room and before you know it they're playing quietly.

*Therapist:* How did you do that?

*Wife:* I just tell them to stay up there and they've been listening. "If you want to fight, go upstairs and fight." But they don't fight upstairs. They play. We also stopped having TV on all the time, which was interfering with their lis-tening.

*Husband:* Things are much better.

*Therapist:* Did you have an opportunity to use the coin?

*Wife:* I've kinda done it without the coin. Like, I've been reading a lot. Last week when Joe came home the house was destroyed and I was sitting there reading. Wow! I just said I'm going to read, and the kids were having a blast.

*Therapist:* You were just reading and relaxing? How did you accomplish this in the midst of all that chaos?

*Wife:* I just said I'm going to sit down and read and ignore them. And I did!

*Therapist:* Wow!

*Husband:* It was nice, but the house was a wreck. Angela had to go out that night and I was left with the mess. I was saying, "Oh man, I've got to pick it all up."

*Wife:* Someone's got to do it. The first weekend, after our last visit, I had to go to the hospital to spend time with my aunt, so he was in charge. And by Sunday night he was acting like me. He was saying, "I feel like I'm going a hundred miles an hour . . . Oh, my god." He was a maniac.

*Therapist:* Did you like that?

*Wife:* I loved it! [everyone laughing] And he did that reflective listening, and I burst out laughing. It was in the morning, and I was trying real hard to not freak out [with the kids] and I see his head peeking out of the bed. It was his morning to sleep in, and he goes, "I can see you're really frustrated . . ." and I ran in and jumped on him and we were laughing. Then all the kids ran in to see what we were laughing about. So when he finally says it, I burst out laughing.

As this example demonstrates, repetition of a sequence of behavior in the office can lead to some useful and humorous results that can arise quite spontaneously. Let's look now at a format for developing tasks in therapy.

# GENERATING HOMEWORK: A POTPOURRI OF IDEAS

Brown-Standridge (1989) has developed a useful structure for designing homework in therapy.[1] My adaptation of her paradigm is shown in Figure 3-1. I have organized tasks according to the client's readiness to take action—that is, the customer, complainant, and visitor positions discussed earlier. The tasks in any of the quadrants can be used with customers; tasks from quadrant B would be most effective with complainants, and those from quadrant D with visitors. Obviously, the best homework tasks are ones that clients generate themselves out of the clinical conversation. For example, with one couple the partners decided to develop lists of ways that each felt cared about by the other. The lists were then exchanged. So now, rather than trying to "read each other's minds" about what they needed from the other, they could simply refer to their list. At times, however, clients do not come up with their own idea for action, and in these instances I will suggest some activity that builds on our conversation together. Over time I have become less directive, offering suggestions and ideas in a more consultative capacity, and leaving the manner of implementation to the clients. I have also become more "transparent" in my presentation of ideas, openly sharing the thinking behind my suggestions.

Tasks can be categorized as either behavioral (*doing* something) or non-behavioral (*thinking* about something). A thinking or "noticing" task may be useful for someone who has not as yet moved into the customer position because it doesn't put pressure on the client to engage in any new behaviors. If you recall, in the transcript of Rose and Tony discussed in Chapter 2, Rose (who was not in a state of customership) was asked to simply *notice*

|  | *Behavioral* | *Nonbehavioral* |
|---|---|---|
| *Direct* | **A**<br>Straightforward homework tasks | **B**<br>Thinking and noticing tasks |
| *Indirect* | **C**<br>Therapeutic suggestions | **D**<br>Messages, anecdotes, stories |

**FIGURE 3-1   Task Construction Paradigm**

Adapted with permission from M. D. Brown-Standridge, *Family Process, 28,* 1989, p. 477.

when her husband walked away from potential conflicts with their son. Thinking tasks are also effective with clients when you want to discourage moving too quickly in a certain direction. They allow clients to mobilize their thoughts and consider their decisions. Tasks are "direct" if offered straightforwardly. "Indirect" tasks simply seed ideas and are presented as possibilities for the client to think about. They do not require action by the client. Direct tasks are useful for people who are at the customer stage, ready to take action. Indirect tasks are useful for people whose goals and levels of motivation are less clearly defined. Figure 3-2 provides examples at each level of task construction.

The suggestions and homework that are presented next are offered as examples of tasks generated out of the clinical conversation and are *not*

---

**FIGURE 3-2    Task Construction Paradigm: Examples**

---

**Behavioral/Direct [A]. Therapist suggests action steps based on the clinical conversation:**

---

1. "Do one good thing for yourself each day."
2. "Surprise your wife by doing something unexpected that she would like."
3. "Keep track of what is happening (what you are doing) on those days when you're *not* feeling depressed."
4. "Allow yourself 20 minutes each evening to worry, making sure you spend the full 20 minutes engaged in this activity" (paradoxical).

---

**Nonbehavioral/Direct [B]. Therapist makes suggestions that do not require action or behavioral change:**

---

1. "Think about something you could do that would be totally different from your usual way of approaching your husband about his drinking, yet might help you worry less."
2. "Notice when your wife is acting in the ways you would like."

---

**Behavioral/Indirect [C]. Therapist encourages the client to find his or her own solutions:**

---

"I wonder if you visited your father's grave and got his advice about this problem, what he might say."

---

**Nonbehavioral/Indirect [D]. Therapist seeds ideas by suggestion:**

---

[Woman coming to see therapist after losing the house she lived in for 50 years]
"Losing your house is like a turtle losing its shell. You're all vulnerable and exposed. I wonder how a turtle goes about growing a new shell."

---

*meant as formulas to apply out of context.* My hope is that these ideas will serve as a stimulus to your own thinking and creativity. As Brown-Standridge pointed out (1989), "When [clients] sense that tasks are just being unloaded on them, as they would for anyone that comes down the assembly line, they may be polite enough to agree to the therapist's wishes, but they may not return for a follow-up visit" (p.472). What follows are examples of direct and indirect behavioral tasks (quadrants A and C in Figure 3-1). The reader is referred to the work of Milton Erickson for numerous examples of indirect, nonbehavioral tasks, including the use of metaphor and story (e.g., see Haley, 1973; Rosen, 1982).

## Giving Permission

Sometimes clients may simply need permission to take steps that in their better judgment they know they need to do but haven't. For example, with a couple who were struggling with the adjustment to having a first child (and getting into arguments when the husband arrived home from work at the end of the day) I suggested the husband consider taking 20–30 minutes after arriving home to "unwind" in a way that would allow him to be more fully present with his wife and child. The wife agreed this would be useful and that she would prefer that he take this time rather than be a "bear" at this important transition point in the day. As it turned out, the husband reported only needing to take this option on two occasions in a 2-week period, but "knowing I could do this made me feel much better." The wife reported that her husband was calmer, more available to her, and more involved with their infant as well.

With another couple in which one of the partners did not want to have sex I offered the idea of engaging in "pleasuring exercises" that did not lead to sexual relations but simply offered a way to have physical contact without any "heavy" expectations. In this situation the partner who did not want to have sex would initiate the process (when, where, how) and the more interested one would follow her instructions. Both members of this couple found the exercise very helpful in making them feel more connected with one another. In some situations I will ask clients to write letters to a deceased parent with the goal of getting the parent's permission or blessing to take some step or make some change in their life.

## Seeking Advice

Some tasks involve asking clients to seek out advice from family and friends or by visiting the grave site of a lost loved one to draw on that person's wisdom. This kind of task is especially useful when the client already knows what steps are needed and simply requires permission to take action. At other times it allows clients to take stock of their situation and reflect on their needs and options.

## Mobilizing

In the clinical illustration discussed earlier, my encouragement of Shirley to "do something that surprises your husband and that is good for you" is an example of a mobilizing task. Other examples include encouraging people to attend an AA meeting or two "just to see what it's about" or to try something new and different in dealing with a "stuck" situation. The goal is to mobilize people to action by encouraging their playfulness and risk taking, and to foster an experimental attitude, seeding ideas and possibilities: "I wonder if you did . . . , how that might impact on your life?"

## Rewarding Yourself

Rewarding tasks take the form "Do something that will be good for you." People often need permission to treat themselves well, and I never fail to get smiles from my clients when I encourage this.

## Marking Change

In many instances, clients can benefit from engaging in structured therapeutic rituals to mark important transitions in their lives (see Imber-Black, Roberts, & Whiting, 1988 for useful discussion of using rituals in therapy). This can take the form of a visit to the cemetery to acknowledge a loss, marking the permanency of a relationship outside of marriage with a celebration or party, marking the end of an affair (e.g., by burning or burying reminders), or simply marking and acknowledging successes and positive changes in some special ways. As we shall see in Chapter 4, the therapy process can also serve to "authenticate" change by marking accomplishments in more public ways.

## Detecting Exceptions

Sometimes the goal is to encourage clients to notice when exceptions to the problem occur. Because exceptions are happening frequently but are going unnoticed, this task allows people to become "competency detectors" in their own lives. Sometimes I might ask clients to notice when "anger, worry, or fear was not able to blind you to your better judgment." This can be effective in helping clients notice when their "better judgment" shows itself. With a client who had a fear her partner would leave her (which she knew was unfounded), I suggested that when she noticed this "fear" beginning to emerge, she do an "evidence search" that "talked back to the fear" and provided support for the strong commitment she and her partner felt toward one another.

With an 8-year-old boy who was struggling with nighttime fears I wondered aloud about whether he could make up a "fear-buster" book that tracked the ways he was not letting the fears run his life. He came back to the next session with a little book he had made up entitled: "Fear buster book: No more Mr. Nice Guy." He systematically kept track of his "victories" and was soon fear-free.

## Setting up Playful Experiments

Doing little experiments can be a useful way to help people notice when change is happening (de Shazer, 1985, 1988, 1991). Most people who are immersed in a problem view have come to expect "more of the same" (i.e., more "bad" days), so a "good" day is a surprising and attention-getting occurrence. To utilize good days as building blocks for further changes, it can be useful to ask clients to make predictions each evening on how the next day will go and then note the outcome. Such experiments can be helpful in opening space for clients to notice when things are going well.

Recently I saw a family in which the 11-year-old was refusing to take his evening dose of stimulant medication. Rather than allowing the parents to get into a debate with the son about the usefulness of the medication as an aid in helping him settle down and do his homework, I suggested an experiment to test the benefits of the medicine. The boy agreed that he would take the medicine on four evenings out of the next eight over a 2-week period (Monday through Thursday) and he would do so in secret without telling his parents. His parents would secretly predict whether or not he had taken his medicine and the results would be shared in our meeting after this 2-week period. The boy agreed that if his parents could guess correctly, he would resume taking his medicine on a regular basis. Viewing this as an experiment helped the son feel some sense of control and agency in the process. If he "fools" his parents into believing he took the medicine when he didn't (by getting his homework done), that is a good outcome. If he gets to see for himself that his behavior is different as a function of taking the medicine, that is also a good outcome.

## Breaking the Cycle

Because many of the issues dealt with in therapy have to do with people having been immersed or caught up in unproductive cycles or patterns of behavior, much of the work of therapy focuses on generating ideas and action steps that will interrupt these patterns and open the way for new, more satisfying ones. These tasks have been referred to as "pattern interventions" (Cade & O'Hanlon, 1994; de Shazer, 1985; O'Hanlon & Wilk, 1987; O'Hanlon & Weiner-Davis, 1989).

Take, for example, the client who when arriving home from work immediately finds herself frustrated and angry with the toys that are strewn about the living room. I might suggest to this client that she come into the house using the back door, go straight to her room, change her clothes, and then enter the family living space.

de Shazer's (1985) coin flip task is also useful in helping people get into a more playful mode that can effectively interrupt old, unproductive patterns. With parents who are dealing with a child's "out of control" behavior, for example, I might suggest the parents flip a coin—if it comes up "heads," they are to do what they normally do in dealing with the situation; if it comes up "tails," they are to "do something different." This kind of task can be effective in encouraging client creativity while "allowing" the client to not entirely give up the old way of managing the situation. Just stopping the action to find a coin can be enough to unbalance the situation in ways that create change.

The following excerpts reflect the usefulness of the coin flip task. In this situation the mother (Sandy) and one of her daughters (Amy, age 6) were getting into numerous conflicts. The mother and her two daughters lived with the maternal grandmother and the client's sister. I invited the mother to bring her mother and sister in to a session.

*Therapist:* One thought I had is to have a coin available, okay? And when a situation happens [where Amy is getting you upset], before you do anything, you flip the coin. If it comes up "heads," you do what you ordinarily would do, okay? If it comes up "tails," you have to do handle the situation in a different way.

*Mother:* Okay.

*Sister* [laughing]: That sounds like a good idea because it'll take a while, at that moment, to find a coin.

*Grandmother:* You [Sandy] are very creative. This should be very interesting.

*Therapist:* In what ways is Sandy creative?

*Grandmother:* She can come up with just what you're talking about . . . finding alternative means to accomplishing things. She's good at that.

*Therapist:* Well, this is a real opportunity to put those creative energies into practice.

*Mother:* This will be fun [all are laughing].

*Sister:* I can't wait to see it in operation!

[We met again 1 month later.]

*Therapist:* Did you have a chance to do any coin flipping over the past month?

*Mother:* I did it a lot.

*Therapist:* So, how did that work?

*Mother:* Pretty well, most of the time. The last time I flipped was just before we came here. When Amy saw me flipping the coin she quickly went to her room. I didn't even say anything . . . .

*Therapist:* You allowed her some space to handle it herself . . . to take responsibility herself.

[The mother then went on to describe several other instances when this approach was successful. I then went on to get the grandmother's perspective on changes that were happening at home.]

*Therapist* [to grandmother]: Were there some times you noticed some things different between Sandy and Amy?

*Grandmother:* I think in the beginning, especially in the first 2 weeks after our last meeting, I definitely saw, and I think her sister would agree, a marked improvement. It was almost pleasant living in our house.

*Therapist:* What was happening differently that made it pleasant?

*Grandmother:* Sandy was trying hard, being conscious of what she was doing . . . working with the children. She seemed more open. But the past week has been difficult again. But the first 2 or 3 weeks went well. And it showed in the kids.

*Therapist:* What did you notice?

*Grandmother:* I'd say for the first 2 weeks Amy didn't lose her temper at all. It appeared like Sandy was acting rather than reacting. She was being much more productive in handling situations. She listened to Amy very well . . . took time to listen, and this made a difference, I think, in her [Amy's] behavior.

*Therapist:* What difference did you see in Amy's behavior?

*Grandmother:* Instead of stomping off or screaming or doing something inappropriate, she flowed right into it . . . and cooperated.

As you can see, the coin flip task can start the ball rolling on a positive track. In this situation the month gap between appointments was too long. In fact, we had an appointment scheduled in 2 weeks, but this appointment was canceled because the mother was ill. Had we been able to meet at the 2-week point it would have been easier to amplify and reinforce the positive gains made. As it turned out, the mother was able to more easily sustain the positive changes made, after she moved out of her mother's house.

Another useful way to break a cycle is to ask that a record of the process (e.g., arguments between spouses, a child's "temper tantrums") be made public by being recorded on audio or videotape, so that the therapist can "get a better idea of what is going on" (Friedman & Fanger, 1991; Rifkin & O'Hanlon, 1989). When people take this task seriously, it never fails to produce interesting results.

## Using Magic and Metaphor

With some children who are experiencing habits that are intrusive (e.g., nail biting, masturbating) I will give them a "magic rock" that has the power to help them avoid these habits.[2] My collection of magic rocks moves from one client to another, which is what gives the rocks their power. As one client achieves success over their habit, the rock grows in power and can then be given to another child. Each magic rock becomes an embodiment of "achieved knowledges" that can aid the next child in the struggle to overcome an intrusive habit. With one adult client who was burdened and distracted by the memory of an unpleasant experience, I suggested she find a heavy rock to carry around in her purse. At that point when she felt ready to "let go" of it, she was to find a special place to bury the rock. After several months of carrying the rock around, she did find a place to bury it and reported some relief in doing so.

With one 10-year-old boy who had kicked a hole in the wall at home after a temper outburst, I suggested he and his parents take a picture of the hole and have the picture enlarged and placed in a prominent place in his room. At times when he felt himself become upset he was to look at the picture to see the "effects of the temper" as a way to remind himself of what he didn't want to do. In another situation (see Friedman, 1994) I suggested that the parents make up a sign saying "Temper in the area" as a way to remind their youngster that there had been a temper "sighting." In a situation in which the parents were concerned that their adolescent son was not "communicating" about his worries, a plan was worked out for him to leave a special object on the kitchen table whenever he was "worried" or needed to talk with his parents. They would notice this and initiate contact with him. The reader is referred to Combs and Freedman (1990) for many useful ideas on generating metaphors and designing ceremonies in therapy.

## Using Paradox

I use paradoxical tasks rarely and only in situations in which any option taken by the client will lead to a positive outcome.[3] For example, I might encourage some clients to move slowly in making changes in their lives because of possible repercussions (e.g., "Shirley," in Chapter 2). If the client decides to move slowly, that is fine; if he or she feels comfortable moving more quickly, that is also fine. By not pushing people to change too fast, I am opening space for them to move at their own pace (Fisch, Weakland, & Segal, 1982).

Over time in my practice I have moved to a position of greater "transparency" with clients. Rather than simply presenting an idea or paradoxical instruction without explanation, I now offer them more insight into my thinking about the task. For example, with one young man who was waking in the middle of the night and then having trouble falling back to sleep I suggested that he create an ordeal for himself (see Haley, 1984) that might help with this problem. If he woke up and 20 minutes went by without falling back to sleep, he was to get up, move to his desk, and do schoolwork for 30 minutes before returning to bed. He was to repeat this until he fell asleep. I explained to him that no matter which option he chose, something good would come out of it. The reader is referred to Madanes (1981) for examples of paradoxical interventions.

Sometimes a straightforward suggestion may be given with the hope that the client will consider the usefulness of taking the step as a way out of an unsatisfying pattern of behavior. For example, with one man who was having difficulties with both his wife and his stepson I suggested that during times of stress, instead of moving toward his wife, who viewed his pursuing her as "neediness," he move toward his stepson with whom he was feeling estranged. I explained to him that doing so would not only improve his relationship with his stepson but would increase his wife's appreciation as well. He acknowledged what I was saying as useful and was prepared to give it a try.

## A Practical Exercise

The following excerpt is from a consultation session with a family. The mother was concerned with her 10-year-old son Ben's negative comments, like "I hate my life . . . I wish I was dead." The therapist, in the course of a conversation with the mother and son, began to understand these comments as related to Ben's recent frustrations at home and not as intentions to hurt himself. The following dialogue ensued. *As the therapist, what task or assignment might you suggest based on the previous discussion?* Also notice how the therapist uses a process of externalizing the problem, to engage the youngster in the therapy process.

*Therapist:* When you say those words like "I hate my life" and those kinds of things, how much is "frustration" talking and how much is Ben talking? Who's saying those words?

*Ben:* It's frustration.

*Therapist:* It's "frustration" saying it, not Ben. And do you have some ideas—I'm sure you do have some ideas—about what Ben can say when "frustration" starts to talk for him?

*Ben:* I didn't mean it.

*Therapist:* So, you can say something to yourself . . . like you didn't mean it.

*Ben:* Yeah.

*Therapist:* Are there other things you can think of when "frustration" takes your voice? Because it really sounds like "frustration" comes around sometimes and sometimes you don't know when it's going to come. This morning, "frustration" just showed up at your doorstep. Maybe there are some ways that you can figure out to know that "frustration" is in the area, so you can keep your voice from being taken over by "frustration." In listening to you, that's what I was hearing—that those words coming out of your mouth—was "frustration" talking and not the words that Ben wants to use.

Before reading further, take a few minutes to develop a simple task for the family that builds on this interaction.

In this situation the therapist asked Ben to keep track of those things he does that keep "frustration" from intruding into his life. He and his mother were to keep a chart of how Ben was doing in preventing "frustration" from taking his voice. As Ben gained increased awareness of his ability to not let frustration dominate his actions, his negative self-directed comments diminished.

Any tasks given will work better if they emerge from the context of the session rather than being mechanically imposed. Although it is tempting to want to use techniques and strategies that others have used with some success, it is important to keep the context in mind and not become enamored with the idea of producing a standard magical intervention that will work wonders. One goal of a task is for clients to carry something with them from the session to their life in the outside world. At times I use a "prescription pad" (a simple, two-part, 4" × 6" form) to jot down several action steps that the client and I have agreed would be useful. I then give the client the original and keep the copy for my records. A letter to the client is another medium for putting ideas in concrete form in a way that the client can refer to over time. The next section will explore how letters can be effectively incorporated into the therapy process.

## THE USE OF LETTERS IN THERAPY

Letters written by therapist to the client can be a very effective way to amplify and reinforce ideas discussed in therapy. These ideas serve as springboards to action, planting seeds that offer opportunities to experiment with new modes of behavior and interaction. People like to receive personal letters, and the letter is a concrete document that can be referred to at later points (reread as needed). Letter writing makes concrete the ideas discussed with clients, further amplifies and highlights exceptions, and opens the door to action possibilities (Menses, 1986; White & Epston, 1990). Although letter writing can be very time-consuming, I find it helps me to articulate my ideas more clearly. Since preparing letters does require an investment of time and energy, I don't write to everyone I see. In some instances I simply write one letter after the initial visit to summarize and expand upon issues discussed. I am more likely to write to a client when I feel I have not clearly enough expressed my thoughts at the end of a session or when I think it will be useful for the client to have the opportunity to refer back to the letter between sessions.

Although requiring time to compose, letters can be a very time-effective way to communicate to clients. A recent survey conducted by Nyland and Thomas (1994) found that "the average worth of a letter was 3.2 face to face interviews" (p. 39), with some participants rating the letter as worth many as ten sessions! Over 50 percent of the participants attributed the gains made in therapy to the letters alone. David Epston (reported in White, 1995, p. 200) found that a letter was worth about 4.5 sessions "of good therapy." A particular benefit of the letter is its value as a written record that documents the clients' preferences and hopes and that can be read and reread as needed. It can also serve as a public and nonpejorative record of the session and can be used in place of other, more private notes. The reader is referred to Epston (1994), Epston and White (1990), and Menses (1986) for other ideas and practices in regard to letter writing.

As we shall see, in the clinical situation discussed in Chapter 6 the client's response to my initial letter was so positive that I felt compelled to continue. That doesn't always happen. In addition, my writing to her inspired her to begin writing to me. This was something I neither anticipated nor initially encouraged. In fact, the client also began writing to her son as a way to allow herself to be heard without getting a defensive response from him. Here are some examples of letters sent to clients followed by an outline of the characteristics or structure for writing a therapeutic letter.

## *Letter to an Individual*

Dear Margie,

I wanted to write after our meeting yesterday to share some thoughts I had. It appears that Sadness and Depression have crept into your life and have tried to take control. However, 70% of the time, you told me, you have found ways to keep Depression from taking over. In light of how powerful these feelings can be, I am impressed with your efforts to keep Sadness and Depression from completely running your life. You also mentioned that you are fortunate to have a positive relationship with your parents, and I was certainly impressed with your mother's efforts to improve her relationship with you.

You said there were times when you did feel happy, like when you had your artwork exhibited and when the literary magazine that you edit was published. This tells me that you have the capacity for true joy. However, right now that joy seems to be restrained and may be sitting just below the surface, waiting for the right moment to show itself. I wonder in what ways you can set the stage for the joy that lies just below the surface to emerge. Please let me know what ideas you have about how this can happen.

When we met I asked you to notice those moments when you do feel happy and satisfied, even if they are quite brief—and to allow yourself to experience, for as long as possible, the good feelings that come with that satisfaction. This may take some effort, since Depression and Sadness have been working overtime to convince you that your life is unhappy and full of problems.

I also asked if you would keep track of your state of happiness on a day-to-day basis (using a 0-10 scale: "10" = happiest; "0" = least happy) so that we can better understand the ways you find to keep Depression from ruining your life. Another idea I had that may help give Depression the boot is to pretend (on maybe 3 days out of 7 in a week—you decide which ones) that the "miracle" happened, and you were experiencing the happiness and sense of energy you desire. You could then keep track of the differences between "miracle" days and other days.

I look forward to meeting with you on _____ .


Sincerely,

Steven Friedman, Ph.D.


## Letters to Couples

Dear Cindy and Bob,

I'm writing to offer some thoughts I had after our last meeting. It seems that the pattern of mutual blaming, suspiciousness, and distrust that has developed has been wreaking havoc on your relationship. My sense is that both of you would prefer a life free from the influence of these forces, a life based on mutual respect and caring. By freeing yourself from the influence of these patterns you will be creating space for new, more satisfying ways of being together.

Men and women are often socialized differently. For example, men often find themselves using power tactics or more aggressive behaviors when under stress. Women tend to more easily put others' needs ahead of their own. I wonder if these ways of relating are ones that are comfortable to you or whether you would prefer to stand up to these societal beliefs in ways that would allow you to grow closer together.

I wonder how your relationship will look when each of you decides not to fall prey to either the influence of suspiciousness and blame or to the gender-trained ways each of you learned growing up. You have both indicated that you want a relationship built on trust and mutual respect—rather than one based on blame and intimidation. When patterns of blame and suspiciousness become a much smaller part of your ways of being together, what benefits do you think this will have on you and on your children?

I would encourage each of you to keep track of what you're doing, and what your partner is doing, to create a life together that is not determined by forces of suspiciousness, blame, or intimidation. By not falling prey to these powerful and potentially destructive patterns you will be creating a new future, one based on mutual respect and caring. I would suggest you keep track of the ways you do not cooperate with these patterns but act to free yourself from their influence over you.

I look forward to hearing about the ways you are working together to create a more satisfying life for both you and your children.


Sincerely,

Steven Friedman, Ph.D.


Dear Lucy and Mark,

I wanted to write to you with my thoughts after having our last meeting.

Under your weight of obligation, Lucy, I sense in you feelings of percolating joy and freedom that have been hiding away. This weight of obligation has had the unfortunate effect of pushing you in ways that have prevented these positive feelings from emerging. What you, Lucy, described as a feeling of "deadness" inside seems to reflect the cumulative effects of the weight of obligation that oppresses and constrains your joy in living and interferes with your feelings of intimacy and connection. I wonder how you can counteract the oppressive constraints that entice you into this trap of obligation. I wonder what you are already doing when you resist the urge to allow obligation to dominate your life. I am curious about how your standing up to obligation (not complying with obligation's demands) will allow you to experience the joy, excitement, and peace of mind that is ready to emerge.

Mark, you described your wish for you and Lucy to again experience a common dream or set of goals. I wonder how the two of you can reclaim your dreams and develop a renewed vision of the future. I would encourage each of you, independently, to spend 30 minutes or so generating ideas about your own dreams and putting this in writing. Then take about an hour or so and share these dreams with each other. I am curious to hear about how you can again weave together your dreams to form a tapestry of hope and connection.

Sincerely,

Steven Friedman, Ph.D.

Dear Fran and Bill,

I wanted to share some thoughts I had after our last session. I was touched by the mutual respect that I observed in your relationship and with the comfort and ease you showed in relating to one another. Although Fran reported that you did have an argument, you were able to "fight fair." I wonder how the two of you created this opportunity to deal with conflict in a nonviolent way.

Each of you seems to be carrying around old dinosaurs from the past. As I was listening to you, Fran, it seemed to me that you've developed an expectancy that when things are going too well, something bad will always happen. In regard to your husband, it's an expectation that Godzilla will reappear and wreak havoc on your life. I wonder what you need to experience that would allow you to give up carrying the burden of this expectation around with you. At what point will this dinosaur become extinct?

Bill, from your past experiences you seem to have generated the idea that you have to be tough or people will walk all over you. By doing this you've successfully submerged your calm, gentle, understanding side. My sense is that you're committed to overcoming those historical restraints that have prevented your calm and understanding side from fully developing. I would be interested in hearing from you about situations where you experience being respected while allowing your gentle side to come out and where you notice yourself standing up to the old dinosaur blueprint.

I know that you, Bill, as you mentioned in our initial meeting together, prefer that your wife feel respected and loved by you rather than intimidated and frightened. You are fortunate to have such a loyal and loving wife who can see through your dinosaur exterior to your gentle, understanding side that seems ready to emerge more fully. You may be ready soon to turn in your Godzilla suit for one that fits you better.

I wonder if you, Fran, would be willing to notice those things that indicate Godzilla is no longer haunting your house and find ways to celebrate his departure with your husband. And, Bill, I wonder if you would be willing to continue to keep aware of what you do that allows you to handle frustrations calmly yet assertively. In doing so you will not only be building trust with your wife but helping her to let go of her old dinosaurs. As your lives become more your own, you will no longer be slaves to old "extinct" expectations and traditions.


Sincerely,

Steven Friedman, Ph.D.

## *Letters to Families*

Dear Mr. and Mrs. French, Myra and Sam,

I wanted to write to you after our last meeting to review some of my thoughts. It seems to me that tension has gotten a stranglehold on the family in a way that creates distance, irritability, anger, and sadness. It is tension that is forming a wedge between people and not allowing the closeness, caring, compassion, and concern that exist in the family to present themselves. It is clear that everyone in the family wants to be free from the oppressiveness of the tension.

I wonder how you can create a life in which the cloud of tension, instead of growing in size and looming in everyone's horizon, evaporates, enabling each of you to more fully experience the harmony and closeness you desire. I'm interested in learning how you can prevent yourselves from becoming slaves to the tension, the ways that allow you to experience the warmth and sunshine that family relationships can provide. I was interested in hearing about Sam's comment to you (Mrs. French) that "you have no life." Tension has a way of distracting us from more important things. Tension can be a powerful force in creating space through alienation, rather than providing space to allow people to be who they are. I wonder how you can team up to dispel the cloud of tension and provide space for the respect, care, and love that your family desires.

I look forward to seeing you on _____ and hearing about the ways you've found to free yourselves from the grip of tension.


Sincerely,

Steven Friedman, Ph.D.

### [One month later]

Dear Mr. and Mrs. French, Myra and Sam,

I wanted to let you know that I was impressed with the glimmers of progress I noticed in your efforts to keep tension from dominating your lives. Sam, you seem to have a special talent at debating, in preparation no doubt for a career in law or public advocacy. This is very admirable, although at times this quality runs you headlong into clashes with your parents and sometimes even with your sister. You should know that a good lawyer reserves his best arguments for those very important issues and avoids "spending himself" over the small stuff.

Myra, you seem to do a good job of not letting the tension push you around. However, at times that means staying outside the house, away from your family. I wonder how you can stay a participating member of the family while still enjoying your outside interests.

In light of your beginning progress, Mr. and Mrs. French, in dispelling the cloud of tension in your household, I would suggest that each of you note when and how you've been able to keep yourselves from being a slave to the tension . . . . I would be curious to see the ways you devise to reclaim your happiness from tension's grip. I also wonder what would happen if you, Sam, or your parents stopped defending yourselves. Please keep me posted on your progress.


Sincerely,

Steven Friedman, Ph.D.


Dear Mr. and Mrs. Jones and Sharon,

I wanted to write to share some of my thoughts after our meeting last week. For one, I was very impressed with how well you, Sharon, did in the month of June in freeing your life from the clutches of asthma. It is not easy to keep the asthma from pushing you around. I know that some of the past months prior to June were particularly difficult ones and that the asthma had you cornered and really put you to the test. Now that you have let the asthma know that you won't give up, you are in an even better position to take back control of your life so that you can enjoy the things that other 13-year-olds do. It sounds like being active (exercising) and having something to look forward to as you did in August are one way to give the asthma the boot.

I am also impressed with the efforts of each of you, Mr. and Mrs. Jones, in preventing the asthma from totally dominating your lives. As parents who are concerned about the health of their children I know that it would very easy to let the asthma direct and determine your actions and activities and become the total focus of your lives. The two of you, however, have somehow been able to give asthma the message that you won't let it prevent you from pursuing and maintaining your own interests and enjoyments.

As I mentioned at our meeting, I am interested in hearing more about the ways each of you has found to free yourselves from asthma's grip. I know that the asthma can really give a family a hard time and that there have been points in the past when the whole family needed to pull together to keep asthma at bay (and did, successfully). As I'm sure you know, the asthma can be very sneaky and come in and take over a family and make their lives miserable with worry and upset. I am pleased to see that no matter how troublesome the asthma has been in the past, your family has had success in maintaining your own life free from asthma's hold.

I look forward to meeting with you on ____ and hearing about the ways you continue to reclaim your lives from the perils of asthma.


Sincerely,

Steven Friedman, Ph.D.

What do all these letters have in common? For one, they all emphasize ways the individual, couple, or family have found to free their lives from a dominant force, be that a medical condition, a pattern that has interfered with the couple's satisfaction, or a feeling state that, on occasion, dominates the client's life (White & Epston, 1990). As a therapist I am constantly looking for "exceptions" to the old story or problem picture. I also ask questions in these letters that encourage clients to notice certain aspects of their behavior, paying special attention to the times and ways the client does not fall prey to the old story or script. This externalizing process places the "problem" as an objectified force that is imposing on the client's life and relationships and asks the client to begin to detect behaviors that are contrary to this old story (in effect, taking action steps toward a preferred future). Also, the letters document the client's preference for generating a life that is free from these imposing forces—a future-oriented perspective. As we shall see in Chapters 6 and 7, other variations on these themes are possible. I would encourage you to experiment with your own personal style of letter writing.

## Practical Exercise

Think about a client with whom you're currently working and draft a letter that (1) externalizes the problem as a force that is oppressing or subjugating the client, (2) maps the influence of the problem on the client's life and relationships (talks about how the problem has been impacting or intruding on various domains of the client's life), (3) outlines the beginning of a new story, and (4) generates a task (action steps) that suggests the client notice behaviors that contradict the problem-saturated story and affirm the emergence of the new story. The ideas listed here are simply one way to organize a letter using a narrative perspective. Obviously, you will have more success with your letters if you write them in your own personal style rather than being constrained by "rules." Doing so will make your sincerity and authenticity apparent to the reader.

## KEY IDEAS IN THIS CHAPTER

- Set the expectation that the client will be an active partner in the change process.
- Encourage an experimental, exploratory frame of mind in therapy in which new actions taken lead to new understandings (knowledge is participatory, not instructive).
- Make each session count: "What can we accomplish today?"
- Build on client competencies, successes, and resources. Encourage the client to track exceptions.
- Introduce opportunities to experiment with novel alternatives and/or give clients permission to act in ways that support their own good judgment. Encourage clients to be "consultants to themselves" (Epston, White, & Ben, 1995).
- Define the change process as hard work. Applaud small steps taken in a positive direction. If the goal is not attained, begin the cycle again.
- When problems or concerns reappear, draw on the client's resourcefulness and expertise in getting back on track.
- Letter writing, although time-consuming, has multiple benefits to both the client and the therapist, providing a permanent, nonpejorative record of the therapy.
- Time-effective therapy in the possibility frame, rather than having a goal of "cure" or "personality reorganization," simply sets the stage for clients to take small steps into a preferred future, opening doors to further change.

## NOTES

1. I wish to thank Simon Budman, Ph.D., for introducing me to this homework structure.

2. I wish to thank Steven Feinberg, Psy.D., for originally suggesting and experimenting with this idea.

3. Paradoxical tasks, when introduced in an atmosphere of understanding and respect, can be especially effective in opening space for client change.

# ▶ 4

---

# Talking Heads:
# The Reflecting Team
# as Consultant

*The creative act . . . does not create something out of
nothing; it uncovers, selects, re-shuffles, combines,
synthesizes already existing facts, ideas, faculties, skills. The
more familiar the parts, the more striking the new whole.*
*—ARTHUR KOESTLER*

You've just completed a difficult session with a family with whom you've
had four previous contacts, with no substantial progress in sight. The MCC
allotted you six sessions to complete the work and now you are feeling
"under the gun" to make something happen. You know from your previous
experience that working under this kind of pressure does not generally lead
to a successful outcome. In fact, it is more likely that your sense of frustration
will only further bog the therapy down. You realize that a consultation
would be helpful in getting yourself and the family unstuck. You can always
grab a colleague in the hallway, or you could go back to your books and consult with the gurus of the field in a search for new ideas. Another possibility
is to recruit a colleague or two and suggest to the family that they come in for
a consultation with this group. Your colleague(s) can serve as an idea-generating resource for both you and the family.

While at first glance, drawing on the time and resources of two or more
professionals may seem to be an expensive option, growing evidence suggests that such consultations can be time-effective. Considering the press for
productivity and resource management, an HMO may seem like a strange

place to do this kind of consultation with multiple professionals. However, my experience has been that, when used selectively and judiciously, such consultations can move the therapy process forward very dramatically. In the setting in which I work, team consultations are scheduled on a twice-a-month basis during administrative team time. So, in fact, these sessions actually provide an additional hour of clinical service beyond what is expected. Even outside of staff model HMOs, therapists can join together to develop mechanisms for clinical consultation that allow for mutual collaboration in complex clinical situations. Such consultation arrangements, while requiring time and effort to establish, will pay off substantially in more efficient clinical practice. A further benefit of these consulting sessions is the building of trust among colleagues and the learning and growth stimulated by joining together in a common endeavor.

In this chapter we'll look at several ways to incorporate consulting teams in the therapy process. Emphasis is placed on a *collaborative* approach using a reflecting team, in which discussions about clients happen in their presence rather than behind closed doors (Friedman, 1995). Before moving into the logistical details of team practice, some theoretical ideas are presented.

## THE THEORETICAL BASIS FOR REFLECTING TEAMS

For people to learn and change, new information is required (Bateson, 1972). How do we as therapists help clients expand their perceptual fields in ways that open new options and pathways? As a possibility therapist, I am constantly on the alert for novel angles or alternative views from which to consider any particular situation.

Looking at a situation from a single angle provides only a limited view and perspective. Early experiments on human learning demonstrated that when people become "fixed" on a particular mode of solution development, they experience significant difficulty shifting to more effective and more economical strategies even when these alternatives appear quite evident (see Woodworth & Schlossberg, 1954). "Tunnel vision" leaves people vulnerable to missing cues and alternatives that are present. As Varela (1989) has stated, "To let go of a fixed viewpoint . . . is the key to human sanity" (p. 22). The therapist must always be thinking of how to help people move out of the "box" (and linear thinking about the problem) and into a new, expanded level of perception and action. Fortunately, humans are "hard-wired" to seek information and to explore for differences (Fiske & Maddi, 1961).

Research has also found that humans and other animals find large changes (the introduction of novel or unexpected information) overwhelming and distressing (Berlyne, 1960; Carpenter et. al, 1970; Hebb, 1946); they react more positively to small changes. People are more receptive to information that is neither too familiar nor too discrepant from their current expectations (Fiske & Maddi, 1961; Hunt, 1965). Engaging in conversations that assist clients to see and acknowledge "news of difference" can generate change (Bateson, 1972). The use of a reflecting team, an "information-generating" approach, can effectively activate clients to consider new perspectives and possibilities on the dilemmas and predicaments they bring to the therapist's office.

Tom Andersen (1987), basing his work on the notion that "stuck systems" require new ideas, developed a mode of therapeutic conversation that offers clients a "polyocular" perspective on their dilemma. This approach involves a team of professionals initially observing an interview from behind a one-way mirror. After about 20 to 40 minutes the observing team and the therapist/client exchange places. The therapist and client go behind the one-way mirror and have an opportunity to listen to an unrehearsed conversation among team members. After this conversation the participants exchange places again, and the therapist inquires about the client's thoughts and perceptions based on the team's conversation.

In contrast to a strategic team whose anonymous group of experts generates messages to send into the therapy room with the goal of supporting, activating, challenging, or provoking the client to change (Papp, 1983), reflecting team members silently observe and listen to the interview. Team members then offer their ideas and thoughts spontaneously and in ways that open dialogue and make room for multiple perspectives. Reflecting team members do not attempt to arrive at a consensus or one "right" point of view, but rather to expand the perceptual field through a diversity of opinions.

The ideas generated in this way can be envisioned as "seeds," some of which will find fertile ground and some of which will lie fallow. By standing outside the therapeutic circle for a period of time, the client gains perspective and is removed from demands of the clinical interview. The pause created by exchanging places opens space for hearing in new ways and being "captured" by new information.

## THE REFLECTING TEAM AS CONSULTANT

How can the reflecting team be useful in doing time-effective therapy? What are the benefits of working this way? While all the answers to these questions are not yet in, growing data support the usefulness of the reflecting process as a consultative resource in a variety of clinical contexts and with diverse populations of clients, including settings such as psychiatric hospitals and schools, medical settings, and outpatient clinics (Friedman, 1995). The following are some of the advantages of using a reflecting team:

- Ideas are offered that open space for new understandings and options for action.
- A support structure is established such that client and consulting team are working in concert, in a more egalitarian and collaborative style.
- Sensitive issues can be raised more easily from a distance, allowing the client to "save face."
- The client is respected as a person capable of drawing his or her own conclusions and making sense of the information in his or her own unique way.
- Ideas are generated in an honest, open, and unrehearsed way, opening the door to increased spontaneity on the part of the client.
- Ideas and options raised by the consulting team can be brought back into the therapy context as a basis for future work.
- Being in the listening position diffuses conflictual interaction in couples and families and allows all parties to gain a better understanding of each other's points of view.

The results of a study by Griffith and his colleagues (1992) demonstrated significant changes on several variables in the 10 minutes prior to and following a reflecting team consultation. Family communication shifted toward more trusting, comforting, and nurturing interactions and away from more controlling, blaming and belittling behaviors. Informal research by Michael White (1995) found that one reflecting team session was worth about 5 sessions "of good therapy!" Although it increases interview time to about 90 minutes, use of a reflecting team can be a valuable and time-effective way to open the therapist-client system to change.

The following are comments solicited from clients in a research project about their experiences with the reflecting team (from Smith, Yoshioka, & Winton, 1993; Smith, Sells, & Clevenger, 1994): "The strength is in the variety . . ."; ". . . hearing them is just like hearing yourself talk."; ". . . no matter how bad something looks, there is always a good side."; ". . . you get a lot more feedback, a lot more angles."; "I think you learn options . . . . In everything the therapists say, you might find one pearl"; "It's like you're outside the problem and can see it differently." Another client reported the following, after a reflecting team experience:

> In looking back on the experience I had with the reflecting team, my memory of the experience itself was that there was a great deal of safety, respect, honesty, a sense of equality, a sense that I was involved in a community of people who were working together. So

I'm left with a very wonderful memory of that experience . . . . The experience has stayed with me, and I feel it changed me in some ways." (Janowsky, Dickerson, & Zimmerman, 1995, p. 180)

The reflecting process, as adapted for managed care, can be understood as encompassing the two mutually interactive elements discussed earlier: a widening of the therapeutic lens to incorporate multiple perspectives and ideas about the client's dilemma, and a sharpening of focus that funnels these ideas into workable action plans. The therapist and consulting team shift between widening the lens, opening space for new narratives and ideas, and sharpening the focus onto solutions and action steps. This continuous, fluid process of adjusting lenses allows the client and therapist to both entertain new ideas and co-construct preferred stories. These activities, while possible to implement as an individual practitioner, gain prominence and influence when the client or family is in a position of overhearing the consulting team's conversation rather than being spoken to directly.

This chapter is organized into two sections. The first section reviews guidelines for implementing the reflecting process and presents a variety of ways you can incorporate this format into your clinical practice. In the second section, other uses of audiences are discussed. At the conclusion of the chapter a format is presented for experimenting with the reflecting team in your own practice. In Chapter 5 you will also see the ways a reflecting team consultation is incorporated as a hope-generating resource in a complex family situation.

## THE REFLECTING TEAM: CLINICAL ILLUSTRATIONS

The reflecting team serves as a springboard for new ideas and options for action, a forum for expanding possibilities and generating hope for change. The goal is to maintain a collaborative, nonhierarchical and transparent stance by recognizing the family's expertise of lived experience. The comments of team members arise spontaneously as they connect with what clients (family members) are saying. Figure 4-1 offers a set of guidelines for putting the reflecting team into practice.

The following examples illustrate the variety of ways the reflecting team can operate in your practice.[1]

### *Altering Perception of a Problem*

The reflecting team can *generate metaphors and images that activate, intrigue, and alter the client's understanding of the problem.* This includes the idea of externalizing the problem (White & Epston, 1990). This example comes from a situa-

## FIGURE 4-1   The Reflecting Team: Structure and Guidelines

### Goals

To provide a diversity of perspectives
To enlarge the client's pool of ideas and options
To introduce ideas that will capture the client's interest and provide "news of difference"

### Structure

A. Therapist and team* meet briefly before client (family) arrives. Therapist provides minimal background information about the client, leaving this discussion for the interview process itself.
B. Team members silently observe the conversation between the therapist and client. After 30 minutes or so, the therapist tasks the client if she is ready to hear from the team. Team members then engage in a conversation among themselves, using the following guidelines.

### Guidelines for Team Conversation

1. *Be positive:* Find something hopeful; avoid hollow compliments; be affirming and compassionate. Look for possibilities: strengths, resources, and successes.
2. *Talk to one another:* Capitalize on the interest created by the client "overhearing" the conversation; when seeing a family, the reflecting team should include everyone in their comments.
3. *Frame comments in tentative,* rather than authoritative, *terms*—e.g., "I wonder . . . . Perhaps . . . . I am curious about . . . . Possibly . . . .; Comments should not be judgmental or evaluative; translate your curiosity into questions.
4. *Engage in sequential talking*—a conversation rather than a monologue; *pick up on ideas generated by others;* ask questions of other team members as a way to embed and amplify ideas (e.g., "I am curious how you came to understand the situation that way . . . ."). The notion is not to put one idea above another ("either/or") but to offer a "both/and" perspective; there is no need to develop a consensus.
5. *Look for and highlight ways the client acted contrary to the problem*—acted in ways that gained control over the problem.
6. *Generate metaphors or images* that the client can visualize and connect with; utilize metaphors that the client generated in the interview and build on these. Look for "openings" (words, cues, or themes) that have special meaning for the client (family).
7. *Use your own voice;* talk personally rather than objectively. Situate your questions/comments in your own life experience. Be transparent; use ordinary language rather than psychiatric jargon.

**FIGURE 4-1**   *(Continued)*

---

### Continuing the Process

---

C. Following 5–10 minutes of team reflections, the therapist and client resume their conversation with special focus on the team's comments. This process can be repeated one or more times during the course of the interview, allowing for a more interactive process between team and client.

---

### Time Frame

---

The interview process requires approximately 90 minutes.

---

Adapted from Andersen, 1991; Hoffman, 1989; Janowsky et al., 1995; Lax, 1995.
*The "team" can simply be the therapist and a colleague having a conversation in the presence of the client.

---

tion in which a 15-year-old (Nancy) had become the focus of her parents' anxieties and fears. The reflecting team consisted of Sally Brecher and the author.

*Sally:* A question that just got raised for me is whether the family has come under the grip of fear and whether fear has begun to take over their lives in ways they haven't been aware of . . . . I'm wondering whether there are times when the fears aren't as strong and the family doesn't get recruited into worrying so much about Nancy.

*Steven:* I like that idea. I think I can see how the fears have gotten a grip and what it ends up creating are detectives for the fears, trying to study and research and understand them better.

*Sally:* Trace their origins.

*Steven:* Trace their origins. And that in a way pulls people into the grip of the fears. That's part of the fears' power of pulling them in . . . . In some ways it feels like the fears can take such control that they can just swallow the family up . . . . Yet, like you were saying, there have been times when the fears haven't taken over completely and that Nancy has not cooperated with the fears. And again, are there some ways she can continue to do that and other ways her parents can help her not cooperate? Though it is always tempting to be a detective, the fears are really so tricky and sneaky and difficult to understand that it could become a never-ending process that could further envelop them.

*Sally:* I got the feeling that maybe the parents and Nancy were becoming exasperated by all the work they were doing on trying to understand the origin of the fears and trying to fight off the grip of the fears. I'm wondering whether it's become intolerable in the sense that they really want to begin to stand up to these fears so they don't take over their lives as you were suggesting and push them in directions that aren't particularly productive . . . . Also, I'd be very interested in how the family might have gotten recruited into this view of fears taking over their lives . . . . I'm also curious about what might be useful in helping them to reclaim their lives fear-free and to stop being recruited into this view of the world as dangerous with the fears about to take over at any point. Also, I would be interested to know what sort of ideas Nancy might have about standing up to the fears. I'd love to be a spectator at her life when she was much younger and be able to have a sense of what it is she was able to do that helped her strengthen herself and be strong in the face of difficult problems that come along . . . . It's funny, when we hear a story that is so filled with a sense of fear, it doesn't allow room for other stories about Nancy's strengths to come out. That would also be important to learn about.

This conversation, which took place while the family listened behind the one-way mirror, captured the attention of the family and altered their sense of where they needed to put their energies. The reflecting team conversation served to shift the focus of the work with the family from being detectives for the origins of the fears to being detectives for ways the family could experience a fear-free lifestyle.

## Highlighting Exceptions

Another function of the reflecting team is *to notice and comment on exceptions to the client's problem-focused view of self or others.* In the example to follow, the 12-year-old daughter was having temper outbursts. This excerpt from the reflecting team discussion involves a conversation between Sally Brecher and Amy Mayer. A full account is given in Friedman (1994).

*Sally:* I was thinking how Rose moved from 'temper talk' to 'Rose talk' and that more and more the temper isn't having a voice in what she says and what she does. First the temper was stealing her voice and now I get the feeling that she's stealing back her voice from the temper. And I'm wondering if the temper is feeling a little unhappy, saying, "I'm losing my place in this family . . . and maybe I want to act up and tempt Rose again . . . because I enjoy bossing her around." When a temper is desperate it tries to pull some dirty tricks, and I'm thinking that we can all fall for a tricky temper.

*Amy:* I was impressed about the times Rose was not letting the temper be in control. But there may be times when she doesn't realize this and that is how the rest of the family can be helpful . . . noticing and pointing out those times when Rose is in charge. The situation with the TV is a good example of how she was in charge, not the temper.

*Sally:* The temper wasn't talking, Rose was talking. I wonder if Rose and her parents can sit down and talk about when the temper isn't in control of Rose and her voice, and when the times are going well for her. Because I think the temper really has her saying things she doesn't mean like "I don't care." That doesn't sound like Rose. And Rose's parents have found ways this week to get on top of the situation and they should be commended. They haven't let the temper push them around, and Rose's not letting the temper push her around. My feeling is we're seeing real progress . . . real change.

[The reflecting team and family change places. The therapist is Cynthia Mittelmeier and the consultant is the author.]

*Therapist:* I wonder what fit for you in what the team said and what didn't fit. Who wants to start?

*Mother:* I will. It's nice to see a different perspective of what you've experienced. It's nice to hear a positive message. One thing I heard was that the real Rose is not the same Rose we see when she's angry. This is important for me to remember because I take it personally.

*Father:* They seemed to be impressed with last night, with Rose cooperating. It was nice and they felt positive about it, which is good. It gives me hope.

*Consultant:* You mentioned the step the team noticed about the TV situation. The fact that Rose had her own voice in this situation and wasn't being influenced by the temper, what does that tell you about the future?

*Father:* Hope! Maybe we can change this around. It was a nice feeling. I went to bed feeling calm. It wasn't an hour of screaming . . . . It was nice to be able to say "No" and get cooperation.

*Consultant:* And you saw that was possible.

*Father:* Yes. Right. It was. It was nice.

*Mother* [to Rose]: What do you remember about what they were saying about your voice and the temper's voice?

*Rose:* They were saying that they heard my voice and not the temper's.

*Consultant:* The goal here is really for your voice to get stronger and the temper's voice to get smaller and smaller. One of the benefits you have is that you are growing and getting stronger but the temper stays the same—so really the temper gets smaller and smaller and your voice gets stronger and stronger [demonstrates with his hands] . . . . I'm wondering if it would be valuable to have a sign. If your parents see the temper sneaking around, they can grab the sign, hold it up, post it up—"Temper in the area."

*Rose:* It would be kinda embarrassing in front of my friends.

*Consultant:* Yeah. Well, it wouldn't have to be up all the time.

*Rose* [laughing]: If my friends were over, I could just see my mother come marching along with a sign . . . .

*Consultant:* What I think would also be useful is tracking those times when Rose's voice is being heard without it being influenced by the temper.

*Mother:* Yeah. I would like to not listen anymore to the temper. Because I feel I get really hurt when I hear that voice. I think I need to say, at that point, for my own self-respect, for our relationship, I don't want to listen to that voice, because it is not you talking. And I'm going to walk away at that point.

## Generating Alternative Stories

The reflecting team can *generate alternative stories (ones different from the client's problem-saturated view) that open space for fresh perspectives.* A mother and daughter were seen for an initial session following the daughter's 3-day psychiatric hospitalization after taking an overdose of aspirin. Maria (age 17) was living with her mother and stepfather. The mother was both concerned about her daughter's behavior and angry at her for keeping things agitated at home. Maria had been "screwing up" in school and would talk back to her stepfather in ways that created friction and upset at home, putting the mother in the middle between her daughter and husband. Maria was upset with her mother for allowing herself to be pushed around by the stepfather.

The reflecting team consisted of Edward Bauman, Naami Turk, and Cynthia Mittelmeier. Madeline Dymsza and the author interviewed the family in front of the mirror. The author also joined the reflecting team. The following is the reflecting team discussion and an excerpt from the conversation with the family following the team's reflections. Notice how the reflecting team offers an alternative view about the issues presented that leads to a well-specified goal.

*Edward:* . . . I was wondering how much change is possible without Maria's stepfather being involved.

*Cynthia:* I think it may be more difficult without everyone in the same room, but I think some things can get worked out . . . in keeping Maria safe . . . so she doesn't hurt herself again. It's too scary for everyone for Maria to put herself at risk—so I think it is important for Maria and her mother to come to some agreement on the safety question. Maybe what is needed are some strategies for what Maria can do when she's feeling desperate. The other thing I was thinking about was about hope and hopefulness. I was struck by the mother's calm and hopeful demeanor. And Maria is her biggest fan. Maria seems to have tremendous love for her mother to be so protective of her . . . .

*Naami:* One thing I was thinking about was that Maria is turning 18, and while I agree with the idea that she is her mother's biggest fan, it seems like she's also trying to say "hello" and "goodbye" in the same breath. Maria and her mother could join together in helping Maria find safe ways to say "hello" and "goodbye," ways that will support her growing up and becoming more independent.

*Steven:* How do you [Naami] think they could do that? Do you have some ideas about that?

*Naami:* I think right now there are some pressing issues—Maria has had it . . . she wants to get out of the house. If staying in the hospital is more appealing than being at home, that's a pretty clear message. Maybe they could chart out a plan on paper, Plan A, Plan B—about how to support each other, and outline some of the options and choices. Since Maria is not yet 18, her mother still has a place there to put in some safeguards so that Maria is safe. What are the things they can do together to ensure her safety? What can Maria do to take responsibility for herself?

*Edward:* I also agree with you about the biggest fan idea. I also wonder whether being such a big fan, Maria has gotten the idea that she can do all kinds of things, maybe more than is reasonable to expect.

*Cynthia:* I get this feeling that Maria's mother has to choose between "my husband or my daughter." It's a very difficult position to be in. I don't really think she has to make that choice . . . but that's a press she might feel.

*Steven:* Is it possible for Maria to respect her mother's choice of a husband while knowing that it's not her choice for a stepfather—to be able to support her mother and maintain an understanding of who he is to her mom?

*Cynthia:* I think Maria was taking a step in that direction when she asked for the family meeting. She was saying, "I don't like this but I'm going to try to live with it." Maybe Maria doesn't need to fight her mother's battles. Her mother can do this on her own.

The family and team switch places. The following is an excerpt from the conversation following the team's reflections. Notice how the team's comments have shifted the mother's understanding of her daughter's behavior, as emphasized in italics.

*Steven:* We wanted to check in on things you were hearing . . . things that hit the mark and made sense to you and things that didn't fit.

*Maria:* I only do it [fight my mother's battles] because she won't do it her-self. I'm not going to let him shit all over her . . . treat her like that . . . that makes me feel worse cause she's my mother.

*Steven:* And you care about her.

*Maria:* She'll just sit there and let him do it. She thinks he'll calm down in a little while and it'll all be forgotten in the morning. And I don't want her to have to go to bed crying and all . . . so I'll say something to him.

*Steven:* So, the team was on the mark about you wanting to help your mother.

*Maria:* Yeah . . . I love her.

*Steven:* But it seems like the helping is getting you into trouble.

*Maria:* I don't care. I feel better knowing I'm sticking up for her.

*Steven:* How can you be living outside the house when you are helping your mother at home right now?

*Maria:* I can't stay there just to protect her. I'd be much happier not living there. If she wants to learn to stick up for herself she can . . . but that's up to her. She starting to [stick up for herself] lately . . . and he's getting pissed.

*Madeline:* You think if you started backing off she [mother] would pick up the ball? What do you think is enabling your mother to stick up for herself more now?

*Maria:* I guess she's sick of it. I don't know.

[Somewhat later]

*Mother:* Maria should not stick up for me. I can fight my own battles. I appreciate her concern and what she does for me, but I'm afraid it's going to hurt her . . . by getting everything agitated.

*Maria:* But it makes me feel better, to open my mouth.

*Mother:* But it doesn't solve anything.

*Maria:* Just going to your room doesn't solve it either.

*Madeline* [to Steven]: It's interesting that each of them wants the other to try their own strategy—Maria wants her mother to be more vocal and the mother wants Maria to be calmer and more diplomatic.

*Mother:* I think Maria needs a job and to get busy with school and with her own life.

*Steven:* Were there things you [mother] were hearing from the team that you wanted to comment on?

*Mother: I never realized that Maria was trying to help me. I thought she was trying to irritate the situation. I can see it now as her sticking up for me . . . .*

*Madeline:* Does it help to realize it?

*Mother:* Yes, absolutely. It makes me think that Maria needs to be focusing on her own life.

*Steven:* So, Maria staying at home is more about worrying about you [mother] than worrying about her . . . . What did you [mother] do to help Maria develop such a strong sense of herself?

*Mother* [laughing]: She used to be quiet . . . .

*Maria:* I just stick up for myself . . . .

*Steven:* I wonder how you learned to do that?

*Mother:* I was a single parent for 10 years, working two jobs and going to school, and she had to learn to be responsible . . . .

*Steven* [returning to the issue of safety]: How are you going to be able to manage in the current situation so there's no need to hurt yourself again?

*Maria:* I'm going to talk with my [biological] father this afternoon about what's been happening and ask if I can move in with him. He might be able to help. He doesn't even know I was in the hospital.

*Mother:* We need to sit down and develop some goals with Maria, her father included.

The session ended with the therapists commenting on the strengths of both mother and daughter in managing under difficult circumstances. Maria and her father and mother did meet to work out a plan in which Maria would live with him temporarily under the condition she find a job and finish school.

## *Identifying Complexities*

The reflecting team can serve to *identify and comment on aspects of self that are hidden, ignored or unnoticed, taking a humble position about the complexities of people's lives.* Often team members have an opportunity to offer thoughts that validate and normalize life's complexities. In one case a father had expressed his upset and anger in a family session. One team member offered her thoughts as a way to let him know that she understands and respects his position:

> I felt somewhat protective of the father, and I think he was trying to tell us that there is more than meets the eye and that this is a long and complicated relationship, and that perhaps we were not valuing some of the unspoken things, the hidden things; for example, the degree of loyalty that they feel toward one another, and even the degree of connectedness that is there but doesn't emerge during the time of removal from one another. I think that his comment was a

signal to us of outrage that we were minimizing in some way the many complex components of this relationship. That we have to stop perhaps at this point and give them time to reassess and absorb some of the things that were said today.

In another situation a team member normalized a difficult transitional period in a family in which the mother and daughter had been engaged in significant conflict:

[This] seems to be a certain transition where the daughter is no longer the mother's little girl . . . where the mother isn't sure how much she needs to protect, should protect, and how she can let go and let the process continue. I think it's a very painful time . . . in a way. It's [also] an exciting time because the daughter is becoming her own person . . . . This is very exciting, while at the same time there is a sadness about the mother losing the little girl that once was more dependent on her. There has been a shift, and that is not an easy time to get through. My feeling from my own experience is that, often trying to be open about things, trying to share more of my inner feelings and concentrate less on rules and limitations, sometimes is a way of maintaining the contact or the closeness while the growing is going on . . . . I think the mother has done an exceptionally good job in bringing Jane to this point. But it's bittersweet. I guess that's what I'm hearing . . . is that it is somewhat bittersweet.

## Authenticating Change

An important function of the reflecting team is to *authenticate change by making comments that embody and embed the changes in observed behavior.* The following clinical example is one that incorporates a larger professional audience in authenticating the changes made by a family over the period of several months while the adolescent was at a residential treatment center. As you read the transcript of this consultation, notice the kinds of questions the therapist is asking members of the audience to help them situate their comments in their own personal experience. By so doing, he brings forth information that amplifies change and generates hope.

Present at this meeting was the mother (Cindy) and two of her three children (Randy, age 15 and Lance, age 10). Also present were about twenty staff from the residential program that Randy had attended for 3 months and from which he recently "graduated" and several members of the child and family team from my HMO who were consulting with the residential program prior to the family being seen on an outpatient basis in the HMO. The author and a member of the residential staff acted as therapists.

*Steven* [to family]: How I thought we might structure this meeting is that we would talk for a while and then stop and hear from the others. I may ask them some questions and you can be listening in on this conversation, and then we will come back and talk again. Is that okay?

*Cindy:* Sure.

*Steven:* Maybe, Randy, you can begin by telling us what you see as your achievements in the program. I understand that you graduated recently. What were you hearing at that graduation ceremony?

*Randy:* What I needed to do was control my anger and learn how to deal with violence in my life. What I heard was what people thought about how I did around this.

*Steven:* What kinds of changes did they notice, that you made?

*Randy:* That I could manage the anger . . . . But there have been some slips here and there . . . but the violent stuff is not happening like it used to.

*Steven:* What have you done to achieve this?

*Randy:* I take a walk or go my room and listen to music. If I get aggravated I take a walk . . . .

*Steven:* You give yourself some time . . . .

*Randy:* Yeah.

*Steven:* So, over time it sounds like you've been able to be a consultant to yourself, giving yourself suggestions that have helped. Have you seen some changes, Lance?

*Lance:* Yeah. A little. He's not breaking my nose anymore.

*Steven:* That's good, cause you've got a nice nose. What else?

*Lance:* He's all happier now. He used to be all mad.

*Steven:* He's calmer now?

*Lance:* Yeah.

*Steven:* How about getting along together . . . do the two of you do okay with that now?

*Lance:* A lot better than we used to.

*Steven:* What's come out of the program for you [mother]?

*Cindy:* A lot of compliments. It's nice to hear Randy take the compliments. I still have a hard time taking compliments. I think they [the boys] definitely get along better. They still have their issues, but Randy seems to be controlling himself a lot better.

*Steven:* So how does that show itself? How does he control himself?

*Cindy:* He walks away, takes his space. We have a sign on the refrigerator that says, "Take a walk . . . listen to music."

*Steven* (to Randy):  Do you check in with the sign or do you already have that in your head?

*Randy:*  I know it.

*Steven:*  What I'm wondering is whether we can hear from the people who were working with you about thoughts that they have. [Turning to the group] I wonder if you could share one thought that would be helpful to know . . . that you've learned about Randy and his family in working with them over the past several months.

*Staff A:*  Cindy called me one night and told me that the boys were hitting each other. She was upset and said, "I don't know what to do." I said, "What did you do?" She said, "I put them each in their rooms." I asked, "Did they go?" and she said, "Yeah." I said, "You did it, then." And she said, "I can't believe after all this time I still have to call you guys." I told her, "It sounds like you set the limits and everybody listened." Looking back on it, Randy could've ended up back here, but instead Cindy set the limits and the children listened. I told her to call me back in half an hour. And she did, and everything was fine. That was impressive to see—Cindy setting a limit and getting a good response. That was a good step.

*Steven:*  What made that a big step?

*Staff A:*  Because we had worked on that—the limit setting and Randy's respecting his mother's limits.

*Steven:*  So, you were feeling like Cindy was gaining more confidence in using her own resources?

*Staff A:*  Yeah. I was really proud of her. Because in the past she wasn't confident of her decisions and Randy wasn't confident of his decisions. And so it was really nice to be able to tell her she did a great job.

*Steven:*  Knowing that Cindy took that step and was effective, what does that tell you about the future, about how this family can work together?

*Staff A:*  Well, I think they're starting to respect themselves and each other more. They are all working together as a team now and, like you said before, slip-ups will happen, but they're not the kind of big slip-ups that were happening before. It's really encouraging.

*Staff B:*  When I first met with the family, violence had a lot of control. I've been most impressed with the strong stance that each family member has been taking to decide what happens in the house in setting limits on violence.

*Staff C:*  One of the things I've noticed is Randy's maturity level. It's progressed from trying to impress other kids with violent talk to being an example for the others in gaining control over violence. He has grown in the program and became a role model. The other kids started to like him more and more. He could be himself and not have to hide behind the mask of violence. He might have a bad evening, but the next day was a new day, a chance for a new start. So he did well in letting go . . . taking space and letting things go.

*Staff D:* Although the violent behavior showed itself from time to time, we never had to put our hands on Randy. He did respond to limits. What also impressed me is how Cindy is able to deal effectively as a single parent with three very active kids. I know because I took care of them for a couple of hours one day. What a job! They can be quite a handful (all three are considered "hyperactive").

*Steven:* As violence plays less and less of a role in Randy's life and in the family's life, how do you envision Randy's life changing?

*Staff E:* I think they are developing a nice supportive system with one another, relying less and less on outside help. I've noticed that the kids are having their friends over to the house more without worrying that things will get out of control.

*Staff C:* Now that violence is not so prominent in the family, there is room for improved relationships. For the future, I would see the relationships growing stronger and closer, now that violence is not standing in the way.

*Staff E:* Things seem promising, not stuck anymore. They're moving forward, putting violence behind them.

*Staff F:* As the violence started to ease a little bit, Randy has become involved in basketball. He's even been organizing the basketball activities, putting energy into sports.

*Staff G:* What I got to see that some of the residential staff might not have is that not only Randy was moving away from violence but so was Lance. He was also taking more responsibility for himself, keeping his room organized and clean. Lance and Randy even painted his room together. Violence has a grip on the whole family and although we had Randy here [in the program], and were working to keep violence locked out, Lance was also making progress on the outside.

[Steven turns to the HMO team for their comments.]

*Sally* (to Cindy): Do you expect that as you get further and further away from violence, that you will be able to recognize more quickly when you've been successful in dealing with the children?

*Cindy:* I know I've grown. I have goals.

*Staff G:* Violence has tricked Cindy into doubting herself and her competencies. Although she frequently reacts very positively as a mother, the violence that has been part of her life can really trick her into thinking she's done something wrong . . . .

*Sally:* . . .Or hasn't been as effective as she's actually been.

*Staff G:* Yes. It's really been a big step for Cindy to recognize, that although "I can pick up the phone and call, I know I've done the right thing."

*Cynthia:* I wonder if we can talk about the violence vaccine that family members seem to have developed to keep violence away. What has helped in developing this violence vaccine?

*Randy:* Going to AA meetings has helped. I think it helps me get along with my brother. It's a twelve-step program. I'm also getting medication after the doctors found a temporal lobe problem.

*Staff G:* I think Cindy's setting limits has also been a vaccine against violence.

At the end of the meeting, Randy agreed to come back to the program, at some point in the future, as a consultant to other children struggling with similar problems.

Figure 4-2 summarizes the variety of ways one can apply the reflecting team.

Although in the material presented here several professionals are involved as a team, it is possible to do this work with one other person in addition to the therapist. In this situation the therapist, following about 20–40 minutes of the interview, would join with the "consultant," who had been observing the interview, and engage in a conversation while the client listens. The advantage of a larger group of people (three to five) serving as a team is the increased diversity of views and perspectives represented. However, the reflecting process is even possible to use when working alone with a client or family (Wangberg, 1991). With this structure the therapist simply stops at various points in the interview and offers his or her reflections while the client listens. During these "reflecting interludes" (Lax, 1995) the therapist can divert his or her eyes from the client and talk to the ceiling or focus

---

**FIGURE 4-2    Functions of the Reflecting Team**

1. To generate metaphors and images that activate, intrigue, and alter the client's understanding of the problem.
2. To notice and comment on "exceptions" to the client's problem-focused view of self or others.
3. To generate alternative stories (ones different from the client's problem-saturated view) that open space for fresh perspectives.
4. To identify and comment on aspects of self that are hidden, ignored, or unnoticed; to take a humble position about the complexities of people's lives.
5. To "authenticate" change by making comments that embody and embed the changes in observed behavior.

---

on an object in the room, creating space for the client to listen without pressure to respond immediately. A solo practitioner could also use the reflecting position by putting his or her thoughts down on paper in the form of a letter written following a session, and then sent to the client. Composition of the letter would follow the same "rules" of conversation outlined for the reflecting team (see Figure 4-1). One other point is worth mentioning. Although the examples presented in this chapter are drawn from work with couples and families, the same process is applicable to work with individual clients (see, for example, Janowsky, Dickerson, & Zimmerman, 1995).

## INCORPORATING AUDIENCES IN THE THERAPY PROCESS: REAL AND VIRTUAL COMMUNITIES

The reflecting team format outlined here is only one of many possibilities for structuring team interventions. Recently my colleagues and I have been experimenting with a new approach in which any observing team member is free to leave the observation room during an interview, knock on the therapy room door, and join the therapist and client for a brief period of time. This format allows team members to spontaneously offer an idea or raise an issue of curiosity. Not all team members may choose to actively participate during any one session, but those that do form an idea-generating "tag team" that provides multiple perspectives around which the client can connect.

Another approach (Seikkula et al., 1995) organizes the observing audience into "voices," each representing one or another family member. For example, one team member listens to the mother's "voice," while another listens to the child's "voice." A dialogue then ensues among team members (while the family listens), allowing all family members to be "heard" and a variety of viewpoints to be presented.

In addition to having professional teams observe and directly comment on the interview process, a number of other innovative possibilities exist for introducing new ideas into the clinical system. For example, Ben Furman (personal communication, July 1994), a psychiatrist in Finland, sometimes interviews a client in the presence of a professional audience. At the end of the consultation, Furman asks members of the audience to each offer, in writing, one idea that the client can take home. The client is instructed to draw on these letters in times of need, opening one at a time. Using this structure, the client leaves the session with a wealth of ideas and resources.

Another idea is based on a "virtual community" of former and current clients who communicate to one another via the therapist. David Epston, a family therapist in New Zealand, has been developing these communities or "leagues" for several years.[2] One of these groups is called the "Anti-Anorexia, Anti-Bulimia League." While not meeting as a group, members of this community are asked to write letters offering ideas on ways they managed to free their lives from anorexia or bulimia. These letters come to the therapist, who then shares this information with a current client. These "leagues" become resource banks or archives of preferred knowledges that can be circulated from one person to another. In this way the indigenous knowledge of the community is accessed in ways that remove the therapist from the role of expert with all the answers. These communities of connection and caring are powerful ways to facilitate the change process.

Another form of virtual community is the Internet computer network, which has the capacity to electronically link enormous numbers of people, all over the world. One client of mine reported that during a recent depressing time in her life she communicated about her sense of sadness on the Internet and ended up receiving hundreds of letters of support and encouragement!

On-site community rituals can also serve to authenticate changes made and offer support. Nichols and Jacques (1995) have applied this idea in a residential treatment center for adolescents. Toward the end of an adolescent's stay at the center a celebration ritual is planned to acknowledge the adolescent's accomplishments and progress in the program. This "rite of passage" takes place in the adolescent's home, and friends, relatives, and members of the community are invited.

## A Practical Exercise

Think of a clinical situation about which you feel stuck. How might a consulting team help in this process? Who could you recruit to be team members? (Remember the team does not have to be made up of professionals: the client's sister, brother, spouse, friend, parent, could also be included as a member of a consulting team.) You might also consider calling on former clients who would be willing to offer their ideas and expertise to your current clients, either through personal consultation or via letters (see Epston, White, & "Ben," 1995; Madigan & Epston, 1995, Selekman, 1995 for more details).

## NOTES

1. The reader is referred to Andersen, 1991; Doan & Bullard, 1994; Friedman, 1993, 1995; Parry & Doan, 1994; and White, 1995 for other examples.

2. See Epston, White, & "Ben," 1995; Lobovits, Maisel, & Freeman, 1995; Madigan & Epston, 1995 for further discussion of leagues.

## KEY IDEAS IN THIS CHAPTER

- Doing time-effective therapy is demanding and complex. The therapist in a managed care practice can benefit from periodic consultation around especially difficult clinical situations. Bringing in a colleague(s) to a session brings a fresh perspective and opens the door to new ideas and possibilities.
- The time-effective therapist, always on the alert for ways to expand options and generate alternative perspectives, can find much value in using a consulting team, especially around stuck or complex cases.
- The reflecting team offers the client a polyocular perspective, a diversity of ideas that relate to the client's dilemma or predicament.
- New ideas (what Bateson called "news of difference") are the building blocks of change. The reflecting team, by offering ideas respectfully and nonjudgmentally, opens the door to change.
- Problems tend to lead us into "tunnel vision"; the multiple views offered by the reflecting team enlarge the client's perceptual field.
- The magic of the reflecting team is embedded in the idea of clients "overhearing" a conversation about them. This process allows clients to take in information that fits and leave what doesn't and respects clients' capacities to choose wisely.
- The reflecting team model is easily adaptable and useful in a wide variety of clinical contexts. It can also be used by a clinician working with another colleague or even, in modified form, when working alone.
- The reflecting team offers opportunities for professionals to use their creativity and imagination in a collaborative context for change. Team collaboration builds morale among colleagues and supports creativity, learning, and growth.
- Audiences, both professional and peer, can be recruited to witness, highlight, and solidify change and to support clients' new, emerging stories.

The Reflecting Team Format Sheet that follows is a tool that can be applied to your practice. Please feel free to modify the format as needed.

### *Reflecting Team Format Sheet*

1. Allow yourself to experience the clinical interview with curiosity and openness. Then, generate an image, metaphor or story that captures your observations.

   _____

   _____

2. Situate your comments and questions in your own personal experience. How does this situation relate to my life? to my own struggles as a person? as a parent?

   _____

   _____

3. When seeing a couple or family, maintain a balanced position by identifying something positive about each participant (regarding their motivation, strengths, coping abilities, intentions, successes, and so on). Positive comment:

   A: _____

   B: _____

   C: _____

4. Allow your strongest reaction to the interview to surface and then translate that feeling into a nonjudgmental, tentative thought or question that can be introduced into the reflecting team conversation.

   _____

   _____

5. Think about ways to frame the issues presented as "both/and" rather than "either/or."

   _____

   _____

► 5

# Managing Complexity: The Pragmatics of Resource Allocation

**STEVEN FRIEDMAN, PH.D.**
*Harvard Community Health Plan*

**CYNTHIA MITTELMEIER, PH.D.**
*Harvard Community Health Plan*

> *When the magnitude of problems is scaled upward . . .*
> *the quality of thought and action declines . . . . [By]*
> *cast[ing] larger problems into smaller, less arousing*
> *problems, people can identify a series of controllable*
> *opportunities of modest size that produce visible results and*
> *that can be gathered into synoptic solutions.*
> *—KARL WEICK*

People's lives are complex; the goal of therapy is not to cure life's ills but simply to provide a medium for the client to take small steps in a positive direction around circumscribed issues. This process involves tailoring treatment alternatives to each unique clinical situation. To achieve this end, the time-effective therapist needs to judiciously allocate resources in meeting the client's goals.

At a minimum, therapy serves as a hope-generating catalyst for change. The difficulties that most people bring to therapy are complicated. A single parent with four children, several of whom are experiencing problems at school, who is trying to make ends meet on a minimum wage job and dealing with an exhusband who has been abusive and still occasionally harasses her is unlikely to find psychotherapy a panacea for her distress, no matter how often she is seen. Being in psychotherapy also does not immunize us from newer problems that may come our way as we move through our developmental journey.

Therapy in any form is a limited arrangement. The sooner we recognize this fact and, by so doing, focus on generating "small victories," the sooner we will experience a higher rate of success and a greater sense of satisfaction. In an HMO setting the therapist must gain comfort juggling a number of complex clinical situations simultaneously.

The following is offered as an example of a complex clinical situation for which there were no magical answers. The therapist, chapter co-author Cynthia Mittelmeier, put in many hours of work with this family to help them find pathways out of the problem-saturated morass in which they were immersed. A significant amount of energy was directed toward accessing and allocating resources in a time-effective manner from both inside and outside the HMO setting. Because of the complexity of this situation, Cynthia called on her colleagues to share some of the responsibility and provide support along the way. There were 66 therapy sessions over 28 months.

As you read this transcript, think about what "time-effective therapy" means in a situation like this one. How would you negotiate the goals for therapy? What resources might you need in working toward these goals? How would you go about accessing resources in ways that support the agreed upon goals? In situations like Nancy's a treatment structure cannot be neatly organized in advance. Resources are accessed as the need arises. Of paramount consideration is what services make the most sense to use at various points in the treatment process. The goal is always to effectively match the intensity of service with the need, and, by so doing, avoid overutilization of resources.

## THE CLINICAL SITUATION: BACKGROUND AND INTERVIEWS

### Background

Nancy is a 16-year-old girl who lives with her mother, father, sister, and twin brother. Nancy was raped while at a girlfriend's house by two males her age. They had been drinking. After the rapes she developed insomnia, headaches, anxiety, irritability, and an inability to concentrate. She also became intermittently suicidal and, at times, physically aggressive with family members. Nancy did not keep regularly scheduled appointments and would appear in crisis. At these times there was often a request by her mother, June, for an immediate evaluation or a hospitalization.

Nancy continued a cycle of running away, doing drugs, attending appointments inconsistently, constantly arguing with family members, and not attending school. She continued to be symptomatic with extreme fear/paranoia, multiple somatic complaints, sleep disturbance, bulimia, suicidality, and polysubstance abuse. Her mother recontacted the mental health department after she found out that Nancy had been raped another time while at a girlfriend's house. Although there were problems before, the situation now became much worse.

Nancy dropped out of school, ran away frequently, used alcohol and drugs, and made multiple suicide attempts. She was psychiatrically hospitalized on six occasions. Her family was, needless to say, very worried about her. On several nights June slept in front of the door to prevent Nancy from running away. Her sister had several friends who tracked Nancy's whereabouts. Both parents were frightened, overwhelmed, and exhausted.

The situation reached a state of crisis in the summer of 1992. As a clinician in a busy staff model HMO this was only one of many situations with which the therapist was involved. June wanted to see Nancy in a long-term residential facility for her substance abuse, while Nancy felt she did not need to come in for treatment. The therapist felt a great deal of pressure from June to admit Nancy to another treatment facility and also experienced significant anxiety about Nancy's safety. For the therapist there was a certain attraction to knowing that Nancy would be safe in a locked or tightly structured setting that offered relief from the stress and anxiety of dealing with this situation on an outpatient basis. However, this thought immediately led to a sense of guilt, since it was the therapist's responsibility to deliver cost-effective services. Even with the hospitalizations the situation was not getting any better. In fact, with each hospitalization the situation appeared to worsen. The parents' and therapist's sense of helplessness also seemed to be increasing.

The family was then approached about coming in for an interview with a reflecting team. The initial reflecting team consultation emphasized the idea of standing up to "fear" and "secrecy," which were externalized as forces that had gotten a grip on Nancy and her family. This externalizing process continued throughout the therapy. A second consultation session was then arranged to focus on treatment planning. At this point, Nancy was continuing to run away and was allegedly still involved with drugs. June was pressing for placement for substance abuse treatment; Nancy was adamant that she did not want or need another facility. The therapist's goal was to prevent a continuation of the cycle of repeated and largely unhelpful hospitalizations.

## Second Consultation Session

Following are excerpts from the second reflecting team consultation, which took place about 6 weeks following her return home from a psychiatric hospitalization. We join the family at a point about 5 minutes into the session.

*Therapist:* How do you think this consultation can be useful?

*Mother:* Nancy was in a pattern before, of every 2 weeks of so of drinking and drugging. It seems the pattern is just continuing. It's just a little bit harder for me to pick up on. I think she needs a lot of structure right now. I have to work. My husband has to work. I can't stay home to babysit her, to be with her.

*Nancy:* I don't need a babysitter.

*Mother:* Nancy, that's what I think. I mean, she went to an AA meeting the night before last, and yesterday she took off again with the drinking.

*Father:* And she hasn't talked to anybody about it [the second rape] , from what I understand, until just recently. I think she has to be treated for the second incident [rape].

*Consultant:* Nancy, how is it that you told your parents about this [the second rape]?

*Nancy:* I didn't tell my father. I told my mother.

*Consultant:* Okay. How is it that you decided to tell her? How did you make that decision?

*Nancy:* I don't know.

*Father:* I think maybe Nancy was getting a sense that things in the house were getting back to the way they used to be, because . . . .

*Nancy:* Oh, I know why! I wanted to let my parents know what was going on, some of the ways I was acting. So they wouldn't think I was like a psycho or something.

*Consultant:* How come you told them at all?

*Nancy:* 'Cause, I started flipping out wicked easily, punching walls and stuff. I was really flipping out, bad.

*Consultant:* Oh, okay. And you wanted them to understand what was bugging you, so they could understand it better and not say, what is this all about?

*Nancy:* Yeah.

*Therapist:* It sounds like some of the things we've talked about before, in terms of fears pulling you away from your family. Here you were trying to work with the family by letting your parents know what was going on.

*Consultant:* Yeah. Not letting the fears continue to just push you out of control. So that was an important thing to do. To let them know, so they could understand what your behavior was about.

[Later in session]

*Nancy:* Yeah . . . Well, she [mother] made me feel horrible the other day. She was like, "Don't you tell anybody about the rape," and blah blah blah. Like wicked mean, like it was my fucking fault or something. And it's not. Made me feel like an idiot, like I had to be ashamed of it or something. I felt so stupid, like I shouldn't have even told anyone in the first place.

*Consultant:* What would you have liked to have heard? What would you like to hear, in telling about what happened?

*Nancy:* I wish my mother would talk to me about it. Give me a hug or something, instead of just totally ignoring me and not talking to me. It's a good way to deal with it. She's acting like I do.

*Mother:* Excuse me. I guess I have something to say. I am just very angry. I am so angry. And I'm tired of her manipulating me and my husband. She does it all the time, because she always talks to my husband. Then my husband will come back on me, say something to me about it. And I'm tired of being manipulated by a 16-year-old. I love her, but I will not sit by and watch her destroy herself anymore (extremely upset). I can't. I'm sorry. [Nancy heads for the door.]

*Therapist:* Nancy, why don't you stay with us.

*Nancy:* No (she leaves).

*Mother:* (crying) I can't fix it. You know. I can't protect her anymore. I don't know how to save her anymore.

*Therapist:* It sounds you're coming to some realization about this.

*Mother:* I know I can't protect her. I know that. I know. As much as I want to, I can't.

*Therapist:* It sounds like learning about this last rape was a . . . a major blow.

*Mother:* It was. She just keeps putting herself at risk, all the time, when she's drinking.

*Therapist:* I know.

*Mother:* And how can I stop her from doing that? I can't.

[Soon after]

(Nancy returns.)

*Consultant:* Can we have an agreement that nobody goes storming out? Can we have an agreement that although things may come up, and you may not like it, that you will stay in the room? Is that agreeable?

*Nancy:* Yeah.

*Consultant:* Okay. Your mom was telling us that she has this sense now that she can't protect you as much as she has wanted to, and has tried to.

*Nancy:* She can't protect me. Nobody can. She says I haven't been really truthful with her lately. I know I used to lie, but I haven't in a wicked long time. I told her about all the stuff I used to do when I used to drink. My father asked me, was I drinking yesterday. It's not like I lied and said, "No, I wasn't drinking." I told them I was drinking.

*Consultant:* So you've been honest about it.

*Nancy:* Mm-hmm.

*Consultant:* Now, you're going to AA meetings? You're [father] going with her?

*Father:* I've been taking her.

*Consultant:* How often are you doing that?

*Father:* I went twice. She was supposed to be going with some other people, and it just never happened. So I figured, the only way she was going to go was if I go. I didn't mind going at all.

*Nancy:* I like going.

*Therapist:* So there are some things that have gotten better, in terms of Nancy not lying, and not letting the fears totally overtake her, and being able to escape from secrecy around revealing this last rape. But yet, you're continuing to put yourself at risk in situations, and your school's not back on track. And each time this happens, it's very alarming and very worrisome.

*Nancy:* I know, but my parents don't talk to me about it. They yell at me, and rip the phones out of the wall, and I can't talk to anyone. So I'll go upstairs and slice my wrists.

*Mother:* I think that's not true.

*Nancy:* Yeah, Mom, last night I wanted to talk to Katy. I was wicked upset. You wouldn't let met talk to Katy. You hung up on her, and you took the phone away.

*Mother:* You walk in the house at 8:30, very obnoxious, very cocky . . . .

*Nancy:* I wasn't cocky! I didn't say one thing to you, or Dad. You were on the phone when I walked in the house.

*Consultant:* (interrupting) Nancy, what would you like from your mother?

*Nancy:* Maybe to talk to me, and just be like . . . she comes in with this stupid attitude. It drives me nuts. "Oh, so, I hope you had fun, nyah nyah nyah." When I'm wicked upset, she's like, "Oh, I hope you had fun." And I'm like, "I didn't have fun." "Well, isn't that too bad."

*Consultant:* What do you want to hear from her?

*Nancy:* Maybe for her to talk to me. I know she looks like she's happy, but I know she's wicked upset, but that's just way she shows it.

*Consultant:* Uh-huh. So you know she's upset.

*Nancy:* Yeah.

*Therapist:* So you'd rather hear the upset.

*Nancy:* Yeah. And not screaming and yelling at me. Maybe talking to me. It's about me. Obviously I'm upset that I did that. I'm not like, "Oh yes, I got to get drunk yesterday. I'm so happy" (said sarcastically).

*Therapist:* So you both felt upset. All three of you felt upset about what happened yesterday.

*Consultant:* Nancy, if you were in your mother's shoes, what would you want to say to Nancy? You know, she came in at 8:30, she had run off. What would you want to tell her? She comes walking back in. What would you say to your daughter?

*Nancy:* Umm . . . . Let's sit down and talk. Or even she could yell at me if she was upset. But let me talk too.

*Consultant:* Okay. So, wanting to talk, letting her know that you're upset.

*Nancy:* Yeah. And let her say whatever she has to say.

*Consultant:* Uh-huh. That would be helpful.

*Therapist:* What would you say to her?

*Nancy:* If I was who?

*Therapist:* If you were your mom. What would you say to Nancy?

*Nancy:* Umm . . . that I was shocked that she went out and drank, and left school.

*Therapist:* And?

*Nancy:* I'd ask her why. And . . . that she can't start drinking all the time again, or she won't be able to live in the house anymore.

*Consultant:* So you think that would be a good idea, to spell that out. To have it clear.

*Therapist:* What are your thoughts, June?

*Mother:* I was too angry to talk to her.

*Father:* We also accepted numerous phone calls from different people, not just one person, saying that she's been drinking all the time.

*Nancy:* I really haven't been.

*Father:* I'm not saying you were. I'm just saying those are the impressions we're getting.

*Consultant:* So you had a lot of information that was getting you stirred up even before Nancy got home.

*Mother:* Well, yeah, because it fit the pattern. The pattern has been that Nancy is not in class. She goes to school and wanders all day long. That was the pattern from last year, this is the pattern that is now. The pattern from last year was when she was wandering all the time she was drinking and drugging.

*Consultant:* It sounds like you switched into a mode of expecting that the old pattern is going to be there in full force. You've seen the signals. Your mom's seen some signals.

*Nancy:* If they think I've been smoking marijuana, I'll get a drug test when I go to see Dr. Jones, and it stays in your system over a month. And I haven't done marijuana since the time when I ran away. So you can see.

*Consultant:* But, the reality of this is not as important as the fact that you [mother] saw some signals that led you to believe that the same old pattern is happening.

*Mother:* Yeah.

*Consultant:* And then you go right down to the bottom. You know what I mean? It's like all your hopes are dashed. And that's where you've gone. Now, Nancy, you're not feeling like it's gotten to that point, even though your mother's responding to it as if it's gotten to where it used to be.

*Nancy:* It hasn't! It's just one incident.

*Consultant:* Okay. The question for me, in the time we have left, is what kind of steps are going to help your mother build some trust, your dad build some trust, and you build some trust in yourself, that things are going to be able to get to and stay at a more stable place? Because your mom has been hurt, your dad's been hurt, *you've* been hurt.

*Nancy:* I don't know.

*Consultant:* And the repetition of these patterns is only continuing to hurt everybody and really pull people apart. Instead of, in the ways you're talking about, Nancy, of bringing people together, so you can talk and be closer and understand one another.

*Therapist:* So your question was what steps need to happen. What steps that Nancy needs to take.

*Consultant:* Yes. To build some trust up. When we met 5 or 6 weeks ago, people were optimistic. Nancy had been home a few days at that time [from a psychiatric hospital]. And it's not surprising that there has been a couple of steps forward, a step back. That's how these processes go. It's not just going to turn around overnight. It's not unexpected that there will be slip-ups along the way. The question is how are those slip-ups going to be managed, so you can get back to some of the better places that you've been.

*Mother:* I still have a real problem with her being home right now. Before, I was practically sleeping in front of the door. I won't subject myself or my family to that again. Maybe a detox. I don't know.

*Nancy:* I'm not going to some detox, Mom. Go ahead and send me there. See what happens. You're not fucking sending me anywhere. (Nancy storms out of the room.)

[While the therapist and consultant are checking in with their team, the mother and father are left alone in the room:]

*Mother:* I don't understand why you can't see—when I mentioned detox and she left—why you can't see that this is a pattern that she had at the hospital, that she had when she was in day treatment, that she had here at family meetings in the past. Why can't you see the patterns coming back again? The last time that she left, 2 minutes before that, was because I said something that she didn't like. And bing—out the door. That's what I mean. She's back to what she was. Or she's on her way. Everybody told me. People in the residential program. People when I got her evaluated, they all said she needs long-term treatment. She needs long-term residential. She needs detox. And where is she? She's at home.

## The Reflecting Team Conversation

Edward Bauman, Ethan Kisch, Sally Brecher, Amy Mayer, and Madeline Dymsza, served as the reflecting team.

*Edward:* The thing that's striking me the most, I think, is the predicament that Nancy's mother is in. It's obvious just how much pain she feels about all of this. Really wanting to help her daughter in any way she can, and yet feeling like it's the same thing all over again. It sounds like there's so much pain there that it's hard to hear something that might be hopeful. Sitting there listening to Nancy, it sounded like what has been happening recently is a little different than what happened in the past. That there was a slip, but not necessarily something irrevocable . . . .

*Ethan:* To look at it from a different standpoint—that is, from the standpoint of where Nancy is—she is very much puzzled by her own behavior. And she's struggling to understand it. I think that's why she said to her parents, "I want you to talk to me. I want you to ask me why am I doing this, why do you drink." She doesn't want her parents to ask her in a way that makes her feel humiliated or on the spot or caught on the carpet. I think it's really because Nancy is struggling with this, and is faced with something bigger than herself. She doesn't know quite where to turn and quite how to understand this. So I think the fact that she is turning to her family, wants her family to ask her those questions, help her to figure it out, is for me a very optimistic sign. I think the situation would be far worse if Nancy were saying just the opposite. You know—leave me alone, it's none of your business, this is my life, you can't make me stop drinking, go away. She's saying just the opposite. She's saying, "Help me figure this out. I don't know what to do."

*Edward:* Along with that, Nancy seems to be saying, "I want to do it by myself, but I want to know when I mess up someone will be there for me." The other thing I was struck by in the session was the comings and goings, in terms of people going in and out of the room. I wonder what they're going to do when they see Nancy next, when they greet her again. I think that may be something that may be very important to think through about how they want it to go differently.

*Sally:* How would you suggest? What lines were you thinking along?

*Edward:* Well, for Nancy in particular, I guess I was thinking about what she had said, and that she understood very well that people would be mad at her. But she was hoping that somebody might put an arm around her, or at least be glad to see her, or be willing to talk to her, to give time for that anger to subside and set up a time to talk.

*Amy:* I think the question that everyone's struggling with in the family is how can we help? And wanting to provide that answer, and knowing that, in some ways, Nancy needs to come to some of that in time. So it's sort of this push-pull that everyone is experiencing—wanting to support each other, but trying to come to terms with what you really can do. Even if you can't come up with the answers, you can support the feelings that people are having. I also want to mention how important I think it is that Nancy was able to share this very difficult piece of information with the family, and how embarrassing that is. And also how frightening it must be for the family to think about Nancy being in situations where she could be hurt . . . . Alcohol is one way to try to push the trauma away. I think Nancy took our suggestion to heart [at an earlier meeting], about talking about the fears. And now she is talking about the fears, and we're seeing the next, very difficult step, once you do start talking about your fears.

*Madeline:* I keep coming back to Nancy's mother, in terms of just how much grief I saw. The relationship's changed, and the grief that a mother must go through in terms of realizing that you can't help your daughter, your child.

*Sally:* It must feel like you're losing a child, that you've lost a child in a way. You haven't in the real sense, but the sense that you can't protect a child. I think it took a lot of courage for this mother to come to the realization that she loves her daughter—that's clear—but she can't protect her. She's tried so hard, and she's been so vigilant in trying to do it, and yet sees that this isn't something that can be done. I think it's a very difficult place to be. There's no pretense. She's not pretending she can. She sees what her daughter is facing.

*Edward:* And yet at the same time I think it's important that she not lose hope. Her mom is still connected enough to want to talk to her about this stuff. There is some hope there, and even if she [mother] may not feel she can protect her, there are still some ways that she might be helpful to her.

## Interview with the Family Following the Reflecting Team Discussion

*Consultant:* We just have a few minutes. I just wanted to follow up on—the team had a lot of different thoughts, and a lot of things to say—whether there was anything in particular that the team said that fit.

*Mother:* (crying) I think it's true—what they were saying.

*Therapist:* What was true?

*Mother:* They just had a really good way of zeroing in on things.

*Therapist:* They spoke to some of your feelings?

*Mother:* Yeah. But I guess it just comes down to trying to keep her safe.

*Consultant:* Trying to keep her safe? But it sounds like the team was saying there are some limits to what you can do, even though you've worked so hard.

*Mother:* I just don't know what to do.

*Consultant:* I wonder if a hug might be a good thing to do, even though you're upset. This whole situation is upsetting . . . . But is there a way to get past that momentarily, to be able to give her a message that you care about her no matter what? Now, caring about her and feeling you can save her and protect her are two different things. The only message that a hug is giving is that you care about her. That's all. And it's a message that it sounds like she's asking for or needing in all this.

*Father:* Well, I think she's had it—that message. She sat here and said that she doesn't talk to Nancy, but she does.

*Therapist:* I know. From what we heard last time, yes.

*Father:* When she walked in last night, June was angry at her. Now tonight, June probably would have said, "Come on, let's go out and get a cup of coffee," or something, and go out and talk to her. That's usually the pattern that I see with June and her. There's a blow-up first, and then they talk about things, and they get things off their chests.

*Consultant:* Yes. People were saying that Nancy's looking to understand herself. She's trying to make sense out of all this. It can feel like she's doing it to you, that she's manipulating, that she's doing things. But I think that she's really feeling some pain in what's going on with her. She's not indifferent or rejecting, but she's in some pain to try to figure things out. She needs her parents as much as you can be there.

*Mother:* I just guess I get tired. I try to get everything going again, and try to be that organizer and get everything together. I'm just having an awful hard time, that's all.

*Therapist:* Maybe your resources are depleted. You're exhausted. This has been going on for a long time now. These crises, and the not knowing, and the uncertainty.

*Mother:* I'm just tired, and I just don't know what else to do, or where else to go. I don't know.

[The session ends with the father offering to take increased responsibility for Nancy at home, and another meeting is scheduled.]

## ESTABLISHING GOALS/ALLOCATING RESOURCES

In a subsequent session the following goals were mutually agreed upon by the therapist, June, and Nancy in regard to Nancy's behavior: (1) to become drug-free, (2) to be able to articulate her feelings in ways that open options other than running away or cutting herself, and (3) getting back on track in completing high school. Figure 5-1 provides an outline of resources allocated in work with this family. They included both managed care resources and outside resources. On several occasions, meetings were organized with the external providers and Nancy and her parents to coordinate planning and clarify goals.

### *Subsequent Interviews*

Nancy continued living at home but agreed to go to a residential drug and alcohol treatment center for a brief period. The excerpt that follows took place right before Nancy was to be discharged from the drug treatment center. Notice how Nancy and her mother are now able to engage in a productive conversation that supports their connection to one another.

*Nancy:* I know I'm not going to be able to go home.

*Therapist:* I don't understand. What do you mean, you're not going to be able to go home?

*Nancy:* Because my parents don't feel safe with me home (crying). No, I'm leaving.

*Therapist* (to June): She's very sensitive to the comments you make, the things you say.

*Mother:* That's all right. I feel like I can't say what I feel, because I'm afraid I'm going to upset her. That's how I feel at home. I just feel like I'm walking on eggshells. I have to be careful what I say. I kind of second-guess myself before I open my mouth, because I don't want to upset her.

*Consultant:* I get the sense that everybody's worried about everybody else here. You know what I mean? Nancy, you're worried about your parents, about how they're feeling. Your parents are worried about you. Your mom was just telling me she's got to be careful of what she says because she's afraid it's going to upset you, and yet she's got feelings about things. So everybody's walking around in this protective mode, when what it comes down to is you all care a great deal about one another, and are trying to get through this very difficult time. What I'm hearing Nancy, is that it's important to have your mother there for you.

**FIGURE 5-1   Resource Allocation: Nancy [1992–1994]***

| Managed Care Resources | Outside Resources Accessed |
|---|---|
| Primary therapist | Psychiatric hospital |
|   Individual therapy |   "Holding bed" |
|   Family therapy |   Inpatient stays |
|   Crisis intervention |   Day treatment |
| Urgent care clinicians |   Trauma group |
|   Crisis intervention (when primary | Short-term residential facility |
|   therapist was unavailable) |   Individual/group therapy |
| Medical personnel | Department of Social Services |
|   Re: rape, drug, HIV screens |   Trauma group |
| Child/family mental health team | Department of Mental Health |
|   Reflecting team consultations |   Aftercare program (6 mo) |
| Community resource specialist | Alcoholic Anonymous/Narcotics |
|   Accessing outside resources |   Anonymous |
| Psychiatrist | |
|   Prescribing and monitoring | |
|   psychotropic medication | |

*Some services were accessed simultaneously (e.g., attendance at trauma group, AA meetings, and outpatient (therapy). Intensity of treatment decreased over time from hospital based to outpatient.

*Nancy:* I know, but I don't want to go home. It's not going to be normal. I hate when my mother acts weird toward me.

*Consultant:* How would you like her to act?

*Nancy:* Like she normally does.

*Therapist:* I think after one of these incidents that your mom is sort of in shock. It takes her a while to kind of get used to the idea again. She goes along, and she trusts you, and she starts to feel this confidence, and then something happens. Maybe she's trying to protect herself a little when these things come up.

*Consultant:* Nancy, just take a minute to tell your mother how you'd like it at home, what you want it to be like at home, when you go home now.

*Nancy:* Just like it was before I left.

*Therapist:* Would you look at your mom and tell her?

*Nancy:* Just what it was like before I left. I don't know . . . just like it was. Without me getting in trouble or anything. I hate when you act weird towards me.

*Mother:* I'm sorry I've been acting weird towards you.

*Therapist:* Can you explain?

*Mother:* When you cut yourself, it's just like a part of me just goes away. I just shut down. I don't know what to do. I don't know how to handle it. Remember how we talked yesterday about how when the dog runs away, when he gets out?

*Nancy:* Yeah.

*Mother:* Everybody in the family was chasing all over the place, looking for him. We ran around in the car, trying to get the dog. Well, Nancy, just multiply that by a billion. That's how it feels when you run away. We go to the police station. We make up forms. We go to court to do what we do to try to get you back.

*Therapist:* Probably the scariest thing you've ever had to deal with.

*Mother:* It's a horrible feeling. I'm afraid I'm going to get a phone call at 2 a.m. telling me that she's dead somewhere. That is my biggest fear. Acting weird towards you, it's almost like self-preservation, Nancy. I want to trust you, but I'm afraid to trust you. I kind of close in on myself. I isolate when I'm in a bad way, when I'm very worried or I'm upset. You know that. I go in a corner. Not literally, but in my mind I guess. It's just a protective thing. Until I can grasp, until I can re-energize and get the energy level back again.

*Nancy:* I just want it to be normal. Like she asks me, "How are you feeling? Let's go for a cup of coffee or something."

*Mother:* That's what I do, Nancy. But you know, remember the night you came home, you said, "I don't understand why people are upset with me." You've been gone for 6 days. We have all these wild . . . you know, when you don't know something, you imagine what's happening. All we could think was, you're dead somewhere. Or you're overdosing. Or you're in some hospital in some god-awful place. I didn't know where you were.

At this point a task was negotiated. It was suggested that June, when she's feeling upset and needing space, would tell Nancy, "I need to go into a corner for a while." Nancy, when she was feeling the need for contact with her mother, would say "Let's go for a cup of coffee." Both mother and daughter were able to do this successfully.

At a point later in therapy, Nancy expresses her fears of having to make a new life for herself without any support. The therapist, understanding that she cannot be there for Nancy every step of the way, reassures her about her continued availability while moving these fears into the family context.

*Nancy:* How long will I see you for? The rest of my life?

*Therapist:* Well, 'til we agree that things are back on track. And when things start to get back on track, we won't have to meet as often. You might not see me for a couple of months and then you might check in.

*Nancy:* What if it's like, I see you for like 2 more years?

*Therapist:* I'll see you graduate from high school. Why do you ask? I'm curious.

*Nancy:* Just to make sure you don't ditch me.

*Therapist:* Is that right? What's that about?

*Nancy:* I don't know, because . . . I mean you're my counselor and I tell you everything, right?

*Therapist:* Mm-hmm.

*Nancy:* So then one day you're just going to disappear, and I'm not going to see you anymore.

*Therapist:* I'm not going to disappear, and I think you have the same worry about your family too. Is my family going to ditch me? Do they really care? Are they going to be there when I need them? And it sounds like you're saying, . . . "If I stay on this recovery path, are we going to all walk this path together, or am I going to be on this path alone?"

*Mother:* I don't think you've been alone yet, Nancy. After everything that's happened, we never ditched you.

*Nancy:* I know.

*Mother:* You might have thought we had when you were in the hospital and stuff, but we never did. I can't see it starting now, either. When you're a mom, and you're the kid, this is kind of like a forever thing, you know . . . .

[Several months later]

*Therapist:* How do you think you're doing, Nancy, dealing with all the fears we talked about, that were influencing you to run away and do drugs and drink, and pushing you away from your feelings. How do you think you're doing managing the fears?

*Nancy:* I think good. A lot of times, when I get upset, I'll be like, "All right, I'm going to call this person and I'm going to go out all night and not tell my parents where I am."

*Therapist:* So you have those voices in your head?

*Nancy:* Yeah. I think like that. Last night I was.

*Therapist:* And then what happened?

*Nancy:* I'll just be like, what am I talking about? 'Cause I think about all the consequences of what would happen. Like my family will be mad at me, and I'll be grounded. And then Joey [brother] will be mad at me if I drink or do any drugs, and my sister will be mad at me.

*Therapist:* So you've been managing those fears.

*Nancy:* Mm-hmm.

*Therapist:* You're getting strong. Toughening up against those fears.

*Mother:* Yeah, she's been doing pretty good that way. She's been doing good, as far as not punching walls and things. She hasn't done that for a while. She's been doing real good.

[Several weeks later]

*Therapist:* Now, are you still using drugs?

*Nancy:* Oh, no!

*Therapist:* So, you're completely clean.

*Nancy:* I've been clean for, I think 64 days today.

*Therapist:* Wow! That's wonderful!

*Nancy:* I have my 60-day keychain.

*Therapist:* Excellent.

*Nancy:* I've been going to meetings every night.

*Therapist:* Wonderful. It sounds like it's been really hard. It's been really painful. A lot of the really sad, depressing feelings are coming up, but you haven't resorted to going back to drugs and alcohol.

*Nancy:* No.

*Therapist:* Are you worried, at this point, about using?

*Nancy:* No. I really have a desire to stay sober. I want to stay sober. I've got to stay involved in meetings. I'm going to a meeting every day. I'm going to join a group, and I'm going to get a sponsor. Because if I don't go to meetings, I'm not going to stay sober. That's all there is to it.

*Therapist:* So what changed? Why did you suddenly want to get sober? Because I know before that you weren't really convinced, and you sort of thought you could still party a little bit.

*Nancy:* Yeah. Oh, I know I can't now. If I pick up another drug or a drink, I'm never coming back. That's the end of me. That'll be the way I am until I die. Plus, I want more than anything for things to work out with me. For me to have all of my dreams that I want to be, go to school, be smart. I know I'm smart. And just act intelligent, go out with my sister and her friends, who are my friends too, and go bowling and go to the beach, and have normal fun without having to do any drugs or anything. Just have fun, like real fun. And be able to get along with my family, so they don't have to worry about me using. If someone calls up for me, one of my druggie friends, I'll just be like, "I can't talk." Because I'm not going to. I don't have to use. Before, I used excuses. I'd be like, "Oh, I got in a huge fight with my mother. I got to get drunk." Those kinds of things would be my excuse. That's not their fault. That's on me, because that's my decision. No matter if I'm an alcoholic or not, it's my decision if I'm going to pick up. So, if I'm going to ruin my life, I'm going to ruin it. I'm not going to let anyone get in the way of it, no matter what. If I have to walk to meetings every night, I will.

.
.
.

*Therapist:* What else do you need at this point? What do you feel is going to be helpful?

*Nancy:* Crying. 'Cause I cry a lot, you know, when I think about things. I cry, and you just need someone to hug. I need to make amends with a few people. Just certain people that I have on my mind. I need to talk to people. Talk to anybody. Even if someone hates me. Even if Ruth [sister] hates me, I'm going to talk to her anyway. I know she doesn't hate me. Even if she's mad at me, or Mom's mad at me, I'm still going to sit down and talk my brains out until I get out what needs to be said.

.
.
.

*Nancy:* I'm sick of talking to people that I don't even know. I'm sick of other people trying to help me out. I'm sick of it. I'm not going to any more places.

I'm not going to day treatment. I don't need hugs from staff. I need hugs from my family when I'm upset. Just like Ruth needs hugs from her family when she's upset. And from my friends. And I can take care of myself at this point. I'm not going to go and slash my arms. If the decision is that my parents don't want me at home, then I'm going to do what I think I need to do to stay straight, and to take care of myself. Not what other people think I need to do. And I'm not going to go out and use. If I'm too much for them to handle, then I'll have to leave.

## Followup

Nancy continued to meet with the therapist intermittently and was able to live more peacefully with her family. She continued to stay sober and off of drugs, and after a while she found a part-time job and completed her high school equivalency diploma. Currently Nancy shares an apartment with a boyfriend, attends AA meetings regularly, and maintains a close relationship with her family. Both her mother and her physician have commented several times to the therapist about how pleased they are with the steps Nancy has taken to get her life on track. There have been no further instances of self-injury. A very recent contact with Nancy, at age 19, revealed that she was now sober and drug-free for 2 years and was attending a local community college.

The following is a letter that Nancy wrote to herself during the therapy process:

Dear Nancy (a greeting card to myself)

Cheer up . . . . You have a right to get upset whenever you want, as long as you don't go overboard and hurt yourself or someone else. You're doing great. Look at all the positive things.

1.   You haven't touched a drink or drug in over 7 months. But you can't expect your family to understand what a daily struggle that is for you.
2.   You haven't hurt yourself. Congratulations! Great accomplishment.
3.   You haven't hurt anyone else! (applause)
4.   You took Mark and John to court (that was a big deal, too).
5.   You are working on all of your issues.
6.   No one else sees how difficult it was for you and all the work you did in such a short time, that's ok. Just keep doing it. And go to meetings.

Love yourself,

Nancy

## KEY IDEAS IN THIS CHAPTER

- In order to provide time-sensitive therapy in the face of complex problems, a range of treatment alternatives must be available (including access to psychiatric hospitals, day treatment programs, in-home family intervention, etc., see Figure 5-2). Planning for treatment alternatives must be tailored to each unique clinical situation.
- People's lives are complex; the goal of therapy is not to cure life's ills but simply to provide a medium for the client to take small steps in a positive direction around circumscribed issues. The sooner we recognize this, the sooner we will experience a higher rate of success and a greater sense of satisfaction.
- Flexibility is required in providing an institutional safety net made up of a team of professionals that can "hold" the client as he or she moves along the continuum from more structured to less structured therapy settings. This safety net draws on the resources of several professionals, including the primary therapist, the prescribing physician, the pediatrician or internist, urgent care clinicians, as well as professionals in facilities with whom the MCC has contracts for service. Treatment is most time-effective when all participants share similar goals and treatment philosophy.
- The hospital should be considered the alternative of last resort. It is not used for purposes of "evaluation" or for respite, but simply as a structured setting that offers safety, supervision, and the opportunity for coordinated treatment planning.
- Complex problems do not necessitate complex solutions. The job of the therapist is to join with the client to generate small, "do-able" goals that can open the door to further changes.

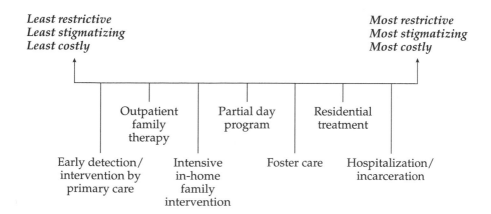

**FIGURE 5-2   A Continuum of Intervention Possibilities**

- Team collaboration in managed care settings allows responsibility to be shared and takes the burden off one clinician to "carry the ball." The reflecting team can be a useful consultative resource to both the clinician and client (family) in complex situations. In addition to the client's primary care physician and other managed care staff, providers from collaborating agencies can be invited to participate in the reflecting team interviews.
- As the number of people hospitalized drops and lengths of stay decrease, a larger commitment must be made to providing outpatient services. Although outpatient therapy may involve substantial investments in time and resources, it is far more cost-effective and significantly less stigmatizing than time spent in the hospital.
- Staff model HMOs provide opportunities for contact with clients over long periods of time. Therapeutic relationships are formed with both the therapist and the institution. These contacts, although sometimes separated by months and even years, allow a level of continuity that is carried from contact to contact. It is much more time- and cost-effective to see the same therapist than to start over with a new one.
- The ultimate responsibility for children and adolescents lies with the family. Too often we have operated "in loco parentis," thinking that we professionals have all the answers. Especially in situations where multiple systems may be involved the treatment team may unwittingly enable the family to abdicate responsibility, making the situation more "chronic" and further demoralizing the family.
- Being effective as a managed care mental health provider requires making significant shifts in attitudes and assumptions about the process of psychotherapy. The therapist needs to accept a humble position about the change process and the impact of formal psychotherapeutic intervention in people's lives. The therapist is a consultant and catalyst for change and as such plays a less central, more facilitating role in the client's life.

# ▶ 6

## Collaborative Practice in Action I: Generating Narratives of Hope

*Sometimes change is directly visible, but sometimes it is apparent only to peripheral vision, altering the meaning of the foreground.*
—*MARY CATHERINE BATESON*

Many of the people we see are immersed in a problem-saturated picture of their lives. How, as therapists, do we set the stage for clients to detect elements of themselves and their behavior that open possibilities for new perspectives? Sometimes just off on the periphery is another story waiting to be voiced. By enabling clients to become "competency detectors," the time-effective therapist sets the stage for change. The clinical conversation becomes a forum for authorizing clients to take steps in redefining a new story of self.

In the clinical situation presented here, Barbara Reynolds, a 42-year-old married mother of four, is struggling with forces from the past that leave her feeling constrained and oppressed and are getting in the way of her being the person (and parent) that she hopes to be. As I listen to her story, I engage her in a conversation that allows her to liberate herself from these oppressive and limiting forces.

## AT THE OUTSET: BARBARA'S PICTURE

Barbara presents her picture of herself as coming from a "dysfunctional family":

> I've been in therapy before, by myself, several years ago. I think I came from a dysfunctional home . . . . I learned that through therapy. It's a cycle and I want to break it [crying]. I feel guilty about being at work when the children come home from school . . . . I do. . . . I always wanted to be the perfect mother . . . . I don't know . . . [cries]. Maybe when he [son John] gets angry at us and he says things to us, which I don't think he really means . . . because I know I say things when I'm not feeling good about myself that come from my childhood. I have to remind myself that I can't do to my kids what my family did to me [cries].

Her husband, who is also present at this session, adds: "She takes the tiniest little things sometimes and blows up . . . and has a temper tantrum. I think John gets most of his temper from Barbara's side of the family. The tiniest little things will set Barbara off sometimes [gives examples]."

*Question:* Based on this client's initial presentation, how might you approach this situation in therapy? As a competency-based therapist, take 5 or 10 minutes to generate your own ideas on ways of working effectively with Barbara.

## AT THE CONCLUSION OF THERAPY

The following are excerpts from Sessions 6 and 7 at the end of therapy (and about 4 months after the initial session). As you read this transcript, notice the changes in Barbara's presentation and the reports of others about her. How did Barbara make these changes? What approach might have helped her to achieve the gains made?

*Barbara* (laughing):  I feel different, you know . . . I've got earrings on . . . .

*Therapist:* I noticed. You usually don't wear earrings? [Barbara's appearance is noticeably changed. She is dressed well, has her hair done, and looks remarkably different than in any of the past sessions.]

*Barbara* (smiling broadly):  No . . . no, I don't. I was wearing these big ones at work and they couldn't believe it . . . .

*Therapist:* Wow!

.
.
.

*Therapist:* I got your letter . . . . You were doing some dancing [with the children] . . . .

*Barbara:* Yes, that hasn't happened in a very long time. Small things like that are happening. It could just be a song on the radio that makes me feel good. It's not anything really big, just smaller things. It's what I used to feel like a long time ago. A few months ago I was in bed all the time . . . going to my room. A couple of times I noticed when the Furies were trying to come back I was getting all upset . . . so I left the situation. Instead of going to my room—months ago I would have done that—I walked away, calmed down, and then went back to the situation and handled it.

*Therapist:* So you came back and approached it differently . . . .

*Barbara:* Yes, calmer . . . .

*Therapist:* That's not easy to do. I'm impressed.

*Barbara:* It takes a lot of work and concentration.

.
.
.

*Therapist:* This whole process feels like you've been finding who you are . . . a person that can be more fun-loving, easygoing, and joyful . . . .

*Barbara:* I have been feeling that for the past few weeks on an ongoing basis, almost to the point that I feel I'm going to wake up one day and it's going to be gone. I haven't had these feelings in a long time.

*Therapist:* With each day this goes on, you really set the stage for more days like that.

.
.
.

*Barbara:* At work, I'm happier with my co-workers, more bubbly. They even noticed. One said, "I don't know if it's the new hairdo or what, but you've changed . . . ." I got new glasses . . . . And she said, "Even the way you walk is completely different . . . ." She sees a complete difference in me . . . . My sister Sharon has noticed a difference, too. I don't call her as much. I was calling her every day—crying. Now I call her to say hello, but it's not that everyday thing. My nails are growing (said proudly).

*Therapist:* I see.

*Barbara:* She [sister] noticed my nails . . . small things like that. She doesn't think I'll go back [to the way I was before].

*Therapist:* I think you're getting stronger and the Furies are not going to be affecting you in the ways they used to. I really admire how you've been able to take these steps . . . so conscientiously. (Therapist gives a compliment.)

*Barbara* (shaking head in agreement): It is, it's work. And my husband and I are closer than we've been in a long time . . . .

*Therapist:* You're on your way. I think there's no turning back now.

## THE MIDDLE PHASE

Let's return now to the middle phase of the therapy and see how the approach taken enabled this client to make the rapid and dramatic changes she did. The session excerpted here took place 3 weeks after the initial meeting and, at Barbara's request, included the whole family. The parents come in ready to tell me about recent positive events. Barbara tells me she requested a change in her work schedule to allow her to be home after school, and her husband Matthew has found a new job! I encourage this talk about change and begin to home in on Barbara's self-perceptions.

*Therapist:* What other changes have happened since we met last? What other things have you noticed that have changed?

*Barbara:* I'm trying to be more in control. I'm trying to really concentrate on it. The day after our meeting the last time, I had to work the next night and I asked John [older son] if he could babysit and he got upset . . . .and I don't blame him. He had youth group . . . and I said to myself, "I'm not going to force him, I'm not going to get upset about this."

*Therapist:* Yes.

*Barbara:* I called Matthew at work and explained [the situation]. We had to work out something and we compromised. He took the younger ones with him.

*Therapist:* You worked out something different . . . .

*Barbara:* Yes.

*Therapist:* How did you manage that? [This question provides an opportunity for the client to "publicize" her resources.]

*Barbara:* It was early in the morning and I said to myself, "I'm not going to get mad at him. He has a right not to want to babysit." We compromised and it worked out okay. But at other times I just get triggered . . . .

*Therapist* (to children): Do you know what your mother means by "triggered"?

*Barbara:* Jane [the 17-year-old daughter] understands.

*Therapist:* We were talking last time about things from your mother's past that come up and get in the way. How can you [Jane] tell when some of the old past stuff is getting in the way?

*Jane:* She's usually angry.

[I begin asking questions in an effort to externalize the "old scripts" that are oppressing Barbara.]

*Therapist:* How does that affect you when you see that old history come up for her . . . when the old history takes control?

*Jane:* I don't take things she says seriously when she's acting like that.

*Therapist:* So you can separate out that something else is going on here . . . outside the situation.

*Jane:* Yeah.

*Barbara:* They'll go off in their rooms. We had company a couple of weeks ago and I woke up in the morning and I felt overwhelmed and I have to have everything perfect. I woke up in the morning and I said to Matthew, "I'm going to really try hard today to have a good day" (crying), and . . . he helps me.

*Therapist:* What would a good day look like? [I make an attempt here to shift the client's attention to the future, hoping she will provide a future vision of where she would like to be. However, the client returns to her focus on the past.]

*Barbara:* Everything just perfect. I can remember my father telling me I'll never be like my mother.

*Therapist:* Your mother kept the house in perfect order?

*Barbara:* Yes. Everything was just perfect, everything. And I can hear those messages and I want to overcome them . . . I just don't know.

I begin to look at the ways the old scripts influence and impact on Barbara's life. These externalizing conversations are an attempt to deconstruct Barbara's constraining narrative and to objectify the old scripts as a powerful force that influences her life. I ask Barbara questions about how this force impacts on her life across several domains and find that she is least vulnerable to their influence in the work setting. This information serves to challenge her "totalizing" descriptions of herself and begins to open up new options and possibilities for change.

*Therapist:* These old messages are powerful. They have a powerful effect on people's lives. They stay with you. I have the sense that you're struggling to get past them and get control of them.

*Barbara:* I want to be able to say to myself, "I know I'm not perfect."

*Therapist:* It's hard to let go of the messages that say you're not doing enough, not doing good enough.

*Barbara:* Matthew helps me. He helps me a lot. I don't mean to be like that.

*Therapist* [mapping the influence of the problem on the client's relationships]: When this old history comes up, how does it affect your relationship with the kids?

*Barbara:* I feel like I'm an outsider from them . . . not as close as I could've been (cries).

*Therapist:* So the old scripts have a way of getting in the way of being closer. The old messages have a way of separating you from your children . . . so that you're not as close as you'd like to be. How about relationships outside the house?

*Barbara:* I work with the elderly in a nursing home and I'm not like I am at home. I basically have a lot of patience at work.

*Therapist:* Somehow you've been able to keep your work from being affected.

*Barbara:* Yes, it hasn't.

[Later in the session]

*Therapist:* You gave an example at the beginning where you didn't let the old messages win out, so it sounds like there are times you can get the upper hand . . . although it takes some effort to do it.

Here I reinforce the positive steps she has taken, while indicating that this is hard work. I then go on to ask for other experiences in which Barbara has gotten free of the influence of the old messages, and she describes other examples of walking away from situations with John and relying on her husband's support to respond in a different and calmer way. I schedule an appointment in 1 month with Barbara and her husband and send a letter to Barbara about 1 week after this session.

## AN EXCHANGE OF LETTERS

The following is the letter that I sent to Barbara after the last session and her response to that letter. In my letter I continue the process of externalizing and objectifying the oppressive forces and give them a name, "the Furies."

Dear Mrs. Reynolds,

I wanted to follow up with some thoughts I had after our last meeting. I enjoyed meeting your children and experiencing their playfulness and their closeness . . . . I was impressed by your report of how you avoided cooperating with the "old scripts" in dealing with John and by the ways you are able to keep the "old stories" from intruding into your work life. It seems, from our discussions, that your husband has been a great source of support to you in your quest to be unburdened by the "old scripts." You are fortunate to have him by your side.

I was thinking of a name for the "old scripts," and one that came to mind was "the Furies." The Furies are forces (from Greek mythology) that represent feelings of guilt. They are part of the irrational world we sometimes carry with us. The Furies are the false, guilt-inducing voices that have been intruding on your life. It seems to me that at times "the Furies" wreak havoc on your relationships with your children and prevent your home life from being more satisfying. In that way "the Furies" are a very powerful force. Somehow "the Furies" have gotten the idea that they have a permanent home with you. The goal will be to avoid cooperating with the Furies and by so doing allow your own voice of inner peace and calm to be heard.

I wonder if you could make a list of the ways that "the Furies" try to direct your life. In this way it may be possible to plan a challenge to the Furies' domination. By giving the Furies the "boot" you will be making space for inner peace and healing.

Please call or write me before our next appointment if you have any thoughts about this. I look forward to seeing you and your husband [about 1 month later].


Sincerely,

Steven Friedman

Two days before to our scheduled meeting I received a letter from Barbara. The letter follows:

Dear Dr. Friedman,

I have been doing a lot of thinking since our last visit. This is the list I have come up with regarding "the Furies."

I am afraid to ask for help outside the immediate family. There was an instance during Christmas that I needed to borrow something from my sister. I was really scared to ask, but I told myself I would not be scared. In the end I couldn't do it. I can remember whenever I asked my father for something, he would usually yell at me and put me down, even in my adult life.

I find fault with everything in the house. At Christmas time I wasn't happy with the way my house looked with all the decorations. I moved the tree three times and still wasn't satisfied. I found myself at one point unwrapping a few gifts because I wasn't happy with the way they looked. I have to have everything perfect if we entertain but will procrastinate to the last minute to get the work done. In my head I know I have the work to do but I always set myself up.

A few weeks ago a person at work gave me a beautiful compliment. I couldn't believe what she said about me could be actually true.

I want my children to be perfectly behaved. Especially when we go visiting. I get very uptight if the boys wrestle on the floor. I remember this because my sister called this to my attention. I can recall that growing up, my brothers, sister and I were always perfectly behaved. It was expected of us.

Dr. Friedman, these are just a few that I could zero in on. I hope this helped you.


Sincerely,

Barbara Reynolds

[The next session (#3)]

*Therapist:* I got your letter . . . and it was a very helpful description of the way what I was calling "the Furies" push you around.

*Barbara:* When I put it on paper it looks so stupid . . . It's like trivial stuff.

*Therapist:* What were your thoughts about my letter . . . how I was thinking about "the Furies"? It seems like there are these forces that make you feel guilty.

*Barbara:* Right, right.

*Therapist:* Did that fit for you?

*Barbara:* Yes, definitely.

*Therapist:* I don't know if you had some other words to describe this force . . . . One of the things I put together, and I'll give you a copy, is the "laws of the Furies."

I then read the laws, which are reproduced here:

### *The Laws of THE FURIES (after Esler, 1987; White, 1986)*

1. THE FURIES feed on attention.
2. THE FURIES like to find a home with people who are experts in self-torture.
3. THE FURIES look to escape from places where they're ignored.
4. Since THE FURIES are always hungry it is possible to starve them by not letting them dominate your thoughts or influence your actions.
5. THE FURIES have one fear (which they try to keep secret). This fear is that people will give up believing in them. When this happens they lose their power and disappear.

I begin asking a series of questions that allow Barbara to re-author her story in a way that places her in control and not the Furies. I also offer Barbara opportunities to tell me how motivated she is to make changes in her life.

*Therapist:* What I'm wondering is when you think you're going to be ready to push these Furies out of your life.

*Barbara:* I want them out now.

*Therapist:* What do you think it's going to be like to have your life back, without these Furies pushing you around?

*Barbara:* Like you said, inner peace. Just accepting me for who I am and letting all that old stuff go . . . . My sister Sharon told me that she remembers our parents telling her she'd never be anything but there was always something in her saying she will be something.

*Therapist:* She fought it then and you're fighting it now . . . and the Furies have had more time to take hold. Does she [sister] have some ideas when you tell her about what's going on with you?

*Barbara:* She understands. It was a dysfunctional family, I know it was. She came out of our childhood hating more that I did.

*Therapist:* She was more angry.

*Barbara:* Angry . . . but able to get out of the house, while we [Barbara and her husband] stayed in the house.

(Barbara explains that she took care of her alcoholic father after he had a stroke. During this period he was very angry and irritable.)

*Therapist* [searching for "exceptions"]: What are your thoughts about how you've prevented the Furies from taking over completely?

*Barbara:* I don't know.

(Barbara explains how her husband helps by telling her to calm down when she gets upset.)

*Therapist:* With some people I would expect their whole life would be dominated by the Furies.

*Barbara:* Yes, right. No, it hasn't.

As a way to increase motivation for change, as well as to highlight the fact that change has already been happening, I explore with the client a worst-case scenario should she give her life over to the Furies.

*Therapist:* What would you anticipate if you let the Furies stay with you, into the future?

*Barbara:* A miserable life. He [husband] would be unhappy.

*Therapist:* What does it mean "being miserable"? What is your picture of this, of letting the Furies dominate your life?

*Barbara:* Maybe getting more depressed. I can remember a couple of years ago when I was in treatment, I was sleeping all the time [this was after her father's death]. But now I have a job. I have to work.

*Therapist:* So, you made some positive changes.

*Barbara:* Yes.

*Therapist:* But you could imagine that if you let the Furies continue, you could go back in that state.

*Barbara:* Could be.

*Therapist* [to Matthew]: What sense do you have about that, if the Furies continued pushing her around?

*Matthew:* Well, like she said, she would just go back into her little shell and start sleeping all day and lose her job.

Barbara describes a change she made in her work hours that will allow her to be home when the children return from school. This required that she make a request to her supervisor, which she did. This change also relieves John of some babysitting responsibilities. Barbara reports a positive change in the household with this arrangement.

*Therapist:* What kind of compliment did you [Barbara] get that you mentioned in your letter?

*Barbara:* I was doing my work. It was just before Christmas and one of the temporary staff stopped me in the hall and said, "Barbara, I just wanted you to know that you're a beautiful person, the way you take care of these people and the way you treat them." I had tears in my eyes. I told her I didn't feel that way. How people perceive me, I don't see myself, though. I said thank you and gave her a hug. But when I went home and thought about it I said to myself, "I don't see myself like that."

*Therapist:* That's where the Furies come in with their negative messages. You see what I mean?

*Barbara:* Uh, uh.

*Therapist:* So a good sign would be your being able to accept compliments . . . and in a way you did accept the compliment.

*Barbara:* Yeah. Right, right.

*Therapist:* But you still had some doubts. And that's the Furies coming in and getting in the way.

*Barbara:* For example, at our last meeting I was getting upset about how Joseph [youngest child] was behaving. Because in our childhood we were like this. (She demonstrates sitting straight up, prim and proper, "perfect children.")

*Therapist:* That stuck with you. One of the ways that you will know that the Furies are going away is when you're able to tolerate those situations in a different way. And these situations will come up again. I was asking before what your picture would be if the Furies stay with you. And I'm also interested in what the picture will be like when the Furies disappear and you have that inner peace. What will life be like at home?

*Barbara:* I think a better marriage.

*Therapist:* When you stop cooperating with the Furies, what else will be different?

*Barbara:* The relationship with my children. I would feel closer to them. Joyful and being happy to be up in the morning.

*Therapist:* What other changes will happen in the family when you decide not to cooperate with these Furies?

*Barbara:* I would enjoy my children more, accept them for themselves.

*Matthew:* Probably there would be a lot less yelling and more cooperation from the kids.

*Therapist:* What needs to happen now is to look at the ways, and I know it happens now, when you don't let the Furies win out. I think the times when they do [win out] are powerful and you tend to notice that, but there are also times when you handle situations calmly.

*Barbara:* I think John has calmed down a lot over this past month, don't you think, Matthew? There haven't been as many confrontations.

*Matthew:* I haven't yelled at him in a while.

*Therapist:* I think that's a sign that somehow you are getting control over these Furies. What I would be interested in is asking you to keep track of the times when you haven't cooperated with the Furies, when you, and not the Furies, are in control of your life. That's the aim here, for you to experience that inner peace; to get a compliment . . . .

*Barbara:* And let it absorb.

*Therapist:* Right . . . let it sink in. And it's going to take some active efforts. You mentioned your sister and how she would say "no" to your parents' demands, would express herself very clearly, and you may need to say that to the Furies, not let these outside forces control your life. Because you deserve that kind of inner peace.

*Barbara:* I know I have four beautiful children.

*Therapist:* Yeah. I was very impressed with them.

*Barbara:* And there again, when you sent the letter, the opening said how you enjoyed their playfulness. And I couldn't accept that . . . . I thought they weren't behaving themselves.

*Therapist:* I took Joseph's exuberance very positively, that he was feeling comfortable being here. It's going to take a little work to let the Furies know they're not needed anymore . . . that you don't want them around. Your sister is a support to you, as is your husband. And maybe there are some things your sister learned how to do that can be useful to you in gaining control over these forces.

*Barbara:* Maybe.

*Therapist* [asking for an action step]: Another idea I have is for you to note, to put into a sentence, what the messages are that the Furies send—for example, "Question the validity of all compliments," "Expect the children to behave perfectly," "Don't ask help from others," et cetera.

*Barbara:* Okay, okay.

*Therapist:* And with that, make me a list of the ways that you've *not* cooperated with the Furies' messages. When you're calm, even momentarily, and find some inner peace . . . .

*Question:* Before reading further, take 10 minutes or so and develop an outline for a letter to send to Barbara based on this session. The goal here is to summarize and amplify the positive steps the client has taken and review possible actions that will support her continued progress.

Four days after this session I sent Barbara the following letter:

Dear Mrs. Reynolds,

    I wanted to write to follow up on our last meeting. I was impressed with the commitment of your husband to helping you rid your life of the influence of the Furies. Working together as a team, as you seem to do so well, is an effective way to gain the upper hand on the Furies. It also sounds like you have the help of your sister Sharon who understands the struggle that you are undertaking to gain inner peace and calm. Your sister seems to have taken on the Furies earlier in her life and maybe her anger served in some useful way in winning over them. This might be interesting to discuss with her.

    Considering your very structured upbringing I am impressed with your flexibility in creating a different and more open family environment than the one you knew growing up. This is not easy to accomplish, especially in light of your great loyalty to your parents.

Your shift in work hours so you can be home in the afternoon for your children is a wonderful gift that you are giving them, that is also working to gain inner peace for you and the family.

You described your ideas for what would happen if the Furies were to take over completely (you would become depressed, sleep all the time, "go back into a shell", etc.). I wonder how you have prevented this from happening. As I mentioned in our last meeting, it might be useful to make a list of those situations when you do not cooperate with the Furies' messages, but make choices for yourself. This may be experienced as feeling some of the inner peace you desire, feeling some happiness getting up in the morning, enjoying your children more (and accepting them as they are), feeling closer to your children, and feeling more joyful and self-confident. One way I can tell that you are winning over the Furies is that John was described as calmer over this past month and that you and your husband were yelling less.

In addition, as we discussed, it might also be helpful to make a list of the messages that the Furies send (for example, "Don't ask for help from outsiders," "Question all compliments as unworthy," etc.). By doing this we can have a better idea of how to counteract the power of the Furies. By the way, by coming to see me you are already not cooperating with one of the Furies' messages!

I look forward to seeing you and your husband [about 3 weeks later] and hearing about the steps you've taken to gain inner peace and calm.


Sincerely,

Steven Friedman


In the next session (#4), 2½ weeks later, I began asking questions that opened space for Barbara to re-author and expand her previously limiting narratives and to experience and express an increased sense of personal agency. She begins to talk to herself in ways that lead to a new sense of empowerment.

*Therapist:* You got my letter.

*Barbara:* And I made my lists (hands therapist the lists she made.).

*Therapist:* These are the messages . . . "anger, negative thoughts, self-pity; unworthy as a person."

*Barbara:* I put "self-pity." Sometimes I feel sorry for myself and cry. And I think sometimes they [the Furies] feed off of that.

*Therapist:* Yes. That's exactly right. That makes you vulnerable . . . .

[Therapist turns to the list of "noncooperation" and spends the entire session reviewing Barbara's successes.]

### Don't Cooperate with the Furies

I calmly approached a situation and remained in control.

I tried to tell myself I am a worthy person.

I looked at the positive things I have done for my children all their lives.

Defending myself against someone who puts me down.

Deserving.

*Barbara* (smiling): The first one I'm the most proud of.

*Therapist:* Tell me about this.

*Barbara:* It was a couple of days after we saw you. And I could have just walked away and let him [Matthew] handle it. And I said to Matthew, "No, Matthew, I'm going to handle this." And I told myself, even before I went to John, "I'm going to be in control and handle this" and I did!

*Therapist* [inviting the client to consider herself as an effective agent of change]: How did you take that step?

*Barbara:* I just said to myself, "I want to handle this and I'm not going to be in control of him. I'm not going to holler at him . . . and make me want to have the last word." And it worked. Wonderful. We compromised.

*Therapist:* So it wasn't just an imposing . . . it was a negotiation.

*Barbara:* I was so proud of myself.

*Therapist:* How did you manage to not let the Furies control your behavior in this situation?

*Barbara:* I didn't want to holler at him.

*Therapist:* What were you doing that was allowing you the freedom to not let the Furies push you around?

*Barbara:* I talked to him like a human being. I don't know. It just worked out.

*Therapist:* You worked with him in a way that felt like a resolution.

*Barbara:* Instead of me controlling and telling him, "You've got to do what I tell you to do."

*Therapist:* I'm trying to understand how . . . .

*Barbara:* How I did it . . . . A month ago I would have probably dragged him out of the bed.

*Therapist:* What were you thinking that was helping you not cooperate with the Furies?

*Barbara:* Was I calmer, or feeling better about myself? I don't know. I did it instantaneously.

*Therapist:* You were feeling ready.

*Barbara:* Right. I was determined. I wasn't going to lose my temper with him. And I did it!

*Therapist:* You surprised yourself about that.

*Barbara:* I've been proud about that for 2 weeks.

*Therapist:* That's wonderful! . . . taking this step, in this one situation, a positive step in a situation where you've, in the past, gotten into some difficulties with the Furies. So, in what ways does taking that step make you more confident about future steps? [Here I invite Barbara to consider what taking this step means for the future.]

*Barbara* (bright smile): I feel like him and I have a better relationship together. I feel it already.

[She then describes another example when she dealt calmly with John.]

*Therapist:* It sounds to me that some of that inner peace and calm is coming through. You're finding it in dealing with John. Who do you think would be least surprised at your taking this step at this time?

*Barbara* (looking confused): Surprised?

*Therapist:* *Least* surprised.

*Barbara:* I don't know. That's a hard one. My sister Sharon maybe. What do you mean?

*Therapist:* Who would be least surprised?

*Barbara:* That I was able to accomplish this.

*Therapist:* Yes.

*Barbara:* Sharon has confidence in me.

*Therapist:* What is it that she's seen in you that would allow her to predict that you would have a successful interaction with John? [By asking this question I am opening space for Barbara to build a new view of self, one based on demonstrated actions that contradict the old script.]

*Barbara* (thinking): Gosh . . . . I don't know. Sensitive?

*Therapist:* So she may see some sensitivity that you have, caring . . . .

*Barbara:* Deep down she knows I'm a caring person . . . and I'm sensitive. We weren't close as siblings. She treated me like dirt. And she recently apologized for taking advantage of my being sensitive. And now we're close. We talked about this about a week ago.

*Therapist:* She may see you as sensitive, caring. Being able to work things out without conflict may be something she would see.

*Barbara:* Yeah.

I ask Barbara to think back to a time in her own life that might have predicted that she would be able to take action in the ways she has done so successfully. She tells me she's always been a "dreamer." I use this idea to help her to further amplify and embody the changes she has made.

*Therapist:* If you think back in your own life, what would have allowed you to predict you would have handled this situation with John in the positive way you did?

*Barbara* (thinking): I was always a dreamer . . . as an adolescent. I was going to tell my children [when she had children] that they were special and unique.

*Therapist:* Being a dreamer, then you were always a hopeful person . . . .

*Barbara:* Right, right.

*Therapist:* And putting in some effort to create better times.

*Barbara:* Our children are not like the way we grew up. I think you put that in the letter. One thing I thought of after I read your letter: My father used to come home drunk practically every night and I remember hiding in the closet. And I was determined that I would never have a father to my children who didn't come home at night after work. And he [Matthew] always has. So I controlled that . . . . I didn't let it happen.

*Therapist:* Yes. That's right.

*Barbara:* Matthew's always been there for me.

*Therapist:* That's certainly working at trying to change those patterns, and very successfully. Well, I'm impressed. I wrote in the letter about the flexibility that you have, that's different from your family growing up.

*Barbara:* It is different. It is. (Barbara describes how in her family of origin she was never allowed to talk on the phone until she was in high school; not allowed to sleep over at friends' houses, etc.)

*Therapist:* You've made a different life for yourself and your children . . . . I want to get to these other things on the list.

*Barbara:* I was writing them down as I thought of them.

*Therapist* [reads next item]: "I try to tell myself I'm a worthy person."

*Barbara:* Lately, I've been thinking about when my children were born. That I was a wonderful mother when they were born, holding them . . . .

*Therapist:* You remember all the care you gave.

*Barbara* (proudly): I am a good mother! (laughing) I still have those thoughts about the past but I have to let it go. I'm almost 42.

*Therapist* [returning to the list]: "I look at the positive things I've done for my children all their lives."

*Barbara:* How proud I am of our children. Our oldest is off to college in the fall. She was accepted to her first-choice school and with a scholarship. She's a wonderful person. She's turning out the way I dreamed that she would. We must have done something right.

*Therapist:* You obviously did something to allow her to get to this point, to take these steps.

*Barbara:* We always paid attention to her needs.

*Therapist:* You listened and it paid off. She seems to take after you [Barbara] in being such a caring person.

*Barbara:* And motivated. Joseph [the youngest] comes in from school smiling and I say, "Joseph, you're always smiling. How come you're so happy?" He says, "I'm just happy" and I said, "What's special about you?" and he said, "Me."

*Therapist:* So, he's got a real positive sense of himself, and there are things the two of you have done to instill that in the kids. Let's go back to the list. "Defend yourself." Tell me about that one.

*Barbara:* There's a nurse that I work with and she can be very demeaning. And she did it to me. It struck a chord in me and very nicely I told her off . . . and that's not like me. But the way she talked to me was the way my father did. And I'm not going to let anybody do that to me . . . .

*Therapist:* You asserted yourself without letting the Furies get to you.

*Barbara:* Or cry . . . or feel bad about myself. I'm the type of person who would cry and go in a corner and feel sorry for myself. But I didn't do that. I'm not going to let her talk down to me.

*Therapist:* You took a stand with her . . . .

*Barbara:* And I think she got the message because she was more friendly afterwards.

*Therapist:* You wrote the word "deserving" [on the list].

(Barbara describes having had the assistance of two aides, which is unusual, one evening at work and thinking to herself, "I deserve this . . . . I work very hard, . . . which is unusual for me to say to myself . . . . I don't need to work hard tonight.")

*Therapist:* Wonderful! How does taking these steps, and you've taken quite a few over the past 2 and a half weeks, affect your picture of yourself as a person?

*Barbara:* You can tell. Today I feel great (beaming). I feel better. I feel positive about myself. I can go home and handle any situation with John or the others. I feel confident.

*Therapist:* What do these steps tell you and tell your husband about what you're wanting your life to be like?

*Barbara:* Happier, closer . . . . Jane gave us a book as a Christmas gift when she was in the fourth or fifth grade called *The Family*. And it's a beautiful poem about what a family is. They forgive each other, they share . . . . That's what I want us to be. For her to have bought this in the fourth or fifth grade, she must have thought our family was like this.

*Therapist:* Yes.

*Barbara:* My oldest one noticed me being a little different. I asked her.

*Therapist:* What did she say?

*Barbara:* She notices a calmness in me. Sometimes I'll get a little upset but catch myself.

*Therapist:* The Furies come in but they don't overtake you.

(Barbara then describes a recent situation in which she made a turkey dinner and left all the dishes piled up. In the past she would have found this worrisome. "I would have gotten mad at myself for leaving them sit." But this time she just laughed and felt comfortable looking at the piles of dishes.)

*Therapist:* You didn't let the Furies get to you . . . .

*Barbara:* I have to concentrate, especially to fight the messages from the past.

*Therapist:* I suggest you continue to keep a list of when you don't cooperate with the Furies. Keep adding to the list. It takes concentration, and your actions are already making a difference. In how many weeks would you like to set the next appointment?

*Barbara:* How about 4 weeks.

About a week after this appointment I sent Barbara the following letter:

Dear Mrs. Reynolds,

I wanted to write to share some thoughts I had after our last meeting.

As a fortune cookie recently informed me, "The first step to better times is to imagine them." Being a dreamer, as you described yourself, seems to have allowed you to imagine a better life for yourself and your family. Not only did you imagine that positive future, you have acted to create it.

Your ability to move from self-pity to self-love is a major step. The examples you presented at our last meeting—how you approached a situation with John, calmly; how you experienced yourself as a worthwhile person; how you saw and accepted the positive things you and your husband have done for your children over the years; how you asserted yourself when you felt demeaned by another person; and how you saw yourself as a deserving human being who is entitled to a life unburdened by self-pity and self-torture—showed me that you are letting go of the past and have made a new future for yourself and your family.

Just to be sure the Furies are on their way out of your life, I would suggest you continue to write down the ways you do not cooperate with their demands. By so doing you will free yourself to step more fully into the future. As you experience the inner peace and calm of this step, your life will become your own again.

Thanks for allowing me to come along on this journey of liberation.

Sincerely,

Steven Friedman

## Followup

In the fifth session, 1 month later, Barbara, although having suffered some setbacks at the hands of the Furies over the month between sessions, had also experienced more positive days when she felt in control. As she put it: "I'm having feelings . . . like . . . I can't explain it . . . just happiness inside . . . inner peace . . . a feeling like I could deal with anything . . . . It was a good feeling." She also reports daydreaming about the future in a positive way, seeing herself going to nursing school and imagining her and her husband "growing old together" with the children off on their own. I normalize the setbacks as "hiccups on the road of life" (Elms, 1986) and encourage her to continue to track these positive feelings of calm and inner peace. At the end of the meeting she tells me, "What I like about calling them the Furies is, it's not blaming anyone . . . . I am an adult and I have to be responsible for myself."

Excerpts follow from two letters I received from Barbara after the sixth session.

Dear Dr. Friedman,

I thought I would let you know how I am doing. . . . I feel like I am handling each situation calmly and being supportive of my children. I have been experiencing more times of inner peace and calm. There was one day the two younger children and I had the radio on and we started dancing together. We were laughing and having fun. There are other times when I just have warm and happy feelings flowing through me.

John has been very good. He seems more happy and content. He did some babysitting for me a couple of days. He really did a good job. I wanted to do something special for him so I bought him a new baseball comforter for his bed. He was really surprised. I wanted to show him I appreciated what he did for me.

There were a couple of times the Furies did try to surface. I did not let them take complete control. I left the situation for a few minutes, calmed down, and returned to do what I was doing.

Matthew and I are growing closer together. We communicate more. I am very lucky to have had a husband who stuck by me and who didn't give up on me. My family is the most important thing to me. A family just doesn't happen, you have to work at it. Thank you for all your help.

.
.
.

I wanted to share some thoughts and feelings while they are still fresh in my mind. The other day I realized for a while now I have not been thinking about my past. I am not as emotional. I know there will be times in my life when my thoughts and feelings will surface. I think I have learned to experience them and let them go. They are part of me . . . . I may write again before our next visit. Thank you for being part of my Journey to Liberation.

Sincerely,

Barbara Reynolds

A followup contact $2\frac{1}{2}$ years after Barbara completed this therapy revealed that she was continuing to function well.

### A Practical Exercise

1. What advantages do you see in using an "externalizing" approach in making your therapy more time-effective?
2. How might you apply this process in your own practice?

## KEY IDEAS IN THIS CHAPTER

- Honor the client's story. Make space for the client's problem-saturated story (internalized description) without making this the focus for the therapy.
- Label and externalize the problem story as a constraining and limiting force that has been closing off other options and other views of self.
- Explore with the client experiences that contradict the problem-saturated story. Bring forth these less prominent descriptions to help the client re-author a new story (one that promotes a revised view of self).
- Strengthen the new story by suggesting the client engage in activities/experiences that offer opportunities to see the self in a new light, to confirm the new, emerging picture.

# ► 7

## Collaborative Practice in Action II: Constructing Time-Effective Solutions

*I think we're all heroes if you catch us at the right moment.*
—ANDY GARCIA as "John Bubber" in the film Hero

Time-effective therapy with children and adolescents requires connecting with the family as the medium of change (Haley, 1976; Minuchin, 1974). Although some individual time in therapy may be usefully spent with the child or adolescent, a majority of energy is focused on the family as a resource to the child. When the therapist works with children and families, the therapy process becomes a laboratory for generating and experimenting with imaginative approaches that open space for change. Rather than being in an expert role, the therapist acts as a consultant, accessing the families' expertise and knowledge. This is especially important in working with families whose cultural context differs from your own, as is the case in the situation presented here. The therapist in these situations has to be exquisitely sensitive to the cultural implications of his or her methods and needs to maintain a sense of openness and curiosity in order to better understand the context in which the family functions.

In the interviews that follow the family is seen for two "rounds" of therapy separated by about 1 year. The first set of contacts were focused on the behavior of the younger son and the second on the behavior of the older son.

The therapist, although not Spanish-speaking, matches his language and phrasing to the style and character of the family's. While serving as a means of initially joining with the family, the adaptation becomes a way to connect with them and to offer ideas in a way that can be heard and understood. If you have the opportunity to audiotape or videotape yourself with different families, you will see how this matching process happens at a level outside awareness.

## THE RAMOS FAMILY

The Ramos family consists of the father Manuel, the mother Marie, and their two sons Rico (age 16) and Luis (age 9). The parents are from Puerto Rico; they immigrated to the United States when they were teenagers. The parents speak Spanish in the home. The referral, which was initiated by the school, focused on Luis, whose behavior was characterized as "aggressive, showing poor impulse control, and poor self-esteem." The school adjustment counselor believed that "it would be beneficial for him to engage in some therapy." This is all the information I had about the family prior to my initial contact.

The initial meeting was with the parents and Luis. The older son did not attend, although the mother wanted him to be there. The father had decided to let him sleep in that morning rather than come to the meeting. Both parents work and arranged to take a day off to make the initial appointment. As you follow this portion of the transcript, notice how the therapist collaborates with family members around *their* concerns; takes the presenting problem seriously, and asks questions that promote hope and point to change.

### *The Initial Session*

*Question:* This is the family's first-ever encounter with a mental health professional, and seeking help outside the extended family system is not usually supported in the community. In addition, as a white, middle-class male, I am not part of this family's culture. Considering all of this, what enables the father, in particular, to connect with me and remain involved in the process?[1]

After making conversation for a few minutes about the weather, the parents' jobs, and the absent older brother, I formally begin the interview.

[I begin with my typical opening question, which is an attempt to move the family immediately away from a problem-focus and toward a focus on goals for change.]

*Therapist:* So, tell me a little about what you were hoping to accomplish here. What were you thinking about why it would be useful to come here?

*Father:* One of the main reasons we've come is because of Luis, he misbehave, he act up . . . Sometimes when we say something to him, he get angry easy . . . he acts quick. And the school sees the same problem.

*Therapist:* Who does he get angry with?

*Father:* Actually, when we say something to him, he can get angry too quick . . . .

[I try to redirect the father toward those times Luis's mood is seen as acceptable.]

*Therapist:* And sometimes his mood is fine and he will listen and there's no trouble . . . .

*Father:* Sometimes he is, but most of the time I have a lot of problem with the reactions . . . . We just switched him from one school to another because he had a lot of angry reactions with teachers.

*Therapist* (to Luis): What grade are you in?

*Luis:* The third.

[When I hear that Luis has recently changed schools, I see an opportunity for framing this as a "new beginning" that does not include the problem]

*Therapist:* And when was that change made in the school?

*Father:* The change was made in the school just last week.

*Therapist* (to Luis): So, you're in a different school now than you were? You've been in the new school now for a week?

(Luis: nods "yes.")

*Therapist:* How was that week? Was it better?

*Mother:* He like it.

*Therapist* (to father): What did you think?

*Father:* He did a little better improvement there.

[I immediately tune in to any mention of improvement that family members have noticed and try to support and amplify this.]

*Therapist:* So, have you noticed recently some changes?

*Father:* In school, he do a lot better. We got a note saying that he behave excellent.

*Therapist:* It's just a short period of time, but it's a good start.

*Father:* Yes

[I then ask the "miracle question" as a way to help the family give me a clear and specific picture of life *without* the problem. The father doesn't understand what I am asking, so I present the question in a slightly different way.]

*Therapist:* Tell me, if a miracle happened, you woke up one morning and everything was the way you wanted it to be, what would things look like? What would Luis be doing? What would be happening?

*Father:* I don't know how to explain.

*Therapist:* What would be going well? How would you like things to be?

*Father:* What I would like, in the house, is for him to listen to us the way he should . . . and to do whatever he has to do in school, the right way . . . and behave in the house. We tell him something and sometimes he listens and sometimes he doesn't. Most of the time he doesn't. He get angry.

*Therapist:* And when he listens, how does he let you know that he's listening?

*Father:* His temper is different. He's calm and does what he's told to do.

*Therapist:* He's calm and pleasant and says "yes" and goes off and does it.

*Father:* Yes. Whatever we tell him he take in the right way. But, we get to a point sometimes when we can't have both [Luis and his older brother] together . . . . They fight a lot. But 2 minutes later they're kissing each other and making up.

*Therapist:* Do you get involved in that or do you let them figure it out?

*Father:* Well, most of the time I try to stop them. I tell Rico, "Leave it alone, go leave it alone." I would rather not get involved in it though . . . .

*Therapist* (to Luis): Can you take care of yourself when your brother starts with you? Or do you need help from one of your parents?

*Luis:* I move to a different place.

*Therapist:* So, if you move away you get some space from him and it's better. So that's what you do.

*Luis:* Sometimes we fight, but then he comes and says, "I'm sorry."

*Therapist:* He will apologize after. Because he really loves you . . . but sometimes you get on each other's nerves or something.

*Therapist* (to mother): Does he [Luis] take you seriously when you tell him to do something?

*Mother:* He doesn't listen to me.

*Therapist:* Who does he listen to the most?

*Mother:* They don't listen to me . . . (laughs).

*Therapist:* His dad?

*Mother:* Yes, his father.

*Father:* Yes, that's a big problem in the house. When she say something to them, it like goes in one ear and out the other. But the only one who has a little bit control of the situation is myself. Because they know I won't take what they want to give . . . .

*Therapist* (to mother): What is it that your husband does that makes Luis listen to him?

*Mother:* I think when he talks loud, they listen.

*Father:* I tell you right now why they listen to me. Cause I tell them once with my loud voice. They don't listen, then I spank. I don't take no crap from them. And she [mother] is so soft.

*Therapist:* So they know you [father] mean business.

*Father:* I tell them once. If I see they pay no mind I tell them twice. The third time there'll be no talking. I don't like to do that myself, I don't like to hit them.

*Therapist:* Who does Luis spend most of his time with in the evening?

*Father:* She work and I work. When we get home I have other things to do, so she spend time with him. I don't get to spend a lot of time with them. The only time I spend time with them is sitting in front of the TV and watching a movie or something.

[In the following segment I encourage the mother to present her picture of change.]

*Therapist* (to mother): So, how would you like things to be at home?

*Mother:* I'm not the boss at home. Nobody respect me, I think. Because of the way that I talk or something like that.

*Therapist:* They don't take you seriously?

*Mother:* No, my husband is like the big man in the house. I say something, nobody respects (laughs). My husband is nice person, but not when he's drinking . . . that's another thing. [The mother raises the issue of her husband's drinking]

*Therapist:* Who's drinking?

*Mother:* My husband.

*Father:* I use to drink a lot . . . on the weekends. I don't drink now. But my temper is still bad . . . . It's like the person who quits smoking, you know, I don't know how to explain it . . . .

[Rather than focus on the father's drinking, I choose to focus on the time he's been sober. I then question him about who decided that he should stop and finally compliment him on his successful initial efforts at sobriety.]

*Therapist:* How long has there been no drinking?

*Father:* About 6 weeks.

*Therapist:* How come you stopped?

*Father:* Because I had to . . . . I was thinking it was no good. I look at it this way. You spend more money drinking . . . . A lot of time when I want to say something to the kids, I can't say it when I'm drunk. Because I know it's no good example to tell them . . . . I can say something and then the next day when I'm sober they will say you told me this . . . . I say, "Hell, no, I didn't say that." And that's when the problems comes up. I also want to lose some weight, and so you've got to cut that stuff out.

*Therapist:* Did a doctor tell you to stop?

*Father:* No, I decided.

*Therapist:* So, you decided to make some changes. (To mother): Are you happy about that?

*Mother:* Oh, yeah. I'm happy but I see the other side too.

*Therapist:* His temper is . . . he's more irritable.

*Mother:* He's different.

*Therapist:* How is he different?

*Mother:* Sometimes he's happy and sometimes he's moody.

*Therapist* (to father): So, you're moody too?

*Mother:* Yes, he and Luis have the same temper.

*Therapist:* The two of them.

*Mother:* Yes. I think so. They're like macho man . . . like "I'm the boss."

[Puerto Rican families have traditionally been patriarchal (Garcia-Preto, 1982), with the husband expected to be the protector and provider for his family. In this segment, Mother is emphasizing her sense of powerlessness in the face of the "macho men" in the household.]

*Therapist* (to Luis): So, you take after your dad that way. You think you're the boss. Except you're only 9 years old . . . .

*Mother:* Rico is like that too. I told my husband I wanted him to come today too. But, my husband said no, let him sleep. Luis doing the same like Rico . . . . (She describes her sense that the brothers talk to one another and that Luis is following in his brother's footsteps in becoming a 'macho man.')

*Therapist* [to Luis]: So, you think you're a macho man, Luis?

*Luis:* I don't think I'm a macho man. It's just my attitude.

[I question Luis about how he would like things to be and ask him to be specific about those changes that would tell him that things are different.]

*Therapist:* So, how would you like your attitude to be? Are you happy with your attitude?

(Luis shakes head "no.")

*Therapist:* No, you'd like it to be different. How would you like to be—give me an example. What would you like to be doing different?

*Luis:* I would like to do better.

*Therapist:* What would "better" mean. What would it look like, what would you be doing that you'd like better?

*Luis:* Listening to my parents.

*Therapist:* If they asked you to do something, you'd listen. What kinds of things do they ask you to do?

*Luis:* Pick up things.

*Therapist:* I see, to clean up around the house. How would you like to answer them when they ask you about that?

*Luis:* Just do it.

*Therapist:* Just go off and do it. And now, sometimes, you don't. You get angry, you say "no."

*Mother:* I do it because they don't.

*Therapist* ( to mother): You end up doing it.

*Mother:* Yes.

*Father:* When we get home, they watching TV. They leave everything all over the place. It's like a tornado hit the living room. And I say, "Will you clean that up"? . . . Forget it. It's like talking to the wall. They don't want to pay attention. Then I scream . . . grab the belt and then they get their ass together.

*Therapist:* Then they get moving.

*Mother:* When they want to do something, they do it . . . when they don't want, forget about it . . . I try to talk . . . .

*Therapist* (to mother): You end up doing a lot, then. You end up doing what they should be doing.

*Mother:* Yes.

*Therapist:* The children have gotten the idea they don't have to help because their mother will do it. (To mother): You're working overtime. (To Luis): Your mother can't do it all. But she does a lot now . . . doesn't she? She takes care of the house . . . .

.
.
.

*Therapist* (to father): It sounds to me like you've begun to make some changes for yourself. And Luis, you've started a new school, and you're starting some changes, too. It's a fresh start, you know what I mean? It's a new school, new teachers . . . Are you happy about that?

(Luis nods "yes.")

*Therapist:* Luis, it sounds like you've started making some changes . . . . And you were getting good progress reports in the new school?

*Luis:* Yes.

*Father:* I asked them to write a progress note each day . . . whether poor or good or excellent and then I sign it. Then I know how he's doing. So up to this point I got pretty beautiful notes on it . . . .

[Again I work to emphasize difference and change from some point in the past to the present.]

*Therapist:* That's a great start! Have you noticed any difference at home during this week at the new school, in Luis's behavior?

*Father:* He's doing a little better, yeah.

(Father describes how he grounded Luis for a week about 2 weeks earlier, not allowing Luis to go out with friends, and this made a difference.)

*Father:* Right now when he come from school, he do his homework before he goes out. I don't have to be really strong to him now. He understands. The last week I don't have to be so strong with him, like I used to be when he was at the other school.

*Therapist:* It was easier this week.

*Father:* Lighter, a little lighter.

*Therapist:* Hopefully, it will get lighter and lighter. And you won't have to work so hard. (To Luis): the harder you work, then your dad doesn't have to work so hard. You don't want him on your back, do you?

(Luis shakes head "no.")

*Therapist:* I didn't think so. (To mother): Somehow the kids don't take you seriously enough. They're not respecting your voice. They think they're macho guys and they're not going to listen to a woman tell them what to do, uh? (To Luis): You know your mother has something to say, too. What she says is important. So it's important to listen to her, too, not just your dad. (To Luis): How come you're smiling?

*Mother* (to Luis): You listen to Daddy, not to me.

*Therapist:* Your mother has a voice too . . . . Is there someone at school who I can speak to who knows Luis?

*Mother:* The school social worker, the principal . . .

*Therapist:* Please have one of them give me a call. What I suggest we do is set up a time when Rico can come in too, so the four of you can come here.

*Mother:* Okay.

*Therapist:* I think you've all made a good start for this 1 week. It's only a week, but that's good. (To father): It sounds like you're in the middle of making changes for yourself. Your moods are changing, too, and you're going to have to look at that and how that affects everybody else in the family.

*Mother:* Yes (smiling).

*Therapist:* It's certainly affecting your wife. And I'm sure it's affecting Luis, too. So, they've got to see that you're going to be able to take care of yourself and deal with this calmly. It's some big changes that you're making. I'm going to take a short break right now to gather my thoughts and I'll be back in a few minutes.

[I give myself permission to step out of the room for about 5 minutes at this point to gather my thoughts before concluding the interview. Doing this allows me to get some distance and perspective and it also allows the family to take a break. Stepping out from the intensity of the interaction is very freeing and allows me to generate ideas that I would not have thought of in the session.]

[*Exercise:* Before reading further, take 5 minutes or so to consider how you might organize your thoughts in presenting feedback to this family. Besides commenting on the changes already made, generate ideas that offer the family ways to continue this progress.]

*Therapist:* I want to compliment you [the parents] on your caring and commitment to Luis in making his life better. It is impressive to see how everyone is trying to make changes in this family. You [to father] are making some big changes in ridding your life of alcohol so that you can be a better father to your children. You [to mother] are making it clear that your voice also needs to be respected in the family. And Luis, you are beginning to show how well you can do in school and in cooperating at home. This is all very impressive. What I'd like to ask you to do is to watch for times when Luis is doing what you'd like him to do . . . when he's listening, following through, doing his homework, keeps getting good reports from school, is calm in the way you described you can be [not so emotional]. Those are good signs. Keep track of those. Sometimes we miss those things and get sidetracked by the times he's not cooperating. But, I'm sure, Luis, that there are times when you're doing the things your parents want you to do, and they need to notice that and tell you, "That's great, Luis!" Try not to get caught up in the times Luis doesn't follow through but to support the times that he does—because I know that there are many times when this happens. Also, would it be possible to keep track of the times when Luis does take you [mother] seriously in the way you'd like? Just jot down on a piece of paper what happened. (Mother indicates her willingness to try this.) I would like for us to set up another time when Rico can join us for a meeting. What if we let about 2 weeks go by to see how things are going? (Parents agree.) I think it was a good time to come in at this point and I will see you in 2 weeks.

## *A Followup Letter*

In order to emphasize the points I made at the end of the session, I put my thoughts in a letter to the parents, which I mailed 4 days after our meeting.

Dear Mr. and Mrs. Ramos,

I enjoyed meeting with you and your son Luis last week. I wanted to write to you so that I could summarize some of my thoughts from that meeting. After a meeting I sometimes get thoughts which I wish I had shared in person, so I am writing them down.

I was very impressed with your caring and commitment to your children and making a better life for Luis and Rico. It was very exciting to me to see how you are both making changes. You (Mr. Ramos) are working on making some big changes in ridding your life of alcohol so that you can be a better husband and father to your children. I know how difficult this process can be, and I admire your courage and strength in making this effort. By ridding your life of the influence of alcohol you are setting an important example for your sons. It is clear to me that Luis looks up to you and that you are a very important person to him. By staying calm and taking care of yourself you provide an example for him to follow. I am still puzzled by how you accomplished this. Can you let me in on your secret?

You (Mrs. Ramos) are making it clear that you also want some changes in the family. You want your voice to be respected. As the only woman in a household with three men, you have your work cut out for you. However, from our meeting last week I have the sense that you are already establishing your voice in new ways. I wonder how you would like to further develop your voice and what ideas you have for doing this.

I was also impressed with your son Luis, who has gotten off to a very good start in his first week at the Corbin School. Luis seems like a very nice young man whom you can be proud of. I know, as you do, that Luis is capable of being calm and cooperative. I know that you both have seen that side of him. I want to encourage you both to keep track of those times Luis is doing what you want him to do. You might write down all the times he cooperates in a positive manner. I would suggest that you (Mrs. Ramos) write down all the times that Luis listens to you (takes you seriously) in the way you'd like him to. I'm sure you will find many opportunities to appreciate his respect. Please let me know in what ways he shows this respect.

When we meet again, I look forward to hearing about the ways you've continued to build on the changes you've already made. One note of caution: I would advise not making too many changes at once. I'll see you on ____ [about 2 weeks later].

Sincerely,

Steven Friedman

## The Second Session

The second session, held about 2 weeks later, included all four family members. When I went to the waiting room to greet the family, Mother gave me a big smile. I began the session with the statement "I hope you didn't make too many changes at once." The mother then began describing an incident in which Luis was not cooperative and his father got angry with him. I moved the focus back to "What's better . . . what has improved?" Father reported that he has stopped "bribing" Luis for his cooperation by buying him things. We talk about how Luis is "testing" his father to see if he means business.

The mother then shows me Luis notebook with the progress reports from school, which indicate that out of the last 10 school days, 7 were viewed by the teacher as "good or great days," meaning that Luis did not get into trouble for talking in class and that he completed his papers. I read the teacher's comments out loud and compliment Luis on this progress. Mother reveals that she, rather than Luis's father, is now signing the progress notebook for school, and that "Luis is listening to me now, not just his father." I compliment the mother on getting Luis to take her more seriously. I then ask the family if they received my letter and how they have continued to make changes. The father discusses his struggle to stay clean of alcohol (which he has now accomplished for over 2 months). I congratulate him on his successful efforts to stay sober and acknowledge how hard this is to do.

An incident is then described in which the father got upset with everyone in the family, stormed out of the house, but then regained his composure and returned home. The following excerpt describes this process. Instead of focusing attention on the storming out, I emphasize instead the strength it took for the father to return home. I frame it as an example of the father's modeling for his sons, that "macho men have a soft side." My aim is to look for evidence of competency and resourcefulness rather than limitations or deficits. Notice how this focus places the father in a position of role model to his sons.

*Father:* I just blew my stack . . . . I had an appointment . . . and everyone take their time . . . and I don't want to be late when I have something to do . . . . I get mad . . . . I just go crazy . . . . I drove off, but when I got to the highway I changed my mind . . . . I cooled down . . . . I don't want to admit it, I was wrong but I guess . . . my attitude was showing . . . .

*Therapist:* That's good that you realized that, and showed Luis and Rico you could do that.

*Father:* That's the bottom line . . . . I was feeling lousy . . . . Since I stopped drinking my temper can be pretty rough.

*Mother:* When he [husband] has a problem, we all get it [his anger] . . . .

*Father:* I've got a lot of stuff on my mind. One day I said to my wife I'd like to have a glass of wine and a beer . . . but then I fight with myself . . . .

(Father described how previously when under stress he would drink himself into oblivion. Now he becomes more irritable and easily upset. It is also clear that his wife draws him out about his worries and serves as a good listener.)

*Therapist:* It's going to be rough, but you're winning . . . . I want to come back to the other situation. You left the house angry and then you came back . . . .

*Father:* When I was driving I was thinking it was the wrong way to act. If we're going to help Luis out, I just got to do this. I saw his [Luis's] face when he saw me angry and . . . no good.

*Therapist:* You wanted to show him a different picture.

*Father:* So I tried to control myself. I was still mad but I shut up.

*Therapist:* It was important that your sons see that, see you do that. Everybody can lose their cool, and that you can be strong enough to come back and say "Let's start this over again" is very important. You know, last time you [mother] were saying that Luis and Rico think they are "macho men" . . . but the kind of thing you [father] did by coming back . . . is really letting all of you know that he can say "I was wrong." You know, macho men have a soft side, too. You know what I mean?

I then ask Luis what will he have to do to keep getting "great days" from the teacher. He tells me, "Finish my work and not talk out in class." I ask if he sees anything that might get in the way of doing this. He says "no." I then ask each family member to predict how many school days out of the next 10 do they expect Luis to have a "good or great day" on his progress note. Luis says 10, Father says 8, Mother predicts 7, and Rico says 5. I ask them to bring the notebook back to the next session so we can see how much progress Luis is making. I then end the session with a statement emphasizing how impressed I am with the work they're all doing. I tell the father that "the more you can keep in control the more you show your sons that they can too." And I compliment the mother on getting Luis to take her seriously and ask her to continue to notice when he does this. We schedule a third session in 3 weeks. All four family members shake my hand as they leave.

## Followup Letter

Three days after this session I sent the parents the following letter as a way of consolidating a picture of this family as in a quest for a better life.

Dear Mr. & Mrs. Ramos,

I wanted to write to you to share my thoughts after our last meeting. I continue to be impressed with the love and caring that each of you show in your own ways in helping your sons grow up right. Somehow the two of you decided to each take different roles with the children—you, Mr. Ramos, being the "tough guy" and you, Mrs. Ramos, being the "easy or soft one." However, I know from our past meeting that you, Mr. Ramos, also have a "soft side" and that you, Mrs. Ramos, can be tough-minded in your own way.

I am impressed with how each of you are trying to let your sons see more of the hidden sides of you. This was demonstrated by how you, Mr. Ramos, responded when you thought of the look on your son Luis's face and decided to return home after being so angry. It takes real strength to be able to show such caring. At the same time, I think you, Mrs. Ramos, are really stronger than you let on. I admire the way you have taken responsibility around Luis's school progress report and are available as a loving wife to listen to your husband's worries.

I like your idea, Mr. Ramos, of using the money you would have spent on alcohol and spending it on records and tapes. I wonder if your love of music could somehow be helpful to you when you are starting to get "stressed out" and upset. Let me know if you come up with any ideas about how this might work. I think Luis has somehow gotten the mistaken notion that you, Mr. Ramos, need to have someone to yell at once in a while (you know, to "blow off steam"). He has decided to be the person to help you do this. I don't think you need his help in this way and that you can handle your upset and stresses with the help of your wife and your music. In order to let him know that you don't need him to do this, I would suggest that you try to <u>catch Luis doing something right</u> and let him know that you noticed. I think your noticing the good things that Luis does will help him know that he doesn't need to worry about you anymore.

Luis is taking you, Mrs. Ramos, more seriously now. He understands that you have an important voice in the family. Please keep track of those times you notice that Luis is listening to you and what you do that makes this happen.

I can tell how hard you both are working to see that your children have a good life and a happy future. I think this may be a transition time in the life of the family as each of you make changes that will make the family stronger. When I think of your family I think of the beautiful smiles I've seen on each of your faces and your children's faces at different points in our last meeting. Share those smiles with each other and let me know what happens. I look forward to seeing all of you on Tuesday ____ at 6 PM and to hearing about the progress you are making. Please bring Luis's progress reports from school so I can see "first hand" how well Luis is doing.

Please feel free to share this letter with Rico and Luis.

Sincerely,

Steven Friedman

## Subsequent Sessions

At the third session, Luis brought in an award he received at school as "Student of the Month." In addition, in the 3-week interval between sessions he received *10 out of 10* good reports from his teacher! Both parents were surprised and pleased with his performance.

At the fourth session (3 weeks later), Luis's mother proudly presented me with Luis's report card. In addition to showing significant improvement in his academic subjects, *all* of Luis's marks for "conduct" ("exhibits self-control," "assumes responsibility," "gets along well with peers") had gone from "minus" ("weakness") to "plus" ("strength"). Following this session I sent the family a letter affirming Luis's improvement and change.

At the fifth session (3 weeks later), Rico noted that he has seen changes in his father: "Instead of yelling and going out to drink, he stays there and listens to music." Although Father did drink on one occasion (and got sick to his stomach), he continued to maintain his sobriety (now over 5 months).

At the fifth session I awarded Luis a "Winning Against Bad Habits Certificate" (Figure 7-1) to affirm his success in reclaiming his life from bad habits. Besides my signature, the father witnessed the process by signing the

**FIGURE 7-1   Sample Certificate**

---

### Winning Against Bad Habits Certificate

This certificate is presented to ____ because he did very well at stopping bad habits from pushing him around.

Because he now knows so much about winning against bad habits, any child who wants help in getting rid of bad habits could ask ____ for help.

Every time that ____ walks past this certificate he will get proud of himself. Every time that other people walk past this certificate they will realize how well he did.

Congratulations ____!

Awarded on the ____ day of ____.

Signed: ____

**Steven Friedman, PhD**

Witnessed: ____

---

Adapted from *Narrative Means to Therapeutic Ends* by Michael White and David Epston. Copyright © 1990 by Dulwich Centre, Adelaide, South Australia. Reprinted by permission of W. W. Norton & Company, Inc.

certificate. Using a document like this serves to acknowledge, validate and celebrate change and can be useful in a variety of situations (see White & Epston, 1990, for other examples).

A followup meeting was scheduled and then canceled when the father had to return to Puerto Rico. After not hearing from the family for over 3 months, I phoned and spoke with the father. He said that Luis finished the school year with both excellent grades and good behavior and that at home Luis's behavior was no longer seen as a problem. The father indicated that he has had some alcohol since we last met but had not been "crazy drunk" like before. The door was left open for future appointments.

The following are excerpts from letters written to Mr. and Mrs. Ramos after the fourth and fifth sessions.


Dear Mr. and Mrs. Ramos,

I was delighted to hear about Luis's successes at school over the past several weeks. His "Student of the Month" award is something a parent can be very proud of. I am impressed with what the two of you have done in helping both of your sons to make the right choices.

You (Mr. Ramos) continue to demonstrate to your sons how you can be strong under pressure. By freeing yourself from alcohol and from the temper, you also show your sons that they can also have that strength to change their lives. I am also impressed with you (Mrs. Ramos) in your ability to support your husband in his process of helping himself and the family. Your faith and love in your husband and children give you a strong voice in helping your family grow in a positive direction.

I was interested to hear how each of you have different ways of thinking about earning respect from your children. You, Mr. Ramos, seem to follow the old world-ideas, while you, Mrs. Ramos, follow the ideas that you learned from your grandparents. I have the feeling that both of you take your responsibilities as parents very seriously. I know that each of you want the best for your children and that means helping them show you "respeto sin miedo" [respect without fear].

.
.
.

I continue to be impressed and admire your efforts to create a better life for your sons and for yourselves. By reclaiming your life from negative influences (e.g., alcohol) you show your sons that they too can make their lives more satisfying and rewarding. I remember something Rico said at the last meeting about changes he sees in his father: "Instead of yelling and going out to drink he stays at home and listens to music." This is a significant accomplishment!

I enjoyed hearing about life in Puerto Rico—and I can better understand how you have developed such a strong sense of family and community and a joy in living.

Your sons appear to be good boys who care about and respect their parents and their heritage. I think they will faithfully carry your values with them as they move on in their lives.

Sincerely,

Steven Friedman

## PART II: THE FAMILY RETURNS

About 1 year later I received a call from the pediatrician who sees Luis's then 17-year-old brother Rico, expressing his concern about Rico's drug use. Rico admitted to using marijuana and cocaine over at least a 3-month period. He had been stealing money and jewelry from his parents to get drugs. Rico and his friends were also involved in stealing cars to get money for drugs. Rico's drug use came to light when the parents became suspicious about money missing from the house and from their bank account. The pediatrician had him take a urine screen, which turned out positive for cocaine. He admitted to the pediatrician that he was using cocaine and marijuana and indicated that he wanted to stop. The pediatrician asked me to set up an appointment with the family, which I did.

As we shall see in this as well as in other clinical situations, clients may have already made changes (and seen improvement) prior to the initial appointment (Weiner-Davis, de Shazer, & Gingerich, 1987). In these instances, therapy becomes a process of amplification of already demonstrated steps toward a positive outcome. The Ramos family was seen for an initial session with a focus on Rico's drug use. In the 2 weeks that had passed from the time Rico met with the pediatrician and the family's appointment with me, Rico reported no drug use. An opportunity existed, therefore, to build on this positive development. As you follow this portion of the transcript, notice how the therapist both builds on the presession change and uses scaling questions to "quantify" behavior and provide direction.

*Questions:* Is Rico a "customer for change," and, if so, what accounts for his being in this state of readiness? What is the advantage of seeing Rico and his parents together in this initial session? What gives you confidence that change is already happening?

### The First Session: Building on Presession Change

*Therapist:* Do your parents know what's been going on?

*Rico:* Yes. I've told them

*Therapist:* What drugs were you using?

*Rico:* Cocaine and marijuana.

*Therapist:* How were you using the cocaine? Was it smoked, injected?

*Rico:* No. Sniffed.

*Therapist:* Not crack?

*Rico:* No. We used to put cocaine in the marijuana. It's called an "ouli."

*Therapist:* How long has this been happening . . . have you been using?

*Mother:* Excuse me, do you [Rico] want to talk alone without us first?

*Therapist:* I know your parents are here and it may be uncomfortable, but . . . it's in the past now and I'd like to hear from you.

*Rico:* About 3 months on and off.

*Therapist:* Your friends are into that?

*Rico:* Yeah. At parties and stuff like that.

*Therapist:* How did this come to light?

*Father:* Well, some things were missing in the house, like money and other stuff. That's the way it started to come up, the whole situation. And he admit it, what, about a month ago or so?

*Rico:* Yeah.

(The parents went on to describe how Rico's drug use came to light. Money and jewelry were found missing from the home. Rico at one point took his mother's bankcard and withdrew $300. The parents, when they became suspicious, confronted Rico about the missing money. Rico acknowledged he took it.)

.
.
.

*Father:* I was ready to beat him up because I was upset. He know what I was going to do. So he had no choice but admit it. And he asked me for help.

*Therapist:* He did.

*Father:* I spoke with a cop friend of mine and he tried to help me out the best he could. He told me to call here. Rico admitted he used the $50 to buy stuff. They taken advantage of him. They only gave him baking powder.

*Therapist:* So he got taken.

*Father:* At that point, at that moment it tied up my hands because he admit it and he asked me for help.

*Therapist:* That's the important thing. So, what are you doing now [to help Rico]? I'm trying to understand what are you doing now. You're watching in terms of the money?

*Father:* We have to. Right now I cannot trust him. No way. With the things going on. Okay, I feel bad, like I said, but I have to hide the money. I have to lock my door because—maybe he is trying to calm down and all—but if he's dealing with friends, I've got to be careful.

[I frame the parents' vigilant behavior as helpful and in Rico's best interest.]

*Therapist:* It's part of what has to happen now. For your parents to help you, they really have to tighten things up here. Stay on top of where you go and what you do. That's got to be done.

*Father:* Well, I don't know if he understands what I try to tell him almost every day, but I wish he just stop and think about what we're going through. Rico, it's not easy, son. Because if you want to believe it or not, I'd like to kick your ass, but you've got my hands tied because you want help. So, if you just give me the opportunity to help you, things will be okay.

.
.
.

*Therapist:* So, what are you doing, Rico, that's helping you to be able to resist that urge to get involved [with drugs]? [I assume Rico *is* doing something useful.]

*Rico:* I've been staying home.

*Therapist:* Just trying to stay home more, so you're not in a situation to be tempted. Yeah. But how about at school? You're going to see some of the kids?

*Rico:* No. They don't go to school.

*Therapist:* So, you don't run into them there.

*Father:* This is outside kids. He been doing pretty good since he had the drug test done.

*Therapist:* When was that?

*Father:* It is almost 2 weeks. If he keeps doing this kind of thing [coming home after school and not using drugs], he'll build up the confidence. I can't say I have confidence now . . . . I can't say that. No.

*Mother:* I give him less money. Before I give five dollars a day, now I give three.

*Therapist:* That's very good. These are the kinds of things your parents have to do.

In the following section I use "scaling" questions (Berg & de Shazer, 1993; Berg & Miller, 1992; Kowalski & Kral, 1989) as a way to both assess Rico's confidence in overcoming his drug use and provide an opportunity for him to amplify his thinking about the benefits of creating a drug-free life. As discussed in an earlier chapter, scaling questions provide a means to assess where the client places him- or herself on some important dimension and a "visible" yardstick with which to monitor progress. In the following segment, Rico expresses his thinking publicly (with his parents as witnesses). By "going public," Rico not only articulates the steps needed to overcome the drug problem, but also gives his parents confidence in his abilities to free himself from drugs.

*Therapist:* Tell me something, Rico, I'm trying to understand how confident you are about your ability to be stronger than these drugs. And let's say a "10" is you have the most confidence you're not going to be a slave to these drugs and a "1" is you've got no confidence at all. Okay? Where would you put yourself at this point? I know it's early in the [recovery] process.

*Rico:* I would say an "8."

*Therapist:* An "8"—okay. That's pretty confident, pretty confident. What gives you that feeling of confidence that you will not be a slave to the drugs? What makes you feel like you're an "8"? What goes into making you feel like an "8" instead of a "5" or a "4"?

*Rico:* I was thinking awhile back when I said I needed help, "What's the use of using it? It's not going to do nothing." I was thinking that. I spoke to a friend of my mother's who told me that he used to use it [drugs] in Puerto Rico. I remember him saying you don't need to use it. It will bring you nowhere. And that's true, you know. I seen a lot of friends of mine that recently got out of jail from using that stuff . . . got caught selling.

*Therapist:* So, you've seen some of the problems you can get into with it [drugs]. What else have you been thinking that makes you as confident as an "8" about not cooperating with the power of those drugs?

*Rico:* I just stopped hanging with those people.

*Therapist:* So, you made a decision not to hang with that crowd, that group.

*Rico:* Uh, huh.

*Therapist:* How can you manage that? Aren't they going to call you, come looking for you?

*Rico:* Well, they have. I do see them. I knew them for so long. I know when they come around, I know what time, so I try to prevent being there when they have money. I remember, two days ago they had a half ounce of weed. I was coming home from school and they asked me if I wanted to and I said, "I can't . . . . I want to stop this stuff."

*Therapist:* You told them.

*Rico:* I told everybody that I know. A few of them laughed. A few said that's good. I told them I was going to a program. And I just told them I was getting a blood test every week. Just to get them off my mind.

*Therapist:* Right.

*Rico:* They said, "Are you sure?" "Yeah," I said. "I'm sure," and then they wanted to go for a ride and I went home. I knew that they would be coming back and I went home and my father was there and he was cooking and stuff and I said to him, "I'm bored, let's rent some movies". That's why. I knew if I didn't do something I was going to have an urge to do it [use drugs]. I would think about it twice.

*Therapist:* Right. Okay. So, you were having that feeling of being bored and where other times you would be tempted to move in the direction toward the drugs, you spoke to your dad.

*Rico:* Yeah. I said, "Let's rent a movie. I'm bored. Let's go somewhere."

*Therapist:* "Let's do something." Yeah.

*Rico:* I knew if I just stood in the house and I was bored, my father would end up saying go outside or go to a friend or something. I know he ain't thinking about what I was going to do. But I would sneak away and they'd probably be smoking the weed, marijuana, and I'd probably end up doing it. So as soon as I got home, my father started cooking, I said, "Let's rent some movies."

*Therapist* (to father): Okay, did you know what was going on with Rico, or did you think he was just asking to rent some movies?

*Father:* No. no. I had a feeling what's going on. So I said, "Yeah. Okay. No problem. Let's go [get the videos]."

*Therapist:* So, you responded. So, that's one way your parents can help you, you know.

*Father:* An example right now that I can think of . . . . I think it was last Saturday. I went to Boston. I see a big group of friends of his in the neighborhood and I tell my wife, "I don't really want to go to Boston but I'm going to go," and I took Rico and his brother with me. I don't like the air there. [The father had a sense of possible trouble in the neighborhood.]

*Therapist:* This beginning time is the hardest. I think you've made a lot of positive steps; telling those kids you don't want to use anymore is a big step. Being able to walk away from a situation like you did. And being sensitive to your own feelings inside that you're tempted and to figure out another plan is another positive step. [I frame the recovery process as hard work and support and acknowledge the positive steps that Rico has already taken to rid his life of drugs.]

*Father:* I said to Rico, "I'll make time, anytime." I say, "Rico, I don't ask you to say goodbye to these guys completely. You cannot do that. To tell them you cannot be their friend because they do that. But when you see that they're going to do something wrong, you get the hell out of there." It's hard. I always expected the best from him . . . .

*Therapist:* Yeah. I know. You're fortunate your parents are in there for you, trying to help in any way they can. At this point the simplest way to go is to continue doing what you and your parents have started. I think you'll be able to manage it at this level and not need a formal program. But there are other options. That you're at an "8" in how confident you feel makes me optimistic. What do you think would have to happen for you to feel like a "9", to get from an "8" to a "9"?

*Rico:* To get to a point . . . that I can make my friends stop asking me to be hanging with them, if they can understand what I'm trying to do. So far some of them have stopped already [putting pressure on me] and two of them are thinking of going into a program, too.

*Therapist:* Okay.

:
:
:

*Rico:* Because one of them had an overdose and I told him I was getting into a program. And he said, "I want to do that too."

*Therapist:* You're helping those other guys too, because they see someone say, "I'm not going to let these drugs ruin my life." So they say, 'If Rico can do it, maybe I can do it.' Obviously, your interest is in helping yourself. But there'll probably be some kids who keep pressuring you.

*Rico:* Yeah. They'll keep it up.

*Therapist:* Because they don't want to be alone in doing this. You know. So, to get to a "9," you stop being asked.

*Rico:* Yes. The thing that I do . . . when they're coming around and when they get money . . . and sometimes I'll hear, "I'm going to get real bombed out today." So I ask, "What time you getting bombed?" So I start to go home. This week they were smoking bomb, weed, strong.

*Therapist:* On the one hand, it's a temptation to know all of this, but on the other, it's making you stronger. Those outside forces will always be there.

*Father:* Yes.

[I then ask the parents to scale their confidence in Rico having a drug-free future. Because their confidence levels are lower than Rico's, I ask Rico what he would need to do to bring their confidence levels up.]

*Therapist:* So, it's going to be your job to figure out how you're not going to get pulled back into it. And you've shown you're able to do that. It takes some strength. So that makes me very confident. . . . Where would you [father] put yourself on a 1 to 10 scale? How confident are you in Rico's ability to not let these drugs push him around, where a "10" is most confident?

*Father:* I don't know. (The father translates my question into Spanish for his wife.)

*Mother:* "6"

*Therapist:* So, you're more skeptical. You're a little more cautious..

*Mother:* Yeah. Right now he's very good. He can do it. But he can also change his mind like that [quickly]. So I give "6."

*Therapist:* How about you [father]?

*Father:* About the same.

*Therapist:* A "6?"

*Father:* Yeah.

*Mother:* I've been very nervous. Not sleeping, because of all this. It's tension. If I get home and I don't find him there, I start worrying.

*Question:* Before reading any further, take a few moments to generate a scaling question that would be useful to ask at this point in the interview. Remember there are many options, only one of which I use in this situation.

*Therapist:* Your parents are at a "6," so they're not as confident as you are. What do you think you can do that's going to help them get to a "7," from a "7" to an "8"? What are they going to need to see that will be helpful to them?

*Rico:* I'm really not sure. So far, what I've been doing . . . is not thinking about what is going to happen tomorrow. I just take it day by day.

*Therapist:* That's important.

*Rico:* I think about my schoolwork when I'm in school, not where are they. I don't be thinking where will they be now.

*Therapist:* Okay. And you used to be distracted by that stuff.

*Rico:* Yeah. At times I could be anywhere and I'd make a phone call and find out, "Oh, we're going to get some stuff," okay.

*Therapist:* The drug stuff was foremost in your mind then, and now you're not thinking that way. What can you do if you come home and your dad is not there, like he was the other time. What can you do?

*Rico:* So far this week he's been working late. So, the only thing I do is be with these guys [an adult and his friend]. They're cool. I'll talk to them, play cards, and then I go home.

*Therapist:* So, instead of being by yourself you go to a friend's house . . . . That makes sense.

*Rico:* Those people know I used to use it and they tell me, "You shouldn't hang with them" [the other kids].

*Therapist:* They support you. You're safe there. Rico is thinking very clearly about this. I'm impressed. I see kids who are trying to get off drugs who don't think so clearly about this. I'm impressed. And you've already taken a lot of steps and done a lot of thinking.

*Mother:* This week . . . I'm more happy.

*Father:* Every night either she or I get up at 1 am or 3 am to check that he's in his room. It's hard . . . because I get up at 5 am [for work].

*Therapist:* I don't think you're going to have to do it for long, but at this point I think you're right. You've got to do it. It's part of what will help Rico. I think the two of you are doing well, trying to help your son. I'd like to set up another time to meet. Okay?

(A meeting is scheduled for 1 week later.)

### *The Second Session*

I met with Rico for most of the session, with his mother joining us for a few minutes at the very end.

 *Question:* How are the issues of Rico getting a drug screen and the money he took from his parents handled in this segment of the interview?

*Therapist:* How have you been doing over this period?

*Rico:* Good.

*Therapist:* Were there situations this week when you were feeling tempted [to use drugs]?

*Rico:* No.

*Therapist:* You were bored sometimes?

*Rico:* Yeah. But not tempted.

*Therapist:* Did that surprise you?

*Rico:* Yeah. Because yesterday I was watching a movie, a Spanish movie. It had kids smoking weed. And I was laughing, camping on them.

*Therapist:* I see.

*Rico:* It shocked me. I thought I would have the urge, but I didn't. I thought, "It's stupid, don't do that." I think I'm doing well with my situation. The movie makes it [the drug scene] look interesting . . . . It's a strong movie. You see the stuff right there and they're sniffin' it.

*Therapist:* So, it was right there in front of you.

*Rico:* I was just laughing.

*Therapist:* You could step back. You didn't feel part of that movie. [I emphasize Rico's ability to get perspective and distance.]

*Rico:* I didn't feel part of it. It was stupid. I was laughing.

*Therapist:* Have you run into any of the guys [who use drugs]?

*Rico:* Yesterday. One of them who use to sell, I saw him yesterday. I was like, "How you doin'". . . and I went off.

*Therapist:* They're letting you be.

*Rico:* Little by little they're letting me be. They use to call and we would get together and we'd just be chillin', just be relaxed, watching TV, and all of a sudden they say, "We'll be right back," and they bring some stuff out . . . coke or something.

*Therapist:* So, now you're just not putting yourself into that situation.

*Rico:* No. As I said, I'm taking it day by day . . . . I tell people I'm in a program and they check my blood. I'm trying to clean myself up. A friend of mine from Puerto Rico told me as soon as they find out you do drugs your respect is just thrown away. That really hurt me. I noticed that some people who knew I was doing drugs were hitting on me, calling me "basehead" and all this stuff. I didn't even freebase [smoke purified cocaine].

*Therapist:* So, you lose respect in the community [by using drugs].

[A new (preferred) story is emerging based on Rico's wish to achieve respect in his community. It would have been useful, at this point in the interview, for me to highlight this new story by asking him to talk about his future hopes and goals—emphasizing possibilities for defining his life in new ways.]

*Rico:* Yeah.

*Therapist:* Would it be helpful to have a urine test once in a while?

*Rico:* Yeah. That would be nice. It would prove the point that I can do it.

*Therapist:* Okay. I'm trusting your word that you're taking these steps now, so it's up to you. If you think it would help to know you have to come in and get checked out . . . we can do it.

*Rico:* Yeah.

*Therapist:* Okay.

*Rico:* My parents were saying it's harder for them to get confidence in me again.

*Therapist:* So, this would help build confidence for them to see some results on a test.

*Rico:* I would like that.

[To further solidify Rico's plan for a drug-free future, I ask him to tell me what advice he would give a friend who was thinking about getting involved with drugs.]

*Therapist:* If you had a friend who was getting involved with drugs, what would you tell them? What advice would you give?

*Rico:* I've been doing this with some people. I would explain to them every detail that goes into it. You would get a little urge and then 5 minutes later you want more. You find something or jump somebody to get it. I could control myself that far. I never hurt someone. So, I tell them everything that is into it and they be like, "It makes you a fiend, you always want more," and I say, "Yeah, man . . . it's real bad for you. Just don't do it."

*Therapist:* What other steps do you think you need to take? What other temptations might come up?

*Rico:* Parties. If I go to a party—I don't go that much. My father doesn't let me. He knows what type of people are there. If I go to a party there's always going to be a group of people smoking marijuana. Probably half of the whole room will leave. Hopefully, I will pull through that.

*Therapist:* Half the group will leave. What do you mean?

*Rico:* All the boys might leave and go outside and smoke weed. They'll go one by one but you know what's happening.

*Therapist:* And there's a group left in the house that doesn't do it.

*Rico:* Yeah.

*Therapist:* What would you do?

*Rico:* I think I can handle it.

*Therapist:* It sounds like you're really giving yourself respect and getting respect from other people by staying off of drugs . . . . Have your parents asked you to pay back any of the money [you took]?

*Rico:* No. But I want to. I feel bad. I want to pay them back every little cent I took.

*Therapist:* You may not be able to do it now, but at another point when you're working you can do it.

*Rico:* I feel real bad about it. I blame the stuff [the drugs].

*Therapist:* It [drugs] can really pull you into doing things you don't want to do.

*Rico:* My parents just want me to clean my system out and do good in school, but I don't feel satisfied by that.

*Therapist:* It will be a nice thing to be able to give the money back to them, besides your being off drugs.

(I excuse myself and go to the waiting room and ask the mother to join us.)

*Therapist:* Rico continues to do well, and it really has taken a lot of energy and effort on his part. We were talking earlier about how important it is for you and your husband to watch carefully.

*Mother:* I still wake up in the middle of the night and look [to see if Rico is in his bed.].

*Therapist:* That's good.

*Mother:* I watch him closely.

(I encourage the mother to continue being vigilant with regard to Rico, and we discuss Rico's wish to have periodic urine screens to demonstrate his progress and build up trust with his parents. Another meeting is scheduled in 12 days to follow up on Rico's progress.)

## The Third Session

*Therapist* (to Rico): How have you been doing?

*Rico:* Great.

*Mother:* Great. Yeah. Very great. (She pats Rico on the back proudly.)

*Therapist:* Let me hear about situations that have come up that you needed to find a way to handle.

*Rico:* A few days ago—I told my father about it—a friend of mine was going to a party and she needed someone to go and babysit. Two other boys said they would go. And I said yes [I'd join them]. Later, they said they were getting weed. I said, "Why are you doing it?" They said, "It's the weekend, why not?" Then she invited me and I said, "Oh, no, I don't want to go . . . they're going to smoke marijuana and I'm in a program." And she said, "That's all right." As soon as I got home I told my father.

*Therapist:* Have there been other situations that have come up?

*Rico:* No. That's the only time I came close. I told my father I could've gone and come back quick. But I left. And the next day I saw them [the boys] again and they were telling me they really got bombed. And I said, "That's good for you."

*Therapist:* So, you could listen . . . .

*Rico:* I could listen but it doesn't affect me.

*Therapist:* That's wonderful. That's really not easy to do.

## Followup Contacts

Another appointment was scheduled with Rico and his parents. However, I received a call from Rico's father shortly before this session telling me that their insurance had changed and that they could no longer see me. The father asked me to recommend other providers who accepted the insurance they now had and with whom they could continue the therapy. A followup call 3 months after our last meeting revealed that, although the family had not connected up with a new therapist, Rico was continuing to be drug-free. Rico now saw himself as "at least a 9" and his parents reported being proud of his accomplishment. Rico had reconnected with a church youth group and was dating a young woman who was supportive of his not using drugs. About a year later I ran into the family in a restaurant. They all gave me a warm hello, and the father let me know that both sons were doing very well.

What is very interesting here is that, although the family never resumed therapy after our three sessions, the meetings we had were enough to get the ball rolling in a positive direction. Had I had the opportunity to continue to see them, I am sure I would have had several additional meetings. However, as we have seen, I would have been prolonging the therapy unnecessarily beyond what was actually required.

### A Practical Exercise

Think about ways to imaginatively apply scaling questions in your work. For which kinds of situations would this be especially useful? How might you apply these ideas to work with young children? Experiment with scaling questions in your next session and see how they work.

## KEY IDEAS IN THIS CHAPTER

- Work with children and adolescents and their families can be both challenging and fun, offering opportunities for the therapist to exercise his or her creativity and imagination.
- Matching your conversational rhythm and style to that of the family facilitates joining.
- Doing time-effective therapy with families requires a focus on "what's working." Parents and children are viewed as well intentioned and doing the best they can under existing circumstances.
- The competency-based therapist serves as a consultant who utilizes parents as resources to their child or adolescent. The role of the therapist is not to take over the parenting function or provide a re-parenting experience, but simply to access those resources in the family that will free them from patterns (stories) that have outlived their usefulness.
- Letter writing can be a powerful medium for making the ideas discussed in the session concrete, giving families something to refer to outside of therapy.
- Taking a break toward the end of the session to gather your thoughts can open the door to imaginative ideas and helpful feedback.
- Certificates, diplomas, and awards can be especially useful as means to recognize, validate and celebrate change.
- Scaling questions provide a language to talk about change that is easily understood by both adults and children. These questions have wide applicability with diverse populations of clients.

- Staying attuned to any mention of change or improvement and then amplifying these changes will lead to a more productive and time-efficient therapy than becoming immersed in the details of past problems.
- Depending on how we view a situation, we can either find ourselves caught in a whirlpool of complexity and problems or find simplicity by staying focused on the strengths and successes of the people we see.
- Families are resourceful; sometimes only minimal therapeutic intervention is required to initiate movement in a positive direction.

## NOTE

1. That is an interesting question and one that the mother commented on at the end of the third or fourth session of our first round of contact. The father had left the room to accompany one of the children to a medical appointment in another part of the building. I was left with the mother to reschedule the next appointment. The mother said that she was surprised and pleased about her husband's involvement in therapy and that she "never expected that he would continue to come." What made the difference, I think, was my early and active attempts to connect with him as an important figure whose behavior directly influences his sons'. I respected his focus on Luis while gently engaging him in discussions around his own life. I tried to be sensitive to cultural norms and always framed my comments in ways that supported the importance of his role as the father in the family.

# ► 8

---

# Collaborative Practice in Action III: Changing Conversations

*[The couple] come into the room to disclose their unhappiness. I send them out to establish their happiness.*
—*MILTON H. ERICKSON*

"[Imagine putting] a small drop of red ink into a beaker of water . . . . You do not end up with a beaker of water plus a small drop of red ink. All the water becomes colored" (Postman, 1976, p. 234). Words and descriptions are like that drop of red ink; they have the power to saturate our thinking and color our perspectives. In just this way, our conversations with couples can serve to open options, create a context of possibilities, and generate a variety of alternate views and ideas that bring each partner into connection with the other in positive and hopeful ways. By assuming a competency-based perspective, the time-effective therapist generates hope. This framework acknowledges the partners as the major architects of their relationship.

Therapists are in a unique position to engage in conversations that build on client resources, amplify client successes, and utilize client strengths in ways that offer hope for change. In turn, that hope inspires a sense of empowerment and personal agency (Friedman & Fanger, 1991). At any moment in a therapy session the clinician can be faced with a choice about the direction of the interview. Depending on the direction the therapist chooses, the conversation can immerse both therapist and client in a whirlpool of problems and deficits or generate a sea a hopeful ideas and possibilities.

Couples therapy poses an especially complex challenge. In contrast to work with an individual client, sitting with a couple requires special agility and balance in connecting with the stories of each partner. In this process the therapist acts as a facilitator who guides and structures the therapeutic conversation in ways that open space for the couple to achieve *their* goals. The intensity of couple relationships increases the likelihood of both volatile (polarized, conflictual) and loving (passionate, emotional) communications. The therapist must gain comfort with these intense emotional processes while creating a collaborative context that supports movement toward a set of mutually agreed upon goals. An opportunity exists to capitalize on the emotional energy in the relationship in ways that lead to constructive outcomes.

This chapter illustrates the application of a time-effective, competency-based framework with couples. In elaborating on this framework, excerpts from a series of interviews with a couple are presented, along with commentary on the process (from Friedman, 1996). In the clinical situation presented, one partner (Janice) initially met with a therapist on her own because she was feeling "depressed." As it became clear that her "depression" was a reflection of the upset she was experiencing in the marital relationship, this therapist suggested that she invite her husband to a couples meeting with me.[1] Prior to meeting with the couple I knew only that they had considered separating after 39 years of marriage.

## THE INITIAL COUPLES SESSION

At the outset there are several minutes of social conversation, mainly related to each partner's job. I learn that Janice is in a "people-oriented" job while her husband Murray designs auto equipment. I then ask a fairly standard opening question that acknowledges, first, that there is something they are wanting from this consultation; second, that they have co-responsibility for any changes that take place; and, third, that our work together needs to be *goal-directed* in a way that will be useful to them.

*Therapist:* Maybe you can tell me a little bit about what you were hoping to accomplish by coming here; how our conversation could be useful to you?

*Janice:* About a month ago our marriage almost came to an end and I asked for a separation. It became a very separate kind of thing, with very little in common and with an undertone that wasn't very healthy. I was feeling there is no hope in this at all. After 3 days he came to me and said, "I'll do anything to save this marriage." During those 3 days I felt a lot of sadness and grieving that I didn't expect to feel. I finally made a decision after all these years and I was very surprised how sad I was. I thought about this [the decision to separate] for 8 or 9 years. I was feeling very good about this decision but I was surprised by my sadness. When he came back, he agreed to go to marriage counseling, and I'm hoping for myself that we can get better communication skills and listening skills to put this [relationship] back together, because it's worth trying.

*Therapist:* So it was a month ago when you made the decision to separate?

*Janice:* About a month ago this all came to a climax.

[My antennae are always tuned to any mention of difference or change. I am particularly curious about comments that point to "exceptions" to the past problem-saturated picture of the relationship.]

*Therapist:* And in this past month, since you decided not to go in the direction of separating . . . and I assume made the decision to try to reconcile things, what has improved over these few weeks?

*Janice:* Everything . . . everything. I think we both worked very, very hard at making things work. More sensitivity . . . more "how was your day." A better quality of the whole marriage.

[I emphasize how important these changes are and then engage the couple in a conversation using scaling questions.[2]]

*Therapist:* These changes that you've already made are very important. Tell me, at the point that you were saying, "This isn't going to work," if you looked at a scale from 0 to 10, where 10 was the most confidence you had in things working out and the marriage going on and 0 being no confidence, where were you at that point?

*Janice:* Zero.

*Therapist:* So you were at zero. And how about you (to Murray)?

*Murray:* I didn't realize that it was that bad . . . that what I was doing was that hurtful to Janice. Because I was going on my merry way. I could best describe it as very self-centered. I'm a passive-aggressive person.

[Murray has just defined himself in a "totalizing" manner. Because my interest and curiosity are tuned to competencies rather than perceived deficits, I redirect the conversation by pleading ignorance.]

*Therapist:* I'm not sure what that means, but go on.

*Murray:* And, as I was saying, I didn't think it was that bad. But there was an undertone that I could feel.

*Therapist:* So, where would you have put yourself on this scale at that point before Janice came to you? Where would you be on that scale in terms of your confidence and good feeling about the marriage?

*Murray:* Probably a "7."

*Therapist:* So, you were feeling relatively okay and going along in your own world in a way.

*Murray:* That is correct.

*Therapist:* And then at the time Janice told you she had made this decision, where were you?

*Murray:* I probably went down to a "0."

*Therapist:* So, you dropped very quickly.

*Murray:* Yeah. Janice said, "Let's take a walk. I want to talk with you." And so we did, and she said she didn't think the marriage was working and she'd just rather terminate it. At that point I said, "Well, fine, if that's what you want." I was out practically every night and had backed off on a lot of things to keep the marriage going. (Murray discusses his involvement in multiple organizations and how he was "ignoring" Janice.)

*Therapist:* When you [Murray] were at a 7, you were going along . . . .

*Murray:* . . . in my own self-centered way.

*Therapist:* What was it like to hear from Janice that she was ready to end the relationship?

[Again Murray defines himself negatively. As a therapist I find little value in exploring these descriptions of self that point to deficits or limitations; I continue to shift the conversation in a positive direction.]

*Murray:* It was devastating. I know I haven't been the easiest person to live with . . . . I am a recovering alcoholic and a very controlling person. For example, if Janice shuts the front door, I need to check it again or ask her if she did it.

*Therapist:* So you're a vigilant person who is tuned into lots of things, which of course can feel intrusive to the other. Where would you say you are in terms of your confidence in the relationship now . . . at this point?

*Murray:* I'm unsure. I'd say a "7." Janice said the other day that she felt things were getting much better. I didn't feel that I was trying that much harder to be good. Evidently something is coming from someplace that's making me act better . . . do better. Truthfully, it isn't 100 percent conscious.

*Therapist:* But you're feeling back up to a "7" in terms of your confidence that things can work out.

*Murray:* Yes. I think so.

*Therapist:* And where are you [Janice] right now on the scale?

*Janice:* Probably a "7."

*Therapist:* Okay. Now, that's a big jump, from a "0" to a "7" in a relatively short period of time.

*Murray:* Yes.

Instead of thinking of the therapist as someone with privileged knowledge about how to create change, it is more helpful to view our clients as the experts. Therapy becomes a more collaborative process when we develop and nurture a sense of curiosity and inquisitiveness about our clients' lives and relationships (Anderson & Goolishian, 1988, 1992). In the segment to follow I simply ask both partners to give me specifics about the steps they have taken to improve the relationship. Because *change is ever present,* I focus on these specifics to further solidify the idea that change is occurring. The opportunity to expound on these specifics allows previously unexpressed "noticings" to emerge and a sense of hope to be established.

*Therapist:* What I would be interested in hearing from each of you is what you've noticed (and it sounds like you [Janice] have noticed a number of changes recently) . . . what are those very small specific things that have helped your confidence go from a "0" to a "7"?

*Janice:* Little "post-it" notes left for me in the morning . . . little love notes . . . a call during the day to say hello and reminding me that he has to do things, whereas before he'd just come home and then go right out again . . . with no communication. A great deal of communication now . . . about his plans. Sharing a walk together that is peaceful with good conversation. More cognizant that some of this stuff is affecting me medically. My blood pressure had gone way up during those weeks. Now he says, "Let's take your blood pressure . . . a walk would be good for you". . . . attention. Maybe seeing a movie I want to see . . . and he did it and enjoyed it in spite of himself. And we had a nice talk about the ending, talking about people's feelings and all that, which we usually don't do. We had our grand-daughter visiting for 5 days and Murray took 2 days off, which was an unusual thing. I had to work one of the days and he said that is okay because "I will be here." I saw a bonding between them that I had never seen before. He showed a real sensitivity . . . . Also a little more latitude with money. That's always been a bone of contention between us. Much freer and more generous with money. There seems to be a "180" happening that seems so positive.

*Therapist:* That's quite a lot of things that you've noticed. And you [Murray] are saying that you weren't trying in a conscious way to make these things happen.

*Murray:* Truthfully I can't put my finger on it. They were done unconsciously and maybe it is better that I wasn't consciously trying to please her so much. But the whole thing came to a head last April when I was supposed to take Janice to the hospital for a test and I had three other things on my calendar and unfortunately she was put last. I asked her to take a cab there and that's the thing that got the whole ball rolling down hill.

[The therapist focuses on the specifics of what each partner has noticed that further reinforces the idea that change is occurring.]

*Therapist:* I'm interested in hearing from you [Murray] about the kinds of changes you've noticed over the last few weeks.

*Murray:* Well, Janice seems more grateful for any little things I do. I had forgotten about notes I leave on the table. But I've been waiting to come here to really start the process. I don't feel like I started it yet.

*Therapist:* It seems to me like you *have* started the process. Many times people do start the process before coming here, and that is why I'm so interested in the steps you've already taken that can be built on and further amplified to help these changes continue.

*Janice:* Before this last month . . . after an altercation or something . . . there would be several days of trying to placate. But what's happening recently I don't see as placating. This is something different. This is entirely different than the usual pattern of placating and patronizing.

*Therapist* [continuing to focus on any mention of differences as a way to amplify change in a positive direction]: How is this different?

*Janice:* Well, I don't know quite how to explain it other than the placating was quite transparent. "Let me do this for you, let me do that for you." This [current behavior] was much more sensitive and paced in a different way. There wasn't the anxiety . . . it was just kind of flowing.

*Therapist:* So this has felt more paced and flowing . . . .

*Janice:* And more natural. It wasn't staged.

*Murray:* That was I think what I was meaning when I said it wasn't a conscious effort on my part.

*Therapist:* The sensitivity has just flowed naturally.

*Murray:* My goal is to make Janice happy and to see our relationship be better than it's been in the past.

*Therapist:* It sounds to me like you got the "wake up call" from Janice when she said, "This is it, the marriage is over." And you've responded . . . . I want to get back to what we were discussing a few minutes ago, the changes you've noticed about yourself, about Janice, and about the two of you over these past few weeks.

*Murray:* When I hug her there's not as much of a rigidity.

*Therapist:* Okay, so she's more responsive.

*Murray:* It feels more comfortable in bed with her now. I feel more welcome.

*Therapist:* Other things that you've noticed?

*Murray:* Just Janice saying that I'm doing better . . . . Is she talking about the same person that I am? I wasn't really trying that hard. I guess I wasn't doing my usual placating thing.

*Therapist:* It sounds like you're doing something differently now that is a surprise to you. It's different than other ways you've related to Janice.

*Murray:* Yes. I'm acting like a real person.

*Therapist:* You're not putting on a facade.

*Murray:* Correct.

*Therapist:* It feels more authentic.

*Murray:* Yeah. (Murray also described cutting back on outside activities. And they have gone out to dinner several times and enjoyed themselves.)

[By taking seriously the couple's request and keeping his attention on their goals for change, the therapist is able to engage the couple in a respectful and collaborative conversation. This is a *request-based therapy* that places priority on the client's preferred outcome. *Success is measured in the client's satisfaction with the results achieved.*]

*Therapist:* What needs to happen now? You've described a lot of very important steps that each of you have taken to improve your relationship over a relatively brief period of time that has increased, for both of you, your sense of confidence in what the relationship can be.

*Murray:* Janice is the one who was pressing for this consultation, and I'm sure she has thoughts about the situation.

*Therapist:* What is it that you'd like her to be talking about?

*Murray:* The reason why we've come . . . why we need help.

*Janice:* I think we both need better listening skills, to communicate more before things get to a peak. I let things build up and I then I explode. I'd like to figure out how to be less explosive.

*Murray:* I would say Janice doesn't usually explode. She talks things out and I feel inadequate when I'm talking with her. To defend myself I sometimes go off on an anger bent. I feel the anger well up inside me very easily. Probably too easy all my life. Within two sentences I can be arguing. I think it's a lack of my skills in talking. Or I feel a righteous anger—"How dare she intrude on my going out!" No matter what she said I would give her a hard time. It takes a lot to get Janice going.

*Therapist:* Over these few weeks have there been situations that have arisen around your communication?

*Janice:* In 4 weeks there's only been one situation. (We discuss this situation, which turns out to be a relatively minor misunderstanding.)

.
.
.

*Murray:* We never have an intelligent argument. I think of Janice as my worst adversary and I stop listening and start reacting angrily.

*Therapist:* Even though you know you can have an argument with someone and still be friends. That would be a good sign I guess if you [Murray] could argue but still be friends rather than feel like enemies. I wanted to go back to that scale again. If you're at a "7" in your confidence about the relationship, what would have to happen to feel like an "8," that would move things a little further along from where you are now? What would you need to see more of that would further increase your sense of confidence?

In the following segment, Murray presents himself as the one who most needs to change. While not accepting his story of himself as the "cause" of the problem, I do accept his willingness to take action to make things better. In terms of Prochaska and DiClemente's change model (Prochaska, DiClemente, & Norcross, 1992), Murray seems to be in the stage of "preparation for action." He can also be viewed as a "customer" (Berg, 1989). My goal, again, is to generate optimism about change, and I do this by assuming a hopeful, future-oriented stance. With change being inevitable and ever present, *change talk* can be promoted by a focus on future expectations about continued change.

*Murray:* The first thought that comes into my head is that I have to change my attitude the most of either of us. I think deep down I'm the person who's the cause of most of the problem. So both my attitude and how I do things have to change.

*Therapist:* What would be an example of a change in your attitude?

*Murray:* If I do have to do something at least plan it with her a little in advance and see if it fits with her needs and our plans. More of a negotiation. I need to grow up and not be childish about things . . . to have an adult mentality. Don't play games or use various ploys but just be a straightforward adult. Try to express my feelings as best I can. I feel like an underdog when I try to express my feelings to Janice and then it escalates into something unpleasant . . . where I know I'll win.

*Therapist:* What about your thoughts on small changes that will increase your sense of confidence about the relationship?

*Janice:* I'd say to have some prime time together. I also need more information about our financial situation. Murray is going to retire in a few years and I would like to be brought up to date on our financial planning. I'd like to see the house improved . . . it needs a lot of work. I'm happy about what he said about the control issue. That would make it a "10" for me, I think.

Toward the end of the session I summarize the issues discussed and give the couple feedback. This feedback contains a compliment about steps already taken to improve the relationship, my understanding of the perspective or "story" that each member of the couple expressed in the session, and an accentuation and amplification of changes that have been identified that increase my optimism about their ability to continue to improve their relationship.

*Question:* If you would like some practice putting together a summary statement, take 10 minutes or so to organize your thoughts on how you would present your ideas to this couple, using the elements mentioned here as a guide.

*Therapist:* I'm very impressed with the steps you've been taking. It sounds like in some ways things were building up over a long period of time. You were going your separate ways. You [Janice] were feeling more of the burden about the relationship and getting more and more upset. You [Murray] were going along focusing more and more on external things and not being sensitive and tuned in to Janice and to things in the relationship. And finally your [Janice] misery level got to the point you thought it would be best to call it quits . . . . And somehow that served as a "wake-up" call to you [Murray] . . . your ears opened up . . . you started hearing in a different way and obviously responding in a different way and not in the old way of "she's upset so I'll be nice to her" . . . the alcoholic mode of "I've been bad, so now I'll make it up to her and be especially good." This is different. A different side of you [Murray] is coming out in the past few weeks. You [Murray] were saying it feels almost unconscious, that it's coming to the surface now and doesn't require that you force it in ways that you have in the past . . . the placating and so on. The fact that the two of you have been able to move yourselves from the bottom up to a "7" makes me optimistic that you can continue to work things out. It seems like the two of you are at a new stage, developing a new foundation from which to build things back again. That's not to say it isn't easy to fall back into old patterns. So you need to be vigilant about that.

*Janice:* I was so doubtful that this was real. In my mind I was saying, "I'm being manipulated here." He was being so good and then I'd cancel the appointment here and we'd go back to the old way. I had a lot of doubt that these changes were real. I said to myself, "This is like a good dream." It's so good.

*Therapist:* You expected it to end after several days and it didn't.

*Janice:* Yes. My confidence was way up. He really means this. It's not another sham.

[Since Murray appears to be a customer for change, I suggest several things for him to do that may further improve his relationship with his wife. I end the interview on a positive note, telling them they are building a new chapter in their relationship.]

*Therapist:* What I'm wondering about, between now and when we meet again, if the two of you would be willing to sit down and discuss some of the things we've been talking about here that need attention, for example the finances and maybe planning a weekend together. And for you [Murray] to be aware of when that child part is coming out and how you can be straight with Janice. And I'm sure there will be issues that will come up that may get an argument going. I'm wondering if you [Murray] can keep in your awareness that you're arguing with a friend . . . this is not an enemy or someone who is trying to hurt you. You will need to argue in a different way than you have in the past.

*Murray:* Yes. I'll try.

*Therapist:* And Janice also, I get the sense, is already arguing in a new way. She's asserting herself more actively. So, the arguments will be different . . . an expression of differences and an opportunity to sit down and listen to one another and come to some understandings. Again, I'm impressed with the steps you've taken and with the way you've been able to turn things significantly around. And now it's a question of building on these things you've already started to begin a new chapter in your relationship. So, if you're interested we can set up another time.

*Murray:* Sure

*Janice:* Yes

*Murray:* What length of time, 2 weeks?

*Therapist:* That's up to you. What would you think would be a useful span of time between now and the next time we meet?

(After Murray and Janice confer, we set the next appointment in $2\frac{1}{2}$ weeks.)

## THE SECOND SESSION

*Therapist:* How have things been going with the two of you?

*Janice:* Strained at times, but I think we're both trying very hard.

*Therapist:* Okay. So, you've noticed the effort but also some rough edges.

*Murray:* A person is trying hard, but when a feeling comes it immediately comes to the forefront.

*Therapist:* You're more sensitive and aware of yourselves and each other right now?

*Murray:* Right. But I'm still holding to what I think I own . . . by that I mean the money . . . the ultimate control. It's difficult for me not to do.

*Therapist:* That pattern seems well entrenched at this point.

*Murray:* Yes.

*Therapist:* Has that been a source of tension, then?

*Murray:* No. But I'm aware that it could be.

*Janice:* I asked him about the finances in regard to getting our kitchen remodeled, and his answer was "the bank." I didn't know what bank he meant. I'm sure between the two of us we can certainly pay back the loan, but he got very upset and said, "I'm the only one working and I [Murray] would have to pay for it." That's not exactly true since I work a couple of days a week and have another job once in a while. He's thinking with a 1940's mentality that this woman hasn't been working. It's just never, "She works too."

*Therapist:* Somehow he sees himself as the sole responsible person in this.

*Murray:* Right.

*Therapist:* It feels like it's all on your [Murray's] shoulders.

*Murray:* It does. It's good that it's coming up at this time, because without this it may have seemed like a smooth life we were having without any problems. And this is a good problem to be working on.

[Murray and Janice are ready to focus in on a "problem" area. Rather than dive straight into this conflict, I redirect their attention to the positive changes they have been noticing since we met last. My goal here is not to discount the problem or to ignore it; I merely want to create space for this discussion in a warm atmosphere where the changes each has made are identified and acknowledged. Later in the session I will come back to this area of concern.]

*Therapist:* Yes. It certainly touches on some of the issues we've discussed. Before we go too far I would like to know what kinds of things . . . in terms of the changes you've been making since I saw you last . . . how things have developed further in a positive direction? I'd be interested in the changes you've made and how you've built on those.

*Murray:* Okay. I was going to go over money matters with Janice and I haven't gotten to that yet. I don't think I'm holding back, but the time hasn't presented itself where I've had all the information together.

*Therapist:* Okay.

*Murray:* There was something else we were working on that we did good with but I can't think of it now.

*Janice:* A concrete thing that was positive was that Murray said, "Let's think about the kitchen . . . and let's go and see some ideas". . . was really nice to hear. Before we talked about finances we had some fun talking about possibilities for the kitchen. Our tastes are pretty much in common. But it got very testy around the possible home equity loan and there was a backsliding that was all the way back to 0 as far as I was concerned. I got a little disheartened.

Because it started out very nicely. I think what we have to do is find some common way to discuss how we're going to do things. I don't feel badly that we haven't gone over the finances. Murray has been working on some projects at work that have kept him pretty late and he's tired when he comes home. And I don't expect instant gratification for any of the concrete things I want to see.

*Therapist:* Okay.

*Janice:* The nice one was that we went out and had a beautiful dinner. We dined . . . and it was lovely. We talked through it about some feelings and some interesting observations he had. He talked about having some feelings after noticing me sitting by myself in church on Sunday while he was helping the minister up front.

*Murray:* Well, with what we've been going through there was the potential that you would be alone and it didn't make me feel good to see you sitting alone at that time in church. It distressed me that you were alone.

*Janice:* I thought that was a sensitive thing to say.

*Therapist:* Yes. So, you [Murray] had a picture of Janice . . . .

*Murray:* . . . as a widowed or divorced person sitting alone. It wasn't that she was sad or anything.

*Therapist:* But it made you sad?

*Murray:* Yes. It made my heart . . . you know the feeling you sometimes have on the inside . . . it's a physical thing . . . a feeling. So I told her about that at dinner.

*Janice:* There was some very nice personal conversation that happened and it was a very happy kind of meal. It was very relaxed. We had planned to do some awful errands at the shopping mall and Murray said, "It's raining . . . . I don't feel like going there . . . let's just dine and relax and then go home." And there was no pressure or tension. It was fun.

*Therapist:* How long do you think you were sitting there?

*Murray:* Two or 3 hours.

*Janice:* It was a candlelight dinner. We just don't do that very often.

*Murray:* It was a spur-of-the-moment kind of thing.

.
.
.

*Therapist:* What other positive things are going on?

*Janice:* Murray has been working late recently and he's been calling early in the day to let me know what time he'll be home. Before he'd call late.

*Therapist:* So, he's thinking about you.

*Janice:* Yes. I would say a lot more positive things happening over the 2 weeks than negative. Each one is looking out for the other person. More awarenesses.

*Therapist* [returning to the area of conflict the couple initially raised at the beginning of the session]: And it's important to keep that in mind in light of the strain that is going to exist as you make changes, and to keep in mind the positives and not let the strain pull you back to feeling you're at point zero . . . which can happen when your expectations are at a high level. I think it's part of the natural process that there will be some strain as you go through these changes and move forward . . . . Now, in terms of the kitchen, what is it that you have to work out, and how do you want to work it out differently than you have in the past?

(We then begin to discuss their plans for remodeling their kitchen. This project serves, in an interesting way, as a springboard for discussion about their relationship. The couple agreed not to move ahead too quickly on the project but to spend time planning to do this right. Janice says that the important thing was "he said let's do it and that was a big, big plus." We talk about how Janice doesn't "pussyfoot" around anymore and won't "walk on eggshells" with Murray. Janice says, "I don't think he likes that." Murray admits that he doesn't take easily to changes . . . . "I like old . . . really." I normalize this feeling by telling them that most people get used to the familiar, so that change can be a bit startling. Murray then describes having put together the original kitchen himself in his own perfectionistic way and being attached to it. Murray says there are areas that Janice will be expert on like colors and that he can be helpful around things like floor covering where he can systematically get information about alternatives. I tell them that they seem to have a way of complementing one another in this process. We then talk about how finances impact on this project in light of Murray's concern about his impending retirement. In the following segment we return specifically to their relationship, and then I ask a future-oriented question. The future provides a blank canvas on which to paint a new picture of the relationship.)

*Therapist:* What are your ideas about how you'd like to work out this kitchen situation? Or would you prefer not to work together on it?

*Janice:* I don't want it all in my lap. I want us to share responsibility for this. I'm worried that there could be major blow-ups on this one.

*Therapist:* You are imagining this?

*Janice:* I guess I'm projecting, but it's pretty much the way it goes.

*Therapist:* Blow-ups of what kind?

*Janice:* I don't know. Maybe some flooring that I picked out Murray is going to be critical of.

*Therapist:* He might comment in a critical way on your choices.

*Janice:* Right. I'm very scared about doing this. It's trying to be compatible . . . but as far as colors, choices, taste, et cetera, we never have a problem with that. We're very fortunate. And, as I said, I don't need "fancy" to be happy. But it's the "getting it off the ground" stuff that's hard, like deciding which contractors to get for what jobs . . . .

*Therapist* [asks a future-oriented question]: So, what do the two of you have to do to get the ball rolling on this thing?

*Murray:* We've got to sit down and make some decisions . . . and keep going forward with our goals . . . and just work together.

*Therapist:* What's your idea of how you'd like it to be on this project . . . your roles in working together?

*Janice:* A pleasant conversation in discussing things . . . not a closing down. I'm not as knowledgeable about some things, and he's got the practical sense about quality and construction and those things while my eye would go to color and a warm look and that sort of thing. Mostly we need to communicate. I need to listen better to what he's saying and I want him to listen better to what I'm saying.

*Therapist:* And how would you know that you're listening better? What would you be doing?

*Janice:* Sort of reiterating it.

*Therapist:* Listening rather than reacting.

*Janice:* Yeah.

*Therapist:* And in terms of Murray listening to you, what would you be looking for?

*Janice:* Staying in the conversation rather than walking away.

*Therapist:* Do you have a sense that there may be situations when you [Murray] feel like walking away in a huff?

*Murray:* Yes. But I worry that I don't know how to assert myself with Janice without going overboard. My communication skills with Janice end up with me not saying anything or trying to overpower her.

*Therapist:* So something in the middle is what you're looking for.

*Murray:* I've pulled that off a couple of times recently where I haven't backed off but I haven't tried to overpower you. I felt good about it. I can't think of specific instances, but I felt like I didn't win the argument but I felt good that I got my point across. It was something that could have escalated in the past into something serious. There was one time I felt unbending about a situation but I didn't go off the deep end or try to shout you down. I feel like I'm starting to learn how to argue correctly with you on a higher plane.

*Janice:* That's promising.

*Therapist:* So, there must have been some satisfaction . . . you clearly noticed that you were doing something differently.

*Murray:* Yes. Maybe it was a 30-percent improvement over the old way.

*Therapist:* So, you were experimenting with a different way . . . from walking away or trying to impose your way on Janice.

*Murray:* Right.

*Therapist:* And you may have to try several different things to see what will be most comfortable. But it's a step in the right direction.

*Murray:* Yes.

.
.
.

*Therapist:* You're really courageous to take this kitchen project on at this point, because it's an area that will really challenge the two of you. It's got the possibility of pulling you back into old ways that are not going to be very pleasant or to challenge you to develop some new ones that will lead to something much more satisfying.

A little later in the interview we talk about how making one change in the kitchen (replacing the sink) impacts on the need to make other changes (replacing the floor tile and cabinets), noting that this is a metaphor for the process the couple is experiencing. This leads to a conversation about the need for flexibility and openness on the part of Murray and Janice. We then discuss how some people have construction projects that go on for years while others get the work done efficiently. They both say they want to see the work completed quickly with the least disruption to their lives. I comment that both of them want to see the changes happen efficiently at this point in their lives and that people can often think about things for years that can be taken care of relatively quickly.

*Therapist:* As I'm listening to you, I was having some thoughts. As you know, there are different ways to remodel a kitchen, the slow way where you replace a little of the old with the new, or the fast way where you have somebody come in and do the work in 3 days. The two of you seem to be looking for some big changes. You don't want this to be a gradual process of a little of the old and some of the new. You want to be rid of the old. You want the new.

*Janice:* Yes.

*Murray:* Yep. That's a great way of looking at it.

*Therapist:* And both of you seem committed to wanting a new relationship.

*Murray* and *Janice* (together): Yeah . . . .
(We set an appointment for another session 2 weeks ahead.)

## THE THIRD SESSION

*Therapist:* So, I'm interested in hearing how the remodeling of your relationship is going.

*Murray:* Very good (except for one unpleasant episode).

*Therapist:* So, there was one conflictual episode?

*Janice:* That's a good word.

*Murray:* Yeah. And again it was over money.

[Once again, in the following, my goal is not to reimmerse the couple in the problem but to have them begin to consider how they can get it to "dissolve".]

*Therapist:* Instead of telling me the details about the episode, I would be interested in hearing how you got past it, beyond it, how did you resolve it? What actions helped this conflict to dissolve?

*Murray:* Just a little bit of effort on my part. Nothing grand.

*Therapist:* Sometimes it is those small things that make a difference. So, I'm interested in hearing what put that episode in the past.

*Murray:* That episode is still lying there ready to break out again probably.

*Therapist:* So, it's somewhere in the background. So, what do you think you need to do to get that to dissolve so that it's not there lurking in the background?

*Murray:* I would say talk it out a bit and come to an understanding.

*Therapist:* Has that talking process started before coming here?

*Murray:* No. I think I'm probably trying to ignore it, hoping that it would go away. But I know that it's still there.

*Therapist:* What kind of talking about this will help it go more into the background?

*Murray:* Having a good conversation directly with Janice about it. But that's difficult for me.

*Therapist:* So, what would be the best way to proceed to help this fade? Because it sounds to me that this is one episode over 2 weeks . . . and I'm wondering other than that, how were things working?

*Janice:* I think well. (Murray agrees.)

*Therapist:* How much did this incident pervade everything else?

*Janice:* It just went underground like it never happened and we just go on with our lives. I would like to give some details about this . . . since it is this one thing that keeps rearing its ugly head.

*Therapist:* Okay.

*Janice:* The underlying thing I think is there's a basic resentment on Murray's part to my stopping formally working in 1992 and taking my social security. It's never been resolved and it's been a sore spot with him. (Janice provides historical background on the issue, having to do with Murray's attitude about money and his upset over Janice's taking early retirement. They both agree that this needs to be discussed and resolved.)

[I engage the couple around this issue by encouraging that they have a conversation that is satisfying, right here in today's session.]

*Therapist:* What I'm wondering about, that might be useful for you, is to have this conversation about what you've been discussing, but to have it in the way that you would like it to go . . . in a way that would not be conflictual . . . that would come out with some feeling that you've both been heard and that your ideas are out on the table with no hurt feelings. Do you think you can pick up the issue and continue the conversation and get it to some kind of closure?

*Janice:* As we speak?

*Therapist:* Yes. Right now. The closure doesn't mean you have to make a decision . . . just replay this conversation so that it comes out in a more satisfying way.

(Murray and Janice engage in a 10-minute conversation in which each has an opportunity both to talk and to express his or her understanding of the other's positions. After this conversation Murray was comfortable agreeing to Janice's request that he not raise again the issue of Janice's early retirement—"to throw it in her face"—when they discuss money matters.)

In the segment to follow, as a way to limit the couple's expectations and normalize their setbacks, I define progress as something that is not necessarily smooth or without rough edges. In addition, I present my view that therapy will not be an interminable process, although I make it clear that *they* will be the ones to decide when they are satisfied with their progress and wish to stop meeting.

*Janice:* I came in very discouraged about that conversation we had over the money. I came in with a heavy heart tonight, but with doing the role playing I can see there is another way to work things out intelligently and in a calm manner.

*Therapist:* I think you've both been working hard at this process and are making progress. Sometimes it may feel like two steps forward and one step back or that the progress is not fast enough, but you're both working very conscientiously at this and I don't foresee an interminable process here. Maybe meeting two or three more times is about what will be required before you're able to go on your way. We might need a little booster session 2 or 3 months down the road. But you'll need to tell me how satisfied you are with the progress you are making. I do think you're moving in the right direction. So, let's set something up.

(We set an appointment for 5 weeks from now.)

## THE FOURTH SESSION

*Therapist:* How have you been doing?

*Janice:* I think very well.

*Murray:* I would agree.

*Therapist:* What has contributed to your thinking that things are going well?

*Murray:* Probably that there isn't any tension.

*Therapist:* What has replaced the tension?

*Murray:* I think just getting along with each other . . . .

*Therapist:* Let's say a "0" would be that things are at the pits, maybe the way it was back in August [when Janice was talking about a separation] and a "10" is that things are super wonderful . . . .

*Murray:* I'd say a "6.5," maybe a "7."

*Therapist:* And what would you have said 3 weeks ago?

*Murray:* Probably the same. But it's more steady. Not so many ups and downs. I can't think of any major conflicts that occurred.

*Therapist:* What's your sense of where things are?

*Janice:* The Christmas season is always stressful and busy . . . but that kind of tension just wasn't present. It's probably the nicest Christmas season I've known in the 40 years I've been married. (Janice then describes how well things went over the holidays; how her husband sent her a beautiful card, and how he put "an awful lot of thought into the presents he bought me.") In August I would have given this marriage a zero chance of going. As a last ditch effort Murray said he would go for counseling, something he always resisted. Up until maybe 5 weeks ago I would have said, "He just doesn't get it. This just isn't working. He's still isn't hearing anything being said." Again, maybe I was at a "5," maybe "4.5." But he does get it. There are wonderful changes, his thoughtfulness, his communication with me . . . . I had given up. I thought, "He's not going to get it." But he does, and I'm very hopeful.

*Therapist:* So, where would you put yourself now?

*Janice:* Maybe a "7."

*Therapist:* So you're both about at the same place. What would be involved in moving to a "7.5" or an "8"? Or does it feel like a "7" is okay and acceptable to both of you?

*Murray:* I don't know what it would take. I'd say probably doing more of the same . . . being consistent would move it up to an "8."

*Janice:* You asked about whether it could go beyond a "7." I was thinking, we've been married almost 40 years—how much better can it get than a "7"? Because life is life. Who could have expectations of a "10"? And I was thinking, "This is a pretty damn good life."

*Murray:* I was also thinking how lucky we are. We're healthy . . . we're very fortunate. We're blessed.

*Janice:* How much more can you have than a "7"? That's pretty good.

[In this segment above, rather than imposing my own view of how much change is needed, I simply accepted and respected the clients' sense of satisfaction with their own level of progress.]

.
.
.

*Therapist:* It sounds like you [Murray] have been very responsive to feedback from Janice over this period. At the beginning it sounded like you [Janice] were asking more of your husband than you [Murray] were asking of your wife in terms of changes. In fact, you acknowledged that there were certain things that you needed to change about yourself. So, you accepted that and have actively and successfully taken a number of very positive steps that Janice has noticed and appreciated. And it's been nice that you've [Janice] been noticing these changes and actively showing your appreciation.

.
.
.

*Therapist:* You [Murray] were saying that doing more of what you've been doing will increase your confidence . . . and move things along that scale a little bit. Are there other things that you'd like to see going on between the two of you that would increase your confidence to a "7.5" or an "8"? Or, as you were saying, you've been married 40 years, you have your health and feel grateful for what you do have, and that a "7" is just fine . . . without setting new heights or raising expectations beyond what is realistic. And that is an individual decision how people think about this. If what's happening now continues, knowing that there will always be some places where there will be some tension, some conflict, but over all there would be the sense of satisfaction that you've both been experiencing recently, would that be satisfying?

*Murray:* I think that if we continue on that way it will snowball into something better and better.

*Therapist:* So, things may naturally evolve into something better.

*Murray:* Yes.

*Janice:* I'm very happy.

*Therapist:* It seems like you've really turned the corner . . . .

*Murray:* I think we're really doing better.

*Janice:* I even went to the doctor last week, and my blood pressure is normal, and I think that says a lot. The doctor commented that I seemed so much more relaxed.

*Therapist:* I certainly admire the work the two of you have done.

*Janice:* It's been worth it.

*Murray:* I think so.

(We set the next appointment for 1 month ahead.)


## THE FIFTH SESSION

*Therapist:* At our last visit we had discussed using this time for a reassessment of our work. Is that okay? Is there anything pressing that you wanted to bring up before we get into this?

*Murray:* Actually, no.

*Therapist:* Did you [Janice] have something you wanted to bring up?

*Janice:* Not that pressing. It's been a very good month.

*Therapist:* So, you've been able to continue the progress you've been making.

Murray and Janice agree that they have continued their progress. In reviewing their progress, I begin to externalize (White & Epston, 1991) the "patterns" they had developed in their relationship as forces outside themselves that have been influencing them. These patterns, rather than the behavior of either member of the couple, have become the "problem." The externalizing process serves to separate "the person from the problem." By working together, they are liberating themselves from the influence of these patterns and moving their relationship to a new level. I then begin to ask "unique account and redescription questions" (Epston & White, 1992) as a way to increase their sense of personal agency and solidify change.

*Therapist:* Let me go over some things as a way of review of what we've been doing. I also have some questions that I can ask you as a way of reviewing where we are. When you first came in here, you [Janice] had spoken about having come to a point, a few weeks earlier, where you were feeling like it wasn't going to work in the relationship and that this feeling had been building over a period of years. At the same time you [Murray] were going on thinking things were okay while at the same time getting involved in outside activities and organizations, spending less time tuning in to Janice and more time in external pursuits. And then Janice hit you with the "wake-up call" of "I've had it . . . it's not working." At that point you realized very quickly that you weren't tuning in . . . that something was very wrong. Over those few weeks, from the time you took a walk and had that conversation until you came for the first appointment, you were already starting to make some changes. And initially you [Janice] didn't trust that the changes you were seeing were real since in the past you had seen Murray get into more of a placating position where you [Murray] would try to be nice after some episode but then the old patterns would return. But this time you [Janice] began thinking this is not the same old style, it was more authentic, real, and you were feeling more confidence . . . . Over a very long period up until you [Janice] confronted this situation head on, there was tension, withdrawal, and this overpowering kind of behavior that wasn't working. And now you've been able to free yourselves from some of those old patterns. What I'm wondering is what you did to reduce the influence of those old patterns of withdrawal, overpoweringness, isolation, tuned-outness . . . so that those patterns would not be able to dominate your lives in the way they had in the past. What did each of you do that prevented those patterns from continuing to dominate your lives in the ways they had?

*Murray:* I think I was the biggest culprit in this thing. I was going around without consideration for Janice. Whatever I did I did without getting Janice's approval, not consulting with her or anything. That was the way I sort of did things. And Janice took a back seat. I would make decisions for the two of us and she would go along with it. I might say, "Let's go out to dinner tonight," and I wasn't really asking Janice.

*Therapist:* So it was this pattern that was in control. You [Murray] decided and you [Janice] went along with his decision. This was something the two of you were caught up in, cooperating with this pattern rather than doing it differently.

*Murray:* That was the basis for all my dealings with Janice. What I do now is try to consider her a little bit. There's still a long way to go. Old habits die hard. It's hard to make changes when you've been brought up a certain way all of your life. When I grew up, I didn't have a choice about anything. All the choices until the time I got married and left the house were made for me.

*Therapist:* So, that pattern was part of your past that you were bringing along with you.

*Murray:* Yes.

*Therapist:* That was baggage you were bringing with you.

*Murray:* Yes. I thought it was okay to yell at your wife, things like that. But then you do grow up and relearn things too. I think I am making changes . . . and I will continue to try to make them.

*Therapist:* How does making the changes that you've made affect your picture of yourself as a person?

*Murray:* In the old days it would have been a weakness, control the family, control my wife. I would have considered it a weakness that I wasn't strong enough to control my wife . . . but I can see that this is wrong. You have to consider the other person.

*Therapist:* In acting in some new ways that have been different from those old patterns, how has that affected how you think about yourself?

*Murray:* As I say, a little bit weaker . . . .

*Therapist:* So, you're still carrying around those old rules, ideas from the past that say a real man is supposed to be in control of the household . . . .

*Murray:* . . . And not to cry . . . and stuff like that.

*Therapist:* What is the impact of thinking of yourself as weaker?

*Murray:* Actually, not bad. It feels good to know that you're considering another person . . . calling to let them know you'll be late . . . .

*Therapist:* I imagine that these steps will change how you think about yourself. Particularly in the face of the strength of the old patterns, it's not surprising that you'd still have some of that old feeling that being considerate represents weakness rather than strength in considering the other person.

*Murray:* Right.

*Therapist:* The steps you have taken, what do they tell you about what you want in your relationship with Janice?

*Murray:* To do things together, to have fun, to talk about things, to be more thoughtful, to comfort one another in bad times . . . support. Things like that.

*Therapist:* From the time that Janice talked to you, you took that walk and she told you how unhappy she was, what have you learned about her over this period of time that's given you some renewed confidence in the relationship and respect for her?

*Murray:* I respect her for how she handles her job . . . I admire her for that.

*Therapist:* What does that say about her, that she's been willing to stick with you . . . .

*Murray:* Yeah, right. She kept the family together, raised the children . . . I admire her for that. And putting up with what I've given her . . . my drinking and all.

*Therapist:* Janice, what's your sense . . . what did you know about Murray, early on, that would have predicted for you that he would be able to take these positive steps, make these changes?

*Janice:* Basically he was a very good person . . . . Before I married him I knew this was a very upstanding gentleman, a good person, a hard worker, ambitious, someone who would provide for his family. In fact, through all the years of his drinking he never missed a day of work . . . . There was a very strong fiber, a very moral man . . . . Knowing that he was a good person . . . . He had a disease [alcoholism] and I understood it as a disease. But there was something underneath that was special and good.

*Therapist:* You saw through to who he was as a person.

*Janice:* Basically a good person with a lot of that other stuff that got in the way.

*Therapist:* So, you were able to keep that in mind, that through the hard times, you knew he was basically a good person.

*Janice:* Yeah.

*Therapist:* You held onto that even in the face of the difficulties. That's not easy to do . . . . What's your [Janice] sense about the future?

*Janice:* I feel very positive about the future . . . . Earlier, as I said, I didn't think this had a snowballs chance in hell. That he didn't get it. But yes, he does get it. And really, really good things have been happening . . . . Affection: This was never too forthcoming in the last few years. But now, an arm around me, a hug, a kiss. And he said something to me Sunday . . . . This is hard (begins to cry) . . . that he was glad that I hung in all those years. And I had never heard that from him before. And it was very special. I don't know what brought it on . . . .

*Therapist:* It just came out of the blue?

*Janice:* He just came up behind me and said it. He never said that to me before. It's just very comfortable now. I can go over to him and give him a hug or vice versa. It's slow but it's coming. It's almost nightly now that we embrace, which to me is very positive. The first year [of marriage] was lovely . . . and I feel like there was always something there that went away because of this damn disease, but feel some great strength that it could come back. Maybe not in that young love intensity, but like an easy chair . . . soft and comfortable.

*Therapist:* Did Murray's comment that he appreciated your sticking by him take you by surprise?

*Janice:* It did, because those years are never discussed, really.

*Murray:* It comes back to the weakness thing. To tell you that would make me in turn look weak.

*Therapist:* This is another example of how you didn't let the old patterns and scripts determine your behavior or dominate your life.

*Murray:* Yeah.

.
.
.

*Janice:* I see the awarenesses now . . . . Light has dawned on Marblehead. I guess it was always there, but what one considers a weakness, someone else might consider a strength. To me it's very manly to be an honorable person and I see great honesty in Murray now. He's able to verbalize some of these things.

*Therapist:* So, you're seeing strength in what he might consider weakness.

*Janice:* Yes.

*Murray:* That's good.

*Janice:* I don't feel angry the way I felt angry. I just feel this inner peace. I've been able to let go of a lot of it [anger]. The changes become contagious, and one becomes more affirmative to the other person.

*Therapist:* I certainly admire what the two of you have been able to do.

*Janice:* It's work!

Therapist: Yes.

I met with Murray and Janice on five more occasions over a period of 4 months. Although experiencing a few "bumps" along the way (when one of the old patterns resurfaced and Janice felt "discouraged and worried"), this couple was able to build on the strengths of their relationship to establish new and more comfortable ways to complement each other.

## KEY IDEAS IN THIS CHAPTER

- Although neither the therapist nor the client (couple) can predict where the therapy process will lead, the therapist can provide direction by opening space for new ideas, perspectives, and possibilities.
- Couples therapy poses special challenges and opportunities. Capitalizing on the emotional energy of the couple relationship, the therapist creates a collaborative context that supports movement toward mutually agreed upon goals.
- Time-effective couples therapy requires significant therapist agility and an openness to multiple points of view. The therapist needs to actively structure the therapy session so that the voices of each partner can be heard and acknowledged. In a way the therapist serves as a solo reflecting team, offering alternative perspectives on the couple's dilemma—i.e., "widening the lens" while "sharpening the focus" in moving toward the clients' goals.
- By staying attuned to the moment-to-moment interaction in the session, the therapist is in a position to notice, amplify, and highlight evidence of the love, loyalty, connection, and commitment of each partner. The therapist serves as a facilitator or catalyst who, through the medium of conversation, enables clients to liberate themselves from problem-saturated narratives and generate alternative stories that support growth and connection.
- Conversations in therapy can emphasize exceptions to the problem (i.e., instances in which the client has taken a stand contrary to the problem) and/or externalize the problem. An externalizing conversation can free clients from negative, internalizing dialogues and provide an avenue for developing preferred stories such that the client (rather than the problem) is in charge of his or her life. In couples therapy it can be useful to externalize the pattern that has "captured" the couple and that is limiting or constraining movement toward their preferred picture or story. In this way the person is separated from the problem and the partners are joined together in a common effort to reclaim their relationship from this oppressive and unsatisfying "pattern."
- Time is an ally; seeing couples on an intermittent basis (e.g., leaving 2 or 3 weeks between sessions) capitalizes on the day-to-day events that impact on change in their relationship. The therapy process serves a catalytic function in promoting and reinforcing change.

## NOTES

1. Although one person may present for therapy, it is useful for the therapist to consider the possibility of inviting the client's significant other to join the process. Many "individual" problems are relationship issues in disguise. At times the person presenting for therapy may be accepting responsibility for a relationship problem (e.g., "It's my fault") or may be experiencing the impact of a relationship problem (e.g., "I'm depressed"). By meeting with the client individually, the therapist may unwittingly collude with the idea that the problem resides in the client rather than in the system (Friedman, 1984). While the client's partner may refuse to participate, it is useful to open the therapy conversation to this possibility. It should be noted, however, that in some instances it is possible to do an effective "couples therapy" with only one of the partners present (e.g., see de Shazer & Berg, 1985).

2. Scaling questions can be a particularly useful medium to assess each partner's level of commitment and energy to work on the relationship. In the current example, since each partner's commitment to the relationship was evident, I did not pursue this line of questioning.

# ► 9

## Often Asked Questions

*The real difficulty in changing the course of any enterprise lies not in developing new ideas but in escaping from old ones.*
—JOHN MAYNARD KEYNES

While doing workshops and trainings over the past several years, people have often asked me questions on how the competency-based approach discussed in this book fits within a managed care framework. In this chapter I respond to these questions, both elaborating on the ideas presented earlier in the book as well as focusing on points not previously touched upon, but deserving attention.

*Question: Managed care/insurance companies often require both a psychiatric diagnosis and data on client social history and psychological functioning after the first interview. How do you deal with this issue using a competency-based approach?*

Rather than being a process that relies on diagnostic criteria to determine treatment options, time-effective therapy is directed and organized by the client's request and goals. Applying diagnostic categories to people's ever changing and multi-possibilitied lives serves to fix and ultimately subjugate the person with an often pejorative and totalizing definition. Applying a diagnosis, based on deficits and pathology, medicalizes the process of psychotherapy in ways that can stigmatize and demoralize a person. Such a view misses the point of therapy—which is to set people free to use their resources to overcome obstacles and move on in their lives.

The psychiatric establishment has generated a potent mythology that pervades both the professional culture of therapy and the ideas that laypeople have about this process. The prominence of the medical model is evident in the ways we talk and think about our work. Acting in ways that do not support this framework is perceived as radical, naive, or downright subversive because it throws doubt on the "truth" of this formulation. Any classification system represents only one limited view of behavior, not necessarily the only view or the "right" view. As therapists, we need to critically question the implications of any models we apply and not feel bound to unquestioningly accept one view as the truth.

Having said that, there are times when a therapist is required to submit diagnostic information in order to get reimbursed for services or meet MCC regulations. In these instances I try to find the most benign yet "accurate" diagnosis that will meet the requirement for reimbursement. I also find it ethically advisable to talk with the client about this diagnosis and its administrative purpose. Then we put the diagnosis aside and get on with the real work of therapy.

At times, MCCs or other monitoring agencies also ask for a comprehensive assessment of the client that requires exploration of a multitude of issues (e.g., drug or alcohol use, family history of depression, etc.) that may not be at all related to the reasons the client is seeking contact. Again, this point differentiates the possibility approach from traditional models. In most cases, going beyond what the client is requesting and wishing to talk about violates the client's right of privacy and defines the process as one in which an expert is going to review the client's diagnostic profile and life history and then prescribe a treatment plan. While this may work when you visit the doctor with symptoms of an illness and the doctor asks about your health history, it is not relevant to the psychotherapy process.[1] The medical model places the client in a passive mode, looking to the expert doctor to diagnose and prescribe. In the case of psychotherapy I see this diagnostic process as more voyeuristic than helpful. However, if this information is required by the MCC, you can frame this portion of the interview as an administrative process that needs to be accomplished quickly and efficiently, and then move on to the therapy.

Some recent news stories have raised concerns about the privacy and confidentiality of computerized medical records (Bass, 1995a,b; Lewin, 1996). At issue is what information should be included about the client's mental health visits and who will have access to these data. It is clear that what is recorded can have significant repercussions on the lives of our clients (Gaines, 1995, Lewin, 1996). Gaines (1995) found that women who were battered were more likely to be denied health insurance later on! Lewin (1996) reported that many people are denied disability and other forms of insurance after the insurance company gains access to mental health information in the person's medical record. It is my belief that anything in a medical record should be discussed with the client. If the therapist is going to record a diagnosis of "borderline personality disorder," for example, he or she should be prepared to openly discuss this with the client. One of the benefits of letter writing (as mentioned in Chapter 3) is the creation of a nonpejorative record of the session that is available for the client's scrutiny. As therapists, while being accountable to the MCC, we must also be open and "transparent" with our clients.

One way to ethically handle the dilemma of meeting the MCCs request for information while respecting the client's right to privacy, is to inform the client of the potential risks that exist as a function of the involvement of the MCC. One psychiatrist (Dr. Jennifer Katze, cited by Tamar Lewin in the *New York Times*, May 22, 1996, p. D1) presents the following warning to her clients: "In the past two or three years there has been a[n] . . . escalation in requests for 'Treatment Plans' by insurance companies which they use to determine 'medical necessity' for treatment . . . . Treatment Plans, as required by Managed Care monitors, are . . . extensive documents which ask personal questions regarding both history and symptoms, as well as diagnoses and the content of treatment sessions. They are clear intrusions into the confidential nature of psychotherapy. Although every patient signs a 'release of information' with his/her insurance company, granting the physician the legal right to answer such personal questions, few people truly may understand the extent of the information requested. When the Treatment Plan is mailed to the Managed Care company, it may become part of a paper trail that is wholly beyond the control of either the patient or the physician. Each company has its own procedures for handling and storing such sensitive and confidential paperwork, and there is no assurance that I can make that it will be handled with utmost discretion."

The area of confidentiality of records is one that will continue to be at the forefront of managed care practice. Ideally, some balance can be found that allows for accountability on the part of the clinician to the MCC, yet does not violate the client's right of privacy. Obviously, if clients cannot trust MCCs to handle sensitive information discreetly, the whole process of psychotherapy is undermined.

*Question: Do you agree with the idea that setting limits, up front, on the number of sessions that a person can receive, increases the potential for a more time-effective therapy?*

Although many managed care companies currently place limits on the number of sessions authorized, this system has significant drawbacks. Limiting benefits up front places the therapist in an impossible position, undermining the therapist-client decision-making process. As discussed earlier, construction of goals for therapy is best done in collaboration with the client based on the client's request. The amount of time needed to complete the work cannot be driven simply by economic factors or by the results of an administrative intake interview based on diagnostic categories.

Calling the client's attention to benefit limitations, rather than simply focusing on satisfying the client's request, is likely to create opposition. By putting clients in a position to defend their need for more therapy, we unwittingly compel them to dramatize their problems. Therapists often find themselves in this same position by having to "make a case" to the MCC about the seriousness of the client's issues in order to have more sessions authorized. This is not a helpful way to do a time-effective therapy. I prefer a system that focuses on helping clients resolve what they have come to therapy for, in the most time-efficient ways possible. As mentioned in Chapter 1, MCCs are now negotiating with groups of providers who are given the autonomy to allocate and manage a finite set of resources as they see fit. While some clinical situations may necessitate 8, 10, or 15 sessions, many others will need only 1 or 2.

My experience in a staff model HMO, where a population-based philosophy has been in practice for over 25 years, is that it is both possible and preferable to provide quality, time-effective mental health services without recourse to imposing artificial and arbitrary limits on the number of sessions a client can access.[2] Population-based practice in a capitated system, with an experienced group of clinicians trained in time-effective therapy, obviates the need for micromanaging resources from above. The clinician in such a system is both more accountable to manage resources efficiently and more autonomous in making decisions about resource allocation, in collaboration with individual clients, that best meet the needs of those clients.

I realize that many clinicians are working in systems that require them to negotiate with utilization reviewers on the number of sessions to be authorized. This negotiation process can be a complex and frustrating one. However, instead of viewing the case manager or utilization reviewer as the "enemy," clinicians need to use their skills at persuasion to make the case for needed services while demonstrating their expertise in working efficiently and effectively. Although representing quite a challenge, especially to those of us who have experienced the freedom of calling our own shots, this negotiation process requires that clinicians put their skills at collaborative therapy into practice. I do believe that utilization reviewers are trainable and that our efforts at advocacy on behalf of our clients can be effective.

*Question: What is your view on the use of psychotropic medication with clients?*

The use of psychotropic medication becomes a viable alternative after other options have been pursued without success. While not denying that there are biological contributions to behavior, my goal is to frame the use of medication, when needed, as only one part of the "treatment plan" and to emphasize the part the individual plays in the change process. Medication can be an "aid" to functioning rather than a "cure for illness."

Sometimes people struggle valiantly to keep "depression" at bay and are not successful. In these instances a referral to a psychiatrist for medication can be useful and effective. It is obviously best if the therapist and the prescribing psychiatrist are in agreement about the way to frame the use of the medication. However, even when the psychiatrist views the problem from a biological perspective, it is possible for the therapist to emphasize, in his or her work with the client, the nonbiological factors that promote change.

At other times the client may see the need to take medication as reflecting personal failure on his or her part. In these situations I frame the medication as a temporary aid to help get things back on track. While not promoting medication as a panacea, I do encourage some clients to consider this option rather than feel they must continue to suffer. For example, with children and adolescents struggling with problems of distractibility and lack of focus in school, I have been impressed with the benefits of stimulant medication. In these situations, after having contact with the school, I will make a referral to an M.D. so that the parents and child can discuss the benefits/ costs of using medication. The ultimate decision of whether or not to take the medicine must rest with the family (client) and not be imposed by the therapist.

While serving as neither the initial nor primary mode of involvement with the client, the judicious use of medication can be an effective adjunct to therapy and can be integrated into the possibility therapy model. Obviously, as psychotropic drugs are powerful agents with potentially serious side effects (e.g., tardive dyskinesia from continued use of some antipsychotics [Butz, 1994]), they require vigilant monitoring (Sargent, 1986). Just as psychotherapy can be abused, by keeping people in treatment longer than is necessary (Jacobson, 1995; Mould, 1994), pharmacologic agents can also be too quickly instituted or used in place of equal or more efficacious forms of psychotherapy.

An important question that needs to be discussed with clients centers around the ramifications of taking medicine. For example, a woman I was seeing in couples therapy requested a referral for a medication evaluation. It had become clear in our work together that she had been making significant compromises to maintain the relationship, at great cost to herself. She had gained a lot of weight, was tearful and sad most of the day, and was having trouble completing her daily routines. Her level of despair and unhappiness was mobilizing her to consider whether to remain in the relationship, and she expressed this to her husband, who wanted to stay together because it offered him "comfort and predictability." Considering that her husband was the major financial support for the family, leaving was understandably a scary proposition.

Several years earlier, when in similar circumstances, she saw a psychiatrist and was prescribed antidepressant medication. She asked me about the usefulness of taking medication at this point because she was feeling so depressed and unhappy. We discussed whether feeling better, by taking medication, would in fact be a useful way to cope with this difficult situation or whether this would simply serve to put off taking needed action in improving her life circumstance. My role was to help her consider the ramifications of her actions, not to decide what would be best for her. She made the choice to take medication and to remain in the relationship in its current state. The psychiatrist who saw her felt she was "depressed" and while prescribing antidepressant medication encouraged her to continue the couples therapy. However, because the husband found the sessions "too upsetting" and didn't want to experience the "negative reverberations" that seemed to follow the sessions, the therapy ended. Although as a therapist I cannot make decisions for people about what is best for them, I can raise issues that allow them to look at their decisions in a broader social context.

Recently, Griffith and Griffith (1994) have proposed an "ethological" approach to pharmacology that embraces a "both/and" perspective. Viewing medication in the context of clients' language and meaning systems, these authors show how psychotherapy and medication can complement one another. For example, the medicine can serve to calm brain arousal systems such that the person is not so distracted by bodily sensations (e.g., panic reactions), which then opens possibilities for engaging in more reflective and useful therapeutic conversations.

An example is given (Griffith & Griffith, 1994) of a woman who was fearful of presenting at a business meeting in which 20 men would be seated around a table. She informed her therapist (Melissa Griffith) of her history of being abused by several men in her life and her panic and dread about placing herself in a closed room with a large group of men. The therapist, after several sessions, suggested a consultation regarding medication. Xanax (an antianxiety agent) was prescribed as a temporary way to "quiet her body's alarm system so she could hear her own voice and could act on her own wisdom" (p. 200). This woman was able to go to the business meeting and successfully do her job. The following conversation took place after the business meeting (Griffith & Griffith, 1994, p.200):

*Sarah:* Xanax took me to the meeting, and now it's going to get me a promotion! Now I can advance in my job and do the work I am capable of doing. I've been sitting so long in that position just because I couldn't talk to men. It is amazing what that Xanax is doing for me! . . .

*Melissa:* Wait! I know the Xanax helps, but what did it do, and what did you do?

*Sarah:* Xanax did all of it! I'd have been under the table . . . fainted . . . on the floor.

*Melissa:* Okay, so it kept you from fainting. As you were then able to sit at the table, what did you do?

*Sarah:* Well, I talked to the man beside me. I did that. In fact, it was when I talked to him that I decided I could go talk to my boss.

*Melissa:* Wow! What was it you noticed about yourself while you were talking to that man that told you that you could talk to your boss?

*Sarah:* That I made good sense . . . . He noticed it, then I noticed it. He was really interested in my ideas. See, I have good ideas about what the company can do. In fact, I have more ideas than most people, because I have collected them in storage for so long.

*Melissa:* So you had them in storage, and you just had to open the door?

*Sarah:* Well, the Xanax opened the door.

*Melissa:* Okay. Then, when the door was opened, did the Xanax bring out the ideas, or did you?

The therapist continued to explore with this woman "decision points" in her life prior to taking the Xanax, revealing multiple examples of how *she* was an effective agent of change. The Xanax was framed as simply a useful aid.

*Question: Although you take a hopeful, optimistic perspective in therapy, aren't there times when the client may be at risk to hurt himself or others and requires an inpatient hospitalization? What role does psychiatric hospitalization play in your approach?*

Although a survey of studies has shown that "in no case were the outcomes of hospitalization more positive than alternative treatments" (Kiesler, 1982, p. 349), it is necessary at times to use this option. In some circumstances (e.g., with people who are threatening to kill themselves and won't contract for safety) I have little recourse but to move toward a hospitalization. Durrant and Kowalski (1993) suggest that the therapist present to the client the "legal and professional responsibilities" he or she feels when hospitalization is being considered so that the client can better appreciate the therapist's position. The hospital does provide a structured and supervised situation that may offer the client some feeling of comfort and safety. The hospitalization may also provide an opportunity to develop a treatment plan that brings together the client's social system.

Hospitalizations sometimes occur for no other reason than that other alternatives are not apparent or available at the time. Taking the time to systematically review alternatives can save a costly hospitalization, in terms of both money saved and psychological stigma avoided. Often being in a hospital setting too long can support client dependency, passivity, and regressive behavior—factors that do not support a positive context for change.

Developing a natural support structure for the client in times of crisis is clearly preferable to institutional intervention. When this is not possible, the hospital sometimes becomes necessary to prevent clients from hurting themselves or others. While it is possible to introduce and adapt principles of solution-based therapy into an inpatient context (Lipchik, 1988) and to use goal-directed treatment planning as well (Nurcombe, 1989), most hospital settings are run in a fairly traditional and problem-centered way that focuses on deficits and pathology, rather than on strengths and resilience.

In these times of managed care, hospitalization admission rates are rapidly dropping, as is the average length of stay. The managed care movement has, in fact, stimulated the development of less extreme and expensive treatment options. Years ago there were not many alternatives in the continuum of care (i.e., outpatient therapy, day treatment, and hospitalization). Today most managed care programs have a variety of partial hospital programs, "holding beds," and emergency and short-term shelters (D'Agostino, McCabe, & Sclar, 1995). These new services, in contrast to inpatient hospitalization, reduce costs while offering clients less stigmatizing alternatives with equal or better therapeutic results (Gudeman et al., 1985). In fact, some HMOs are contracting with agencies to offer intensive home-based services (e.g., 2-hour visits two times a week) as a way to prevent hospitalizations with families facing complex social problems.

The topic of hospitalization raises the bigger issue of the therapist as an agent of social control. When I report a parent to the Department of Social Services for suspected child abuse, as I am mandated to do by law, I have moved into the realm of social control. In some instances this is absolutely necessary to ensure the child's safety. In other instances the need to take action is in more of a "gray area," leaving openings for the therapist to make decisions that can support people's independence and good judgment rather than bringing in others to take responsibility for their lives.

For example, one 17-year-old I was seeing reported in a session that he had recently purchased a machete from a friend. This young man had a history of impulsive behavior and academic problems, although he had never been in any serious trouble. As he told me about the machete, he asked if I would not tell his mother because she would take it away and he had paid "good money" for this knife. I asked him to tell me what he had in mind to do with this machete, and whether he thought having it was a good idea. He thought about this for a moment and said, "I probably shouldn't have this in the house" and then promised he would find a way to get rid of it.

Should I report him to his mother for safety's sake, or should I trust his statement that he will take responsibility for this himself? Do I act as an agent of social control, seeing him as irresponsible and needing an external authority to take control, or let him know I have confidence in his good judgment? I chose the latter route. When he returned to see me about 3 weeks later, he offered, without my asking, that he had given the machete to the worker from the Department of Social Services when she came to visit the home a few days after our last meeting. I complimented him on his good judgment and used this as an opportunity to support his growing maturity and sensible thinking. Obviously, there are circumstances that would require me to disclose information. In this instance, if the young man had a history of previous violent actions, I would have felt compelled to notify his mother.

*Question: Do you support and encourage client involvement in self-help groups (for example, AA, Al-Anon, Overeaters Anonymous, Tough Love, etc.)?*

Too often we overestimate the power of therapy and underestimate outside forces for change (Bennett, 1984). As a possibility therapist I am always looking for outside resources in the client's everyday world that can support change. With that in mind, I do encourage involvement in self-help groups. These groups can be very useful supports to people during periods of difficulty. I have known many people who have clearly benefited from these groups, and I therefore have no hesitation in recommending them. The story-telling structure of these groups is in many ways similar to Erickson's style in which the client is exposed to a series of stories with which he or she can associate without any direct advice being given about what to do or ways to behave. Telling your story in a supportive atmosphere can be an affirming and validating experience. On the other hand, people can, unfortunately, immerse themselves in these groups such that they begin to define themselves in a totalizing manner based on one problematic area of their lives.

In addition to self-help groups I will sometimes recommend physical exercise or reading as a useful activity. Reading or "bibliotherapy" can be particularly beneficial.[3] For people who require continued contact over extended periods of time (e.g., people who have had multiple hospitalizations) a therapy-group format can be an especially helpful and efficient mode of service delivery (Sabin, 1978). Short-term focused and structured groups, can be time and cost-effective with both children and adults (Brandt, 1989; Budman & Gurman, 1988; Daley & Koppenal, 1981; Donovan, Bennett, & McElroy, 1981; Hoyt, 1993), serving as forums for clients to develop coping skills (Mittelmeier & Meyer, 1994) and generate new stories about their lives and relationships (Adams-Westcott & Isenbart, 1995).

*Question: What are those situations in which your approach is not effective? What do you do then?*

No single approach will work with everybody; flexibility is paramount (Alexander & French, 1946). When my approach does not appear to be working, it is best if I relinquish loyalty to the model I am using and re-establish myself in a listening mode. However useful, techniques should not be applied blindly but must be tempered by a sense of timing and a focus on the therapist-client relationship in the here and now. As a therapist I need to avoid becoming wedded to any one way of approaching a situation and to maintain a readiness to shift gears when my approach does not match the client's experience. As the expression goes, "If the only tool you have is a hammer, then everything begins to look like a nail." Psychotherapy, as Erickson so creatively demonstrated, is invented in the therapeutic conversation. Language is generative (Anderson, 1993); when the therapist stays tuned to the conversation and to the client's story, ideas and solutions will emerge.

Several months ago I met with a family of seven, six children and their mother. The children, ranging in age from 10 to 18, had all been living in different foster homes for many years. The mother brought the family into therapy because since they were reunited there had been a significant degree of conflict among the children. In the initial two sessions with this family I became immersed in the sibling conflict and felt relatively ineffectual. After introducing a variety of solution-focused ideas (e.g., the "miracle question") without success, I decided in the third session to shift gears and simply ask the mother what steps she took to win back her six children. I expressed my respect for how difficult a task this must have been. As she spoke of her accomplishments in gaining custody of her children, she seemed to become more confident and assertive. Her love for her children and her wish to make a life with them was clearly evident in her comments. As I asked her one question after another about how she overcame various obstacles to achieve her goal, the children became more and more attentive and involved. In contrast to the previous sessions, the children listened respectfully. This session was pivotal in creating a shift in the family. So, the short answer to this question is "When stuck, explore competencies and listen to the client."

*Question: How does the kind of positive approach you outline work with a client who has just suffered a major loss and is actively grieving?*

Rather than a problem to be solved, grieving is a process to be experienced. In the traditional view of therapy, grief is something to be "worked through" in cutting the ties with the deceased person and moving on in your life (Stroebe et al., 1992). However, grieving is a process that is culturally defined. In many cultures the relationship with the deceased loved one remains strong and "alive," and the person may look to the ancestor as a source of wisdom, knowledge, and advice (Stroebe et al., 1992). Clients may simply need permission to grieve, understanding that this will be a process over time. I sometimes encourage clients to visit the cemetery or engage in other rituals that mark the passing of the loved one while supporting their connection to him or her (see Friedman & Fanger, 1991, pp. 176–178, for example). As always, flexibility is required. The goal is not to "cheer up" grieving people but to put grief in context while allowing clients to get on with their lives.

*Question: How do you deal with situations in which a client comes in requesting weekly psychotherapy?*

By engaging the client in a discussion of the goals of therapy and the steps needed to reach these goals, I define the process more broadly than what takes place in the room with me. As the client comes to understand this, the idea of weekly treatment loses its appeal. In doing time-effective treatment, you must actively re-educate the consumer about the process of psychotherapy as it differs from more traditional therapy. The client needs to know up front that therapy in a managed care setting is not a condensed or briefer form of what one might get in a private practice setting, but that it represents a shift from an open-ended model to one that emphasizes a short-term focus on specific issues.

Recently an outside therapist referred a 7-year-old for individual weekly therapy, telling me the child needed the consistency of a weekly relationship with a nurturing male figure to recover from traumas he had experienced several years earlier. This view of therapy is not consistent with time-effective work in a managed care setting. My goal is not to re-parent this youngster, but to work with him and his parent to help him move on in his life and not be defeated by the things that happened to him in the past.

As it turned out in this situation, I met with the child and his mother on three occasions (over a 2-month period), with a focus on ways the child was finding to successfully deal with the events of the past. I did not ask him or his mother to detail everything that happened to them but rather left it to them to tell me what they wished to share. Interestingly, at one point in the first session when the mother began talking about some of the traumas they had experienced (e.g., the physical abuse of the mother by the father that the child witnessed), the youngster commented that he felt too much time was spent talking about problems and events that happened in the past and that this wasn't helping him (he had already done this with a previous therapist). At the third session it was clear that the child was doing extremely well, was showing no behavioral problems, and had in fact been very resilient in moving beyond the past traumas. We agreed to stop meeting, with the understanding that the mother could call me at any time should the need arise.

Intermittent therapy, in which the client is seen over periods of time separated by intervals of no face-to-face contact, is a model that I have found effective. Seeing people weekly and/or making longer-term contracts for a specified number of sessions anticipates that therapy will take a long time and sends the wrong message about the possibilities of rapid change. Alexander and French (1946) understood that when they said, "There is no logic in assuming that only a misfortune can have a permanent effect on one's personality. A single equally intensive beneficent experience can also leave its mark" (p. 164).

*Question: How do you apply a competency-based approach when working with families facing complex social problems, like poverty, violence, alcohol and drug abuse, etc.?*

The clinical situations discussed in Chapters 5, 6 and 7 are ones in which multiple stressors were in play, yet the therapists focused their energies in ways that opened the door to small successes. In complex situations the goal is getting movement in a positive direction with the hope that one success will lead to other successes. Time-effective therapy in the possibility frame is not a panacea for life's ills; it is simply a framework that can help both the client and the therapist not to become overwhelmed and demoralized by a large array of issues and problems. The therapist's job is not to sort out and reorganize the life structure of the individual or family, but rather to facilitate small changes in areas that the client is most ready to pursue.

In especially complicated situations the issue of hope becomes even more prominent. With this in mind, I work to maintain a focus on the client's concerns, keep my expectations realistic, and generate conversations that allow clients to get in touch with those strengths, resources, and competencies that are part of their personal history or cultural heritage. I am constantly on the lookout for signs of hope that can be nurtured, allowing clients to move on in their lives with a renewed sense of optimism and increased feelings of control. In situations that seem overwhelmingly complex the goal is to create "small wins" (Weick, 1984). "Much of the artfulness in working with small wins lies in identifying, gathering and labeling several small changes that are present but unnoticed" (Weick, 1984, pp. 43–44). By emphasizing hope and competencies and by keeping an unremitting focus, the therapist can open possibilities for clients to experience themselves as effective agents of change in their own lives.

As a time-effective therapist, I view my role as generating conversations that highlight clients' adaptive strengths and survival strategies. By viewing clients as resilient and strong, rather than as deficit-ridden and incapable, we can enable people to reclaim a sense of hope. No matter how overwhelming a situation may look, there are always possibilities for hope and change. It is this belief that enables the possibility therapist to function effectively in the face of the complexities and obstacles that clients experience in their lives. By focusing on how people cope with adversity rather than succumb to it, we open the doors to hope and future possibilities.

We live in a culture in the United States in which poor people are made to feel responsible for their plight, leading to a downward spiral of demoralization and hopelessness. As Mario Cuomo, the former governor of New York, acknowledged (March 12, 1995 episode of *60 Minutes*), current conservative political trends in the United States have "made the denial of compassion respectable." As therapists, we need to avoid being recruited into this view, to maintain our compassion, and to look for and access the survival strategies and adaptive behaviors that enable clients to survive and stay resilient in the face of external pressures.

*Question: What role does history play in your therapy? When would you explore the client's past history?*

Some people have a need to tell their story and it is obviously important for the clinician to listen. The question becomes, to what aspect of the conversation should the therapist attend—the problems of the past or possibilities for the future? It is easy to become mired in the client's problem-saturated view, unless you actively listen for those parts of the story that are discrepant with the client's dominant picture. It is these "exceptions" that are the building blocks for change. While it is important to attend to the client's story and to be empathic around past struggles and painful life events, the content of the therapy does not consist of the client bemoaning a difficult past or blaming family members for his or her current state.

The approach outlined here focuses on amplification of successes and competencies rather than excavation of past hurts and pain. Rather than a model that promotes catharsis, therapy in the possibility frame views "problem-talk" as serving to immerse the client in a problem-saturated reality that leads to feelings of helplessness and inhibits the generation of solutions. An exploration of past struggles and their successful resolution sets the stage for movement in the present. Another way to use the past to help the client move ahead in the present is to ask a client what advice a relative or friend who died might give to the client (Mittelmeier & Friedman, 1993). In this way the significant figure with whom the client feels a connection becomes a repository of wisdom and advice, an archive of knowledge. When clients do feel the need to talk about the past, I sometimes ask how the past events discussed have been influencing their current lives and relationships. Thus the past is brought into the present in a way that can then be dealt with.

*Question: In many clinical settings it is necessary to do time-effective therapy with people who could be characterized as "chronically stuck," cycling from psychiatric hospital to day treatment and back to the hospital. In what ways can one apply the principles of competency-based therapy with this population?*

Milton Erickson was one of the first to show how even so-called chronic problems were amenable to time-effective intervention (see Haley, 1973, for numerous examples). Part of Erickson's success was based on his steadfast belief that change was possible and even inevitable in the lives of the people with whom he worked. Also, by listening carefully to the client, he was able to utilize the client's frame of reference to create change. While Erickson was a particularly "uncommon therapist," much of his thinking is applicable to our work in managed care.

A competency-based frame can be especially helpful with clients who have long histories of contact with mental health services. The challenge is to generate hope that change is not only possible but already happening. The therapist needs to create a sense of positive movement in time by focusing attention on how the present is different from the past. As Agnetti and Young (1993) point out, "If the temporal dimension is lost in one's view of the world, then the possibility of hope, growth and change is also lost" (p. 69). By amplifying and highlighting even minute differences between past and present in the client's life, opportunities are created to generate hope and movement. Future-oriented questioning like the "miracle question" opens the possibility of change in moving from the present to some future vision. Because change is constant and ever present, the therapist needs to encourage the client to notice change. Besides employing the "change-detection" tasks discussed in Chapter 3, it is useful to focus on how clients' histories of overcoming adversity have affected their state in the present. For example, you might ask, "How have your successful efforts to manage over the years, considering what you've experienced, affected your sense of yourself now?" or, "What learning came out of those years of struggle and hardship that have made you a more understanding and hopeful person?" or, "Considering the changes you've already made in your life, and we have already talked about several, what does that tell you about the possibilities for further changes down the road?"

Not long ago I did a consultation with a client who had been cycling through the hospital and day treatment system for a number of years. She was also seen as being of limited intelligence and as requiring a significant amount of support. We met in front of a group of about 80 people, many of whom knew her. I approached this client from a naive, "not knowing" perspective (Anderson & Goolishian, 1988), focusing my attention on times in the past that she acted contrary to the dominant problem saturated story about her life. As we talked, it become clear that this woman had many strengths (for example, she completed high school with A's and B's and was obviously not limited intellectually) and had a number of good ideas about what she needed to move on in her life. As it turned out, no one had bothered previously to inquire about her resources, competencies, and past successes. By the end of the consultation the members of the audience had their preconceptions shaken and were so impressed with her that they were talking about inviting her to become a member of the agency's board of directors! So, the crucial factors in working with people who have been perceived as chronically impaired are (1) maintaining a position of openness and a naive, "not knowing" perspective, listening for alternative stories; (2) not falling under the domination of the client's history of "dysfunction" or the size of the client's mental health chart; and (3) maintaining a perspective that generates hope by focusing on how clients have overcome obstacles and made their way in life. By not falling prey to constraining and limiting assumptions, we can have a positive impact on the lives of the people we see.

In many instances, cycling between home and hospital can be offset by recruiting family members to play more prominent roles in the individual's care. In one recent situation a 26-year-old woman living at home with her parents was struggling with the residual effects of multiple traumatic events in her childhood and adolescence. The flashbacks and nightmares became so severe that Angie became actively suicidal. In one year she spent all but 6 weeks institutionalized in either a hospital, day treatment, or other residential setting. While the inpatient experiences provided a safe place to be, they were tremendously costly in more ways than simple dollars and cents. With each placement Angie became more and more demoralized and hopeless, seeing herself as incapable of living a normal life.

A meeting of providers was held to develop a new treatment plan in collaboration with Angie and her parents. The new plan (1) placed Angie and her parents in charge of Angie's safety; (2) involved an experienced psychiatric nurse who would be available (both by phone and in person) on an as-needed crisis basis should Angie or her parents require assistance; (3) incorporated family therapy sessions on a twice-a-month basis; (4) involved Angie in an outpatient group meeting weekly for women who experienced childhood trauma; (5) encouraged and supported Angie's interests in horseback riding, playing the guitar, and cooking; (6) included regular appointments with a psychiatrist to oversee the medication she was taking; and (7) involved individual therapy sessions in dealing directly with the trauma.

Over a period of 6 months, with this plan in operation, Angie has not been hospitalized or needed placement in any alternative care facility. While there have been crises during which the visiting nurse made daily visits to the home, Angie, with the help of her parents, has been able to successfully manage outside the hospital. This ability to function at home has been encouraging and hope-generating for both Angie and her parents. The important point here is that it is possible to develop effective treatment plans that can successfully offset the need for more costly alternatives and to do this in a way that supports the personal agency and efficacy of the client and his or her family.

*Question: What place do normative or developmental models have in your approach?*

Norms reflect a belief in an established set of objective criteria against which a person can be evaluated. Norms are set up as objective "truths." Behavior varies significantly by culture and even within cultures; therefore, normative models require close scrutiny. "[D]iverse groups of people engage in different patterns of action and share different meaning systems within which their actions are understood. Thus, actions deemed aberrant, maladjusted or pathological in one cultural milieu may be fully acceptable in another" (Stroebe et al., 1992, p. 1210). Rather than applying normative values for what is or is not good adjustment, I find I am more effective tailoring my approach to the client's specific cultural values and realities. The goals or outcome criteria for therapy are developed directly from the client's request.

Setting up all-encompassing criteria for "healthy functioning" misses the point of the diversity of human behavior and tries to impose categorical definitions on behavior. This question relates to the one discussed earlier on doing a comprehensive assessment as a way to "objectively" determine what needs to be done. This presupposes a model of the therapist as a structural engineer who will assess the situation and generate a blueprint for change. As you can see, this model is unidirectional rather than reciprocal and places the therapist in the role of expert. By staying request-based, therapy matches the client's position and avoids imposing objectively derived assumptions.

In some instances, however, drawing on "expert knowledge" or normative information (e.g., regarding the impact of parental divorce on a child's behavior) can "free people from their isolation" (Fraenkel, 1995, p. 115) by helping them view their situation in a broader context. In these circumstances I am very comfortable offering information to help alleviate anxiety, increase understanding, and promote action.

*Question: How would you apply the process of externalizing the problem in situations in which a child was showing fears and having temper outbursts as a result of being sexually abused?*

At times, children may present with behaviors that reflect a reaction or "protest" to something currently happening in their lives—for example, sexual or physical abuse, a parent's alcohol abuse, witnessing physical violence, or marital separation. In these situations the therapist needs to understand the child's behavior in the context of these stressors. Action in these situations initially focuses on reducing the impact of the stress in ways that ensure the safety of the child and decrease the influence of "worry" on the child's life. These are situations in which I do not initially externalize the problem, but rather respect and respond to the child's efforts to signal that something is wrong. In these situations I work with the family to reduce the negative impact of these stressful events on the child and normalize the child's reaction as understandable considering the circumstances. It is very helpful and relieving to parents and children to appreciate that what they are experiencing is a normal reaction to a set of external events.

*Question: What are some ways the telephone can be used to stay in touch with clients between sessions?*

The telephone can be an efficient means of communication with clients around specific issues. It serves as a bridge between face-to-face meetings and provides access for rapid consultations in times of crisis. Clients generally initiate calls when in crisis or when some agreed upon plan of action seems not to be working. Clients may call when they're feeling discouraged and need help to refocus on "what's working" rather than on "what's not working." Phone contact can be helpful in simply allowing clients to sort out their thinking and gain perspective.

I will sometimes ask clients to call me between scheduled appointments with updates on their progress. In some situations I will suggest, by phone, that the client experiment with a particular approach or strategy (e.g., in dealing with a child who has been having trouble sleeping) and then encourage another phone contact to follow up. In some instances a whole "therapy" can be accomplished via a series of relatively brief (5–15 minute) telephone contacts, avoiding the use of valuable in-office time. Because the mental health practice in which I work is located in a medical setting, clients are already used to calling for advice. Listening carefully to what is being requested, giving the client an opportunity to talk about the issue or event, and then offering some practical advice will often be all that is required for the caller to feel satisfied. I am not reluctant to give advice when I am clear the caller sincerely wants my input and is eager to put it into action. I frame my suggestions as "experimental" and encourage clients to modify or vary these ideas as needed. Sometimes I will even get calls from exasperated parents requesting that I speak directly to their child, which I generally do if the child is amenable to talking with me.

While the phone is a useful medium for client–therapist communication, I anticipate that, with the rapid development of electronic communications ("e-mail"), other forms of non–face-to-face contact will also become available, offering both clients and therapists additional ways to connect outside the confines of the therapist's office. The therapist can also become an 'archivist," storing information in the form of letters and other communications that detail the steps that people have taken to free themselves from problems. The results of these efforts can then be shared, with the writer's permission, with others who face similar problems (see Epston, White, & "Ben," 1995, for examples).

*Question: What is your view on the advantages or disadvantages of having one therapist involved with a whole family, considering situations in which the couple may be asking for marital therapy and the child is also experiencing problems? Do you ever "split the case" with another clinician, or do you find some benefit to doing it all yourself?*

In most situations it is more time-effective to have a single therapist involved with a client or family. Many times after a family is seen, one parent may request to be seen individually around personal concerns. In most of these cases I will see the parent. In one recent instance three young adult daughters came to therapy after they each confided in the other that their father had sexually molested them. All three were furious at their father, who brushed off the incidents as related to his drinking. A few days later the mother called and asked if she and her husband could come in to speak with me (the daughters had mentioned my name to the mother). I agreed to see them, and for a period of time I was meeting with each group separately. The father, feeling totally estranged from both his children and his wife, finally acknowledged the abuse and approached each daughter with an apology. I think I was able to be helpful because of my connection with all family members.

In especially complex family situations, other clinicians may need to be involved in the way of crisis management or medication monitoring. In an HMO setting, working with a team of colleagues who have similar philosophic orientations about therapy is an efficient way to manage complex situations. For example, if someone is in crisis and my schedule does not permit me to see that person frequently, I can call on a colleague to share this responsibility.

*Question: How long do your sessions last? Do you see people for 30-minute time periods?*

My sessions are scheduled mostly in blocks of 1 hour, with some 30-minute slots. A session is over when 50 minutes have elapsed or if the client and I reach a reasonable stopping point sooner (i.e., positive results are evident and/or a plan of action has been established). The client does not "own" the 50 minutes scheduled for the appointment. There are many situations in which a useful stopping point occurs 35 or 40 minutes into a session. To continue after that is to open space for "backtracking," or ending up back where you started, re-immersed in negative problem-talk. I find it more useful to end on a positive, hopeful, and successful note than to have the client leave the office feeling further immersed in the problem.

When I find myself going overtime (i.e., beyond 50 minutes), I usually am inducted into a unhelpful set and am trying desperately to dig my way out, all too often unsuccessfully. It is better to stop a session that is not going anywhere (and take a short break to recalibrate your thoughts) than to fumble around trying to "make something happen" before the client leaves the session.

In some instances, useful followup work can happen in 30 minutes— when an initial plan has been developed and put in motion and good progress has been made in reaching the goal. However, with couples and families I usually schedule 1-hour slots even though the total time may not be needed. In this way I allow myself some flexibility to use the extra time to write notes, return phone calls, consult with colleagues, and other tasks.

*Question: What do you do with people who complete a piece of work and then call back in 6 months or so saying that they have "relapsed"?*

The need for followup contact is anticipated in time-effective therapy. From time to time, people may need to come back for "reinstatement" experiences[4]—opportunities to reinforce and support client resources in getting back on track. So-called "slips" or "relapses" that reflect the re-emergence of the "old story" are commonplace and should be expected by the therapist. While I would not suggest setting the stage for a "relapse" by predicting it (in effect, creating a self-fulfilling prophecy), I do want to leave the door open for future contact should the need present itself. I always tell clients when they depart from therapy that they are welcome to call me at any time to set up an appointment or simply talk by phone, should they feel the need. In doing therapy in the context of managed care, there is no such thing as "termination." One benefit of an intermittent model of therapy is the increasing reliance placed on clients' own resources as they negotiate and navigate the winding rivers of their lives.

## NOTES

1. There are circumstances in which I will ask questions that are not specifically part of the client's request. For example, when I'm meeting with a couple and the wife seems intimidated and constrained to speak freely in her husband's presence, I will see the wife individually and ask directly about issues of physical violence/spouse abuse. When meeting with adolescents, I will usually ask about their drug and alcohol use. With children I might inquire about issues at home that may be upsetting them, as a way to understand the child's behavior in context. At times I might ask about sexual abuse as well.

2. Cummings (1986) also found that "targeted treatment approaches," focused on specific presenting problems, make limit setting on benefits unnecessary.

3. Some of the books that my colleagues and I often recommend to clients include the following (other useful books and audiotapes can be found at your local bookstore): D. Burns (1980), *Feeling Good: The New Mood Therapy*, New York: Penguin Books; D. Greenberger and C. A. Padesky (1995), *Mind Over Mood: A Cognitive Therapy Treatment Manual for Clients*, New York: Guilford Press; H. G. Lerner (1989), *The Dance of Intimacy*, New York: Harper & Row; E. Mazlish and A. Faber (1980), *How to Talk So Kids Will Listen and Listen So Kids Will Talk*, New York: Avon Books; H. C. Parker (1988), *The ADD Hyperactivity Workbook*, Plantation, FL: Impact; D. Tannen (1990), *You Just Don't Understand: Women and Men in Conversation*, New York: Ballantine Books; J. Wallerstein and J. B. Kelly (1980), *Surviving the Break-up: How Children and Parents Cope with Divorce*, New York: Basic Books; and M. Weiner-Davis (1992), *Divorce Busting*, New York: Fireside/Simon & Schuster.

4. Reinstatement is defined as "periodic partial repetition of an experience such that it maintains the effects of the experience through time" (Campbell & Jaynes, 1966, p. 478).

# ▶ 10

## Putting It All Together: Principles for Effective Practice

*The ethical imperative: Act always to increase the number of choices.*
*—HEINZ VON FOERSTER*

This book has articulated a set of principles that can help clinicians function more effectively and with a sense of integrity in a managed care environment. Managed health care, and more specifically the HMO movement, has been growing at a rapid rate in the United States (Rosenthal, 1995). HMOs, as integrated systems of care, have the potential to be cost-effective health care alternatives. With this emphasis on containing costs, HMOs are asking mental health professionals to work in more time-effective ways (Friedman & Fanger, 1991; Hoyt, 1994a; Kiesler & Morton, 1988). In order to achieve positive outcomes while managing resources, a shift in perspective is needed on the very nature of the psychotherapy process (Cummings, 1993, 1995).

From a competency-based perspective, therapy is viewed not as reconstructive surgery, but as a catalytic process in which the therapist plays a consultative role, facilitating change by accessing and activating resources in the direction of clients' goals. Rather than concentrating resources on a small number of people, as is the usual pattern in private practice, therapists working in managed care settings are asked to allocate limited resources in working with a large population of people requesting service.

## CHANGING OUR ATTITUDE

Therapist attitudes and assumptions about change are critical in making the shift to a competency-based, time-effective practice. Unfortunately, current graduate training too often does not prepare clinicians for work in managed care settings (Austad, Sherman, & Holstein, 1993). Recently I heard the following from a clinician, after she was told she would be allowed only three or four more sessions to see a "depressed" client: "The ingrained nature of her problems are so characterological that it will be impossible to deal with them in such a short period of time. If I begin working with her under the managed care agreement I will probably only make things worse by adding to her sense of mistrust." As is evident from this comment, the clinician is bringing to bear a set of assumptions that work against generating a time-effective outcome.

To become a time-effective therapist, you must be willing to give up the kinds of assumptions and preconceived ideas that inhibit possibilities for rapid change. If we are not expecting change, we definitely won't find it. At many points, both inside and outside of the therapy room, opportunities for change may present themselves. We have all witnessed, and possibly even personally experienced, changes that seem to occur abruptly and spontaneously (e.g., the alcoholic who "hits bottom," the person who finds out from the doctor that he or she has a medical condition that requires major lifestyle changes, etc.).[1] We have all experienced "single session successes" in which the therapeutic conversation has enabled clients to move forward after feeling "stuck" (Bloom, 1981; Hoyt, 1994; Kelman, 1969; Talmon, 1990). In this regard, Carl Whitaker tells the story (Whitaker & Bumberry, 1988) of a policeman "who was trying to talk a man down from a bridge . . . . The man was not interested in this talk at all. Finally, the policeman couldn't stand it anymore, so he drew his gun and said, 'You son of a bitch, if you jump, I'll shoot you!' So the man came down. Now, that's real psychotherapy" (p. 221). The time-effective therapist is constantly alert for opportunities to facilitate change, either in the therapeutic conversation or by setting the stage for clients to take action outside the therapy room.

By becoming attuned to natural change-promoting events and attending to resources and competencies, we can become a less intrusive, more facilitating presence in our clients lives. Traditional Native Americans understood this in regard to their beliefs in the circle of life, a continuous and renewing force that joins all things together in a natural balance (Wall & Arden, 1990). Respecting and working with natural/seasonal cycles, rather than actively trying to alter or control these events, their lives were enriched and made easier. Instead of trying to control the balance of nature and place themselves above the elements of the circle (in a more hierarchical arrangement), they joined with that balance to achieve harmony. To achieve that harmony in psychotherapy, we must begin to see ourselves as consultative resources, who stand somewhat on the sidelines, respecting the natural cycles of people's lives. As Nicholas Hobbs (1966) pointed out over 30 years ago, "Time is an ally," and therapists would do well to "avoid getting in the way of the normal restorative processes life" (p. 1110). As clinicians, we need to become comfortable with a "minimalist" philosophy. This requires giving up the satisfaction of "being there" each step of the way, as your clients make changes, and instead, finding satisfaction in the opportunity to offer consultation to large numbers of people.

By respecting people's resources and resilience and the natural healing abilities contained in clients' social networks, we shift from the role of "expert interventionist" to "participant-facilitator." Durrant and Kowalski (1993) reported data from a survey showing that 90 percent of the people sampled had been successful in overcoming significant psychological problems *without* professional intervention. To respect this finding is to embrace a time-effective, competency-based perspective. If nothing else, we need to avoid what Don Meichenbaum (June, 1994: personal communication) refers to as "becoming a surrogate frontal lobe" for the client.

As discussed earlier, a change in attitude and practice style is required in working in a managed care network. Clinicians working in an HMO reported significant shifts in their theoretical orientations over time, moving from more psychodynamic perspectives to more cognitive/behavioral and eclectic methods of practice (Austad, Sherman, & Holstein, 1993). This shift is consistent with the growth of competency-based therapies, which focus on generating effective outcomes in the present, rather than analyzing the past, and the utilization of client strengths and resources, rather than trying to "fix pathology." Using these methods, clinician and client collaborate in designing treatment processes that build on competencies in ways that lead to achievable outcomes.

The framework presented in this book exemplifies a time-effective, collaborative, respectful, and competency-based therapy. The collaborative, time-effective therapist (after Friedman, 1996):

- *Believes in a socially constructed reality* in which client and therapist co-construct meanings in dialogue or conversation.
- *Maintains empathy and respect* for the client's predicament and a belief in the power of therapeutic conversation to liberate suppressed, ignored, or previously unacknowledged voices or "stories."
- *Co-constructs goals* and negotiates direction in therapy, placing the client in the driver's seat as an expert on his or her own predicaments and dilemmas.
- Searches for and *amplifies client competencies,* strengths, and resources and avoids being a "detective for pathology" or reifying rigid diagnostic distinctions.

- *Avoids a vocabulary of deficit and dysfunction,* replacing the jargon (and distance) of pathology with the language of the everyday.
- *Is oriented toward the future* and is optimistic about change.
- *Views time as an ally,* understanding that events outside of therapy significantly and positively impact on people's lives.
- *Is sensitive to the methods and processes used in the therapeutic conversation.*
- *Is sensitive to the factor of time in therapy.*

These assumptions can be translated into five major processes—("The Five C's")—that define time-effective therapy (see Figure 10-1):

1. *Cooperation* with the client
2. *Curiosity* about the client's life and relationships, resources and competencies
3. *Collaboration* in developing goals or a future vision
4. *Co-construction of solution ideas,* direction, and action steps
5. *Closure,* concluding therapy or recycling.

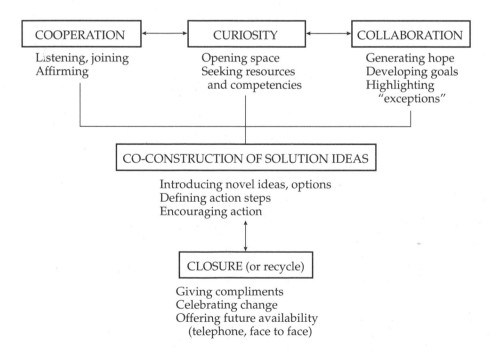

**FIGURE 10-1    A Competency-Based Model of Time-Effective Therapy**

## MANAGING YOUR PRACTICE: FROM POSSIBILITIES TO OUTCOME

Our perceptions of people are reflected in the way we maintain our clinical notes and records. Forms used in agencies often emphasize deficits, pathology, and diagnosis, rather than strengths, resources, and goals for treatment. Scaling questions, for example (similar to those used in Chapters 7 and 8) are a simple and effective way to track change over the course of a therapy. The client, in this instance, serves as the evaluator of progress, which makes a great deal of sense since it is the client's level of satisfaction that determines when therapy has been successful. Another useful way to stay goal-directed and monitor client progress is presented in Table 10-1 and 10-2 which closely follows the competency-based

**TABLE 10-1   Clinical Record**

Client Name: _____.

Date of Initial Contact: _____.

Quick Genogram of Extended Family Support Systems:



Client's Strengths and Resources/"Exceptions" to the problem:

_____

_____

_____

Client's Goals (*in positive and behavioral terms*):

1. _____

2. _____

3. _____

Feedback Statement (including positive steps already taken):

_____

_____

_____

Action Steps (or experiments developed with client):

1. _____

2. _____

3. _____

**TABLE 10-2    Record of Followup Sessions**

Client Name: _____; Session #: _____

Action Steps taken:                    Outcome

(1 = min progress; 5 = max progress)

1. _____        1        2        3        4        5

2. _____        1        2        3        4        5

3. _____        1        2        3        4        5

**New Action Steps?**

1. _____

2. _____

3. _____

framework discussed in this book. (A more elaborate system for measuring outcome is presented later in this chapter.) Berg (1994) has also developed a form for working with families that focuses the therapist's attention on strengths and competencies. Another advantage of competency-based record keeping is that you can give the client a copy of the form at the end of the session!

While such forms and scales can help direct and focus your clinical work, how you allocate your time is critical. For an initial appointment a longer session (e.g., 90 minutes) may allow you to "hit the ground running," reducing the need for additional visits. You might find that, by having a long first session, a treatment plan can be generated, with a followup visit scheduled for 2 or 3 weeks later. Rather than getting into a set that everyone must be seen for 50 minutes on a weekly or every-other-week basis, what is vital is the flexible and creative use of time. For example, as mentioned earlier, if I have scheduled someone for a 50-minute appointment and we can comfortably and satisfactorily complete our work in 35 minutes, I will end the session. The minutes saved can be spent in other useful ways.

Using time flexibly is a necessity when practicing in a managed care environment, as is demonstrating positive outcomes. Although many managed care organizations initially subjected therapists to "inspection-based systems" (Berwick, 1995) in which utilization reviewers carefully allocated the number of sessions that any client could have, the current emphasis is toward outcome-based systems. Under an outcome-based system, MCCs contract with the most cost-efficient and time-effective providers. Rather than spending significant amounts of money monitoring and scrutinizing clinicians' practices, these companies are investing in practices that can be trusted to do therapy in ways that offer quality service while maintaining a sensitivity to time. What this means is less intrusive monitoring by utilization reviewers, more autonomy for the clinician in making treatment decisions, and increased accountability on the part of clinicians in demonstrating the efficacy of their work (Meredith & Bair, 1995). An outcome-based system requires therapists to demonstrate their time-effectiveness with clinical data. Many MCCs already profile providers on several dimensions, including client satisfaction and clinical outcomes achieved (Sleek, 1995). In the next section we shall look at a flexible and adaptable way to systematically measure outcomes in a wide range of clinical situations. This structure offers therapists a means to generate data on the efficacy of their practices.

A focus on outcomes and accountability will help improve the status and respect of psychotherapy as a field. Effective clinical practice "will be rewarded with less stringent oversight of providers and more liberal practice standards" (Meredith & Bair, 1995, p. 44). Since effective psychotherapy can significantly reduce unnecessary medical costs, employer groups will see investment in these services as advantageous.

## MEASURING CHANGE

As Jacobson (1995) articulated, "Criteria for determining progress should be part of a dialogue initiated by the therapist and regularly addressed by both therapist and client. When therapy isn't working, the therapist has an ethical obligation to try something else" (p. 46). In addition, clinicians need to collect outcome data that establish themselves as providers of *quality* mental health services (Noble, 1995; Stromberg & Ratcliff, 1995).

Thomas Kiresuk (1973; Kiresuk & Sherman, 1968; Kiresuk, Smith, & Cardillo, 1994) has developed a simple but elegant structure for evaluating change in psychotherapy that not only offers flexibility for use with individual clients but also can be used as a tool for looking at outcomes across groups of clients. *Goal attainment scaling* allows therapists and clients to collaborate in formulating a set of goals that fit the client's unique situation and allow for assessment of outcome as therapy progresses. Using this system, therapists can generate data on therapy outcomes for groups of clients, providing outcome information for MCCs and opening the door to a systematic understanding of what works with whom. Figure 10-2 illustrates the application of this structure with the client "Nancy," discussed in Chapter 5.

Although the format of the scale remains consistent, content can be flexibly tailored to each client's unique set of goals. One useful guide is that goals should be constructed in ways that allow for behavioral measurement. In addition, it is best whenever possible, to define goals in positive terms, i.e.,

## FIGURE 10-2    Goal Attainment Guide: Clinical Illustration—"Nancy"[2]

# = Level at initial visit

* = Level at end of therapy

(Check Yes if scale has been mutually negotiated between client and therapist:)

| FOCUS | Scale 1 DRUG USE Yes ✔ (W = 40) | Scale 2 RUNNING AWAY Yes ✔ (W = 20) | Scale 3 CUTTING SELF Yes ✔ (W = 20) | Scale 4 COMPLETING H.S. Yes ✔ (W = 10) | Scale 5 CRISIS CALLS TO HMO Yes ___ (W = 10) |
|---|---|---|---|---|---|
| BEST OUTCOME [5] | Maintains sobriety × 3 mo * | Speaks to others when upset; no running × 3 mo * | Speaks to others when upset; no cutting × 3 mo * | Completes H.S. * | Manages crises without calling × 3 mo * |
| [4] | | | | | |
| SOME SUCCESS ACHIEVED [3] | Achieves periods of sobriety (1–2 wks) | Has thoughts of running away, but no action taken | Has thoughts of cutting, but no action taken | Obtains-information on what is needed to graduate | Contacts therapist 2–3× in 2 mo |
| [2] | | | | # | |
| LEAST POSITIVE OUTCOME [1] | Uses drugs regularly (4×/week) # | Runs when upset # | Cuts self when angry # | Takes no action to finish H.S. | Calls in crisis 1+ times/wk # |

W = weight

as movement *toward* a preferred outcome. Weightings for each goal can also be developed that focus therapists' attention on client priorities. In this way, goalsetting becomes a collaborative and public process in which the direction of treatment is not hidden or imposed by the therapist but mutually negotiated. Should goals change over the course of therapy, as they often do, priorities can be re-evaluated. Many clinicians have an aversion to research, but this simple methodology offers a way to generate useful information in a nonintrusive and potentially helpful way. In addition, this system, by offering clients the opportunity to actively participate in monitoring their own progress and play a more integral role in their own therapy, will likely increase "consumer satisfaction."

## POSSIBILITY THERAPY IN ACTION

A competency-based approach that utilizes and builds on client resources and successes offers a wide range of therapeutic possibilities that can be flexibly and easily adapted and integrated in a clinician's practice.

### *Ten Steps to New Possibilities—A Summary*

1. Maintain a position of naive curiosity, optimism, and respect for the client via active listening to the client's story.
2. Tune in to the client's affect and experience; acknowledge and support the client's struggle/pain.
3. Stay simple and focused, listening for exceptions (i.e., contradictions to the problem-saturated story). When a problem seems to have taken on a life of its own, engage in externalizing conversations, defining the problem as an outside force that is oppressing, subjugating, or constraining the client's forward movement.
4. Be on the lookout for evidence of change/success; listen for stories that offer hope.
5. Stay tuned to the client's goal: "What does the client see as reflecting a positive outcome?" "What does the client hope to accomplish?"
6. Negotiate with the client to frame the outcome or goals in clear, observable terms.
7. Build on client competencies, successes, and resources; Invite the client to tune in to exceptions to the problem; encourage the client's creativity.
8. Introduce ideas that create space for the client to "do something different"; encourage small steps; As Alexander and French (1946) pointed out: "In a well-conducted therapy, as much or more happens in the intervals between interviews as in the interviews themselves" (p. 91).
9. Encourage action/practice in the real world. Define the change process as hard work and applaud small steps taken in a positive direction.
10. Support changes made. Ask questions that embed changes in the client's experience; compliment the client on positive steps taken. If the goal is not attained, begin the cycle again. Leave the door open for future contact.

## STAYING SANE IN MANAGED CARE

The managed care environment can be both exciting and pressurized, requiring the therapist to maintain a balanced footing in dealing with complex situations in time-effective ways. Juggling the requests of clients with the expectations of the MCC makes the therapy process a challenging job. Here are several ideas for surviving and thriving in managed care and for avoiding "burnout."

### *Tips for Survival in Managed Care*

- Establish a good working relationship with your case manager. Maintain a nonadversarial (collaborative) posture while educating the case manager on effective clinical practice. Be ready to advocate and negotiate.
- Form a group practice or affiliate with other providers who offer a set of diversified and integrated services. Integrated service delivery means efficiency.
- Cultivate and nurture linkages/collaboration with groups of primary care providers. Better yet, establish a practice within a medical group, offering on-site consultation; People are quicker to use mental health services when these services are easily accessible as part of the health care setting.
- Develop expertise in one or more specialized areas (e.g., child and family therapy; group therapy; chemical dependency; geriatric services, etc.). Find a marketable niche that suits your skills and interests.
- Design treatment plans that utilize community resources (e.g., AA, ADHD parent groups, etc.). MCCs are more likely to authorize your services if they see that you are maximizing outside ("free") resources.
- Stay tuned to current business developments in the managed care marketplace by reading relevant books and newsletters.[3]
- Get involved in continuing education activities that enhance and refine your skills in time-effective therapy and help you develop special expertise.
- Document how outpatient therapy saves money in offsetting medical and hospital costs.[4]
- Systematically monitor outcome and client satisfaction; By so doing you will be able to concretely demonstrate to the MCC the time-effectiveness of your approach.

### *To Avoid Burn-out . . .*

- View the therapy process as a laboratory for change; Encourage yourself and your clients to experiment with new ideas and options for action. Act contrary to old habits that constrain your creativity.

- Never work harder than your clients (never be the most motivated person in the room for change). Notice when you are sitting on the edge of your chair and your client is sitting back in a relaxed position—something is wrong with this picture! Find out what the client is a customer for and stay focused on this goal.
- Be aware of your unique burnout signals. Develop a supportive treatment team; share responsibility with teammates for difficult clinical decisions. Join a peer support network that provides an opportunity to talk about your work. Set up reflecting team consultations with colleagues around "stuck" cases.
- Develop a hobby completely outside of the therapy field (e.g., dancing, photography, biking, tennis, coin collecting).
- Track your own levels of irritability and move to do something good for yourself (dinner at a nice restaurant, a weekend in the country, etc.) when the need is indicated.
- Take up whittling or just spend some time on the bluff of a hill lying on your back and watching the clouds roll by.
- Give yourself credit for what works and be gentle with yourself when you hit dead-ends.
- Beware when you start seeing a client as "resistant" or "unmotivated." This is a signal that your frustration level is high; seek consultation.
- Trust your clinical judgment. Use yourself in therapy. Be personal and real—allow yourself to laugh and cry. This will be therapeutic for both you and your client.
- Don't take yourself too seriously. As Carl Whitaker (1976) said, "Develop a reverence for your own impulses and be suspicious of your behavior sequences" (p. 164).

## KEY IDEAS IN THIS CHAPTER

- Managed care is here to stay in one form or another, requiring clinicians to develop and refine their skills in doing time-effective psychotherapy.
- Working under constraints of time and limited resources and carrying responsibility for defined populations (members belonging to an HMO) require a shift in attitudes about the process of psychotherapy.
- Time-effective therapy includes a mindset for thinking and acting that is based on a revised set of assumptions about the process of therapy and a sensitivity to time.
- Clinicians can be effective in managed care settings by working smarter, not harder.
- More therapy is not necessarily better; better is better (Austad & Hoyt, 1992).

- Therapist expectations and client hopefulness are pivotal elements in the change process. Positive outcomes are more likely when clients experience a sense of hopefulness and a positive expectancy about change (see Whiston & Sexton, 1993).
- Understanding the client's state of readiness for action can make the therapy process more collaborative and ultimately more time-effective.
- Time is an ally. Leaving space between sessions (i.e., seeing clients on an intermittent basis) capitalizes on the normal restorative processes of life and by so doing establishes clients as the major architects of change in their own lives.
- Clients' active participation in goal setting and evaluating progress is an essential component of the therapy process. A collaborative stance on the part of the therapist increases the likelihood of achieving a positive outcome (see Whiston & Sexton, 1993).
- People's lives are complex; the art of doing brief therapy is to appreciate that fact yet not be distracted from finding gentle leverage points for change (Gurman, 1992).
- The time-effective therapist appreciates the idea that helping people reach their goals as efficiently as possible is both practical and ethical.
- Think small.

The managed care movement continues to challenge therapists to modify and refine their skills in making their therapeutic endeavors more time-effective. My hope is that this book has offered you an opportunity to rethink your assumptions and practices in successfully meeting this challenge. By maintaining a hopeful, optimistic frame of mind, by working collaboratively on your *clients'* goals, and by acknowledging and utilizing your clients' resources and strengths, you can make the therapy process a more creative, respectful, and productive enterprise.

### *Questions to Consider*

**1.** What two or three major ideas in this book did you find most useful and applicable to your work? How might you apply these ideas in your next clinical encounter?

**2.** What assumptions do you hold dear in your work? Which of these assumptions make your work more time-effective? Which of these assumptions constrain or limit your effectiveness?

**3.** What changes do you need to make in your practice to increase your time-effectiveness?

## NOTES

1. As the story goes (Koestler, 1964), the Greek scientist Archimedes was asked to determine the amount of gold contained in the king's crown. After giving this problem much thought, he became frustrated and upset as he encountered repeated dead-ends. One can imagine how stuck Archimedes felt about how to solve this problem without melting the crown down. One day, soon after grappling with this problem, he prepared himself a bath, and, as he sat down in the water, he shouted "Eureka!" (I found it!). What Archimedes had "found" was that he could determine the weight of the crown by simply observing how much water it displaced. Archimedes solved his problem creatively by putting together ideas from two different frames of reference. As Briggs and Peat (1989) point out, "The target or solution . . . doesn't lie in the same frame . . . of reference as the problem" (p. 193). In line with chaos theory, Archimedes' frustration led initially to an increasingly erratic search for solutions. "At a critical point in this bubbling of thoughts, a bifurcation is reached where a small piece of information or a trivial observation (such as the rise of the level of the bath water) becomes amplified, causing thought to branch to a new plane of reference—a plane that in fact contains the target" (Briggs & Peat, 1989, p. 193).

Possibilities exist for discontinuous change whenever random events enter the territory. The natural world is in constant flux such that, in spite of the attempts of humans to impose order, a high degree of unpredictability exists (Briggs & Peat, 1989). This unpredictability creates the potential for small perturbations to have major impacts even in systems that appear stable. It is this unpredictability and randomness that can trigger radical transformations or "change through leaps" (Hoffman, 1981). The reader is invited to review the story of Jean Valjean from Victor Hugo's *Les Miserables* for an example of a dramatic change in "personality" as a function of one positive experience (see Alexander & French, 1946, for discussion of this experience).

We need to appreciate the "auspicious moment," that confluence of events that can precipitate rapid change, or what Kelman (1969) called "kairos." See Kelman (1969) for numerous examples of people making rapid changes at critical points in time.

2. I wish to thank the students in my class at the Massachusetts School of Professional Psychology (Summer, 1996) for their constructive ideas on organizing the information for this table. Ways to quantify client change can be found in Kiresuk (1973), Kiresuk & Sherman (1968) and Kiresuk et al. (1994).

3. Several useful publications are: *Practice Strategies* [published by the American Association of Marriage and Family Therapy: 202-452-0109]; *Psychotherapy Finances* [407-747-1960]; and *HMO Practice* [716-857-6361].

4. In one recent situation, I demonstrated how in-home crisis services provided on a 2–3 times/week basis, and costing about $8000/year, was a cost-effective alternative to hospitalization. In the year prior to implementing the in-home crisis program, this client cost the MCC over $65,000 for hospital and related services.

# For Further Reading*

## COMPETENCY-BASED THERAPIES: THEORY AND PRACTICE

Andersen, T. (Ed.). (1991). *The reflecting team: Dialogues and dialogues about the dialogues.* New York: Norton.

Berg, I. K. (1994). *Family based services: A solution-focused approach.* New York: Norton.

Berg, I. K., & Miller, S. (1992). *Working with the problem drinker: A solution-focused approach.* New York: Norton.

Cade, B., & O'Hanlon, W. H. (1993). *A brief guide to brief therapy.* New York: Norton.

de Shazer, S. (1985). *Keys to solution in brief therapy.* New York: Norton.

de Shazer, S. (1988). *Clues: Investigating solutions in brief therapy.* New York: Norton.

de Shazer, S. (1991). *Putting difference to work.* New York: Norton.

de Shazer, S. (1994). *Words were originally magic.* New York: Norton.

Dolan, Y. (1991). *Resolving sexual abuse.* New York: Norton.

Durrant, M. & White, C. (Eds.). (1990). *Ideas for therapy with sexual abuse.* Adelaide, Australia: Dulwich Centre Publications.

Durrant, M. (1993). *Residential treatment: A cooperative, competency-based approach to therapy and program design.* New York: Norton.

Epston, D., & White, M. (1992). *Experience, contradiction, narrative and imagination.* Adelaide, Australia: Dulwich Centre Publications.

Freedman, J. & Combs, G. (1996). *Narrative therapy: The social construction of preferred realities.* New York: Norton.

Friedman, S. (Ed.). (1993). *The new language of change: Constructive collaboration in psychotherapy.* New York: Guilford Press.

Friedman, S. (Ed.). (1995). *The reflecting team in action: Collaborative practice in family therapy.* New York: Guilford Press.

Friedman, S., & Fanger, M. T. (1991). *Expanding therapeutic possibilities: Getting results in brief psychotherapy.* San Francisco: New Lexington Press/Jossey-Bass.

Furman, B., & Ahola, T. (1992). *Solution-talk: Hosting therapeutic conversations.* New York: Norton.

Gilligan, S., & Price, R. (Eds.). (1993). *Therapeutic conversations.* New York: Norton.

Griffith, J. L., & Griffith, M. E. (1994). *The body speaks: Therapeutic dialogues for mind-body problems.* New York: Basic Books.

*The following bibliographic resources are recommended for those interested in pursuing further study of competency-based perspectives in psychotherapy.

Hoffman, L. (1993). *Exchanging voices: A collaborative approach to family therapy.* London: Karnac Books.

Hoyt, M. (Ed.). (1994). *Constructive therapies.* New York: Guilford Press.

Hoyt, M. (Ed.). (1996). *Constructive therapies 2.* New York: Guilford Press.

Hudson, P. O., & O'Hanlon, W. H. (1992). *Rewriting love stories: Brief marital therapy.* New York: Norton.

McFarland, B. (1995). *Brief therapy and eating disorders: A practical guide to solution-focused work with clients.* San Francisco: Jossey-Bass.

McNamee, S., & Gergen, K. J. (Eds.). (1992). *Therapy as social construction.* London: Sage.

O'Hanlon, W. H., & Weiner-Davis, M. (1989). *In search of solutions: A new direction in psychotherapy.* New York: Norton.

O'Hanlon, W. H., & Wilk, J. (1987). *Shifting contexts: The generation of effective psychotherapy.* New York: Guilford Press.

Parry, A., & Doan, R. E. (1994). *Story re-vision: Narrative therapy in the postmodern world.* New York: Guilford Press.

Selekman, M. (1993). *Pathways to change: Brief therapy with difficult adolescents.* New York: Guilford Press.

Waters, D. B., & Lawrence, E. C. (1993). *Competence, courage and change: An approach to family therapy.* New York: Norton.

White, M. (1995). *Re-authoring lives: Interviews and essays.* Adelaide, Australia: Dulwich Centre Publications.

White, M., & Epston, D. (1990). *Narrative means to therapeutic ends.* New York: Norton.

References

Adams, J. (1987, Jan./Feb.). A brave new world for private practice. *The Family Therapy Networker*, pp. 19–25.

Adams-Westcott, J., & Isenbart, D. (1995). A journey of change through connection. In S. Friedman (Ed.), *The reflecting team in action: Collaborative practice in family therapy.* New York: Guilford Press.

Agnetti, G., & Young, J. (1993). Chronicity and the experience of timelessness: An intervention model. *Family Systems Medicine, 11*(1), 67–81.

Alexander, F., & French, T. M. (1946). *Psychoanalytic therapy: Principles and applications.* New York: Ronald Press.

Andersen, T. (1987). The reflecting team: Dialogue and meta-dialogue in clinical work. *Family Process, 26*(4), 415–428.

Andersen, T. (1993). See and hear, and be seen and heard. In S. Friedman (Ed.), *The new language of change: Constructive collaboration in psychotherapy* (pp. 303–322). New York: Guilford Press.

Andersen, T. (1995). Reflecting processes: Acts of informing and forming. In S. Friedman (Ed.), *The reflecting team in action: Collaborative practice in family therapy.* New York: Guilford Press.

Andersen, T. (Ed.). (1991). *The reflecting team: Dialogues and dialogues about the dialogues.* New York: Norton.

Anderson, H. (1993). On a roller coaster: A collaborative language systems approach to therapy. In S. Friedman (Ed.), *The new language of change: Constructive collaboration in psychotherapy* (pp. 323–344). New York: Guilford Press.

Anderson, H., & Goolishian, H. A. (1988). Human systems as linguistic systems: Preliminary and evolving ideas about the implications for clinical theory. *Family Process, 27,* 371–393.

Anderson, H., & Goolishian, H. A. (1992). The client is the expert: a not–knowing approach to therapy. In S. McNamee & K. J. Gergen (Eds.), *Therapy as social construction.* Newbury Park, CA: Sage.

Austad, C. S., & Hoyt. M. F. (1992). The managed care movement and the future of psychotherapy. *Psychotherapy, 29*(1), 109–118.

Austad, C.S., Sherman, W.O., & Holstein, L. (1993). Psychotherapists in the HMO. *HMO Practice, 7*(3), 122–126.

Bass, A. (1995a, Feb. 22). Computerized medical data put privacy on the line. *The Boston Globe*, pp. 1, 5.

Bass, A. (1995b, Mar. 11). AG's office examining privacy of HMO files. *The Boston Globe*, pp. 13, 15.

Bateson, G. (1972). *Steps to an ecology of mind.* New York: Ballantine Books.

Bennett, M. J. (1984). Brief psychotherapy and adult development. *Psychotherapy: Theory, Research and Practice, 21,* 171–177.

Bennett, M. J. (1988). The greening of the HMO: Implications for prepaid psychiatry. *American Journal of Psychiatry, 145*(12), 1544–1549.

Bennett, M. J. (1989). The catalytic function in psychotherapy. *Psychiatry, 52,* 351–364.

Berg, I. K. (1989, Jan./Feb.). Of customers, complainants and visitors. *The Family Therapy Networker,* p. 21.

Berg, I. K. (1994). *Family based services: A solution-focused approach.* New York: Norton.

Berg, I. K., & de Shazer, S. (1993). Making numbers talk. In S. Friedman (Ed.), *The new language of change: Constructive collaboration in psychotherapy* (pp. 5–24). New York: Guilford Press.

Berg, I. K., & Miller, S. D. (1992). *Working with the problem drinker: A solution-focused approach.* New York: Norton.

Berlyne, D. E. (1960). *Conflict, arousal and curiosity.* New York: McGraw-Hill.

Berwick, D. (1995). Quality comes home. *Quality Connection, 4*(1), 1–4.

Binder, J. L. (1993). Observations on the training of therapists in time-limited dynamic psychotherapy. *Psychotherapy, 40*(4), 592–598.

Bischoff, R. J., & Sprenkle, D. H. (1993). Dropping out of marriage and family therapy: A critical review of research. *Family Process, 32*(3), 353–375.

Blakeslee, S. (1993, Nov. 7). Beliefs reported to shorten life. *New York Times.*

Bloom, B. L. (1981). Focused single session therapy In S. Budman (Ed.), *Forms of brief therapy* (pp. 167–216). New York: Guilford Press.

Brandt, L. (1989). A short-term group therapy model for treatment of adult female survivors of childhood incest. *Group, 13*(2), 74–82.

Brecher, S., & Friedman, S. (1993). In pursuit of a better life: A mother's triumph. In S. Friedman (Ed.), *The new language of change: Constructive collaboration in psychotherapy* (pp. 278–299). New York: Guilford Press.

Brehm, J. W. (1966). *A theory of psychological reactance.* New York: Academic Press.

Briggs, J., & Peat, F. D. (1989). *Turbulent mirror.* New York: Harper & Row.

Brown-Standridge, M. D. (1989). A paradigm for construction of family therapy tasks. *Family Process, 28*(4), 471–489.

Bruner, J. (1986). *Actual minds, possible worlds.* Cambridge, MA: Harvard University Press.

Budman, S. H. (1990). The myth of termination in brief therapy: Or, it ain't over till it's over. In J. K. Zeig & S.G. Gilligan (Eds.), *Brief therapy: Myths, methods and metaphors* (pp. 206–218). New York: Brunner/Mazel.

Budman, S. H., Friedman, S., & Hoyt, M. (1992). Last words on first sessions. In S. H. Budman, M. Hoyt, & S. Friedman (Eds.), *The first session in brief therapy* (pp. 345–358). New York: Guilford Press.

Budman, S. H., & Gurman, A. (1988). *Theory and practice of brief therapy.* New York: Guilford Press.

Butz, M. R. (1994). Psychopharmacology: Psychology's Jurassic Park? *Psychotherapy, 31*(4), 692–699.

Cade, B., & O'Hanlon, W. H. (1994). *A brief guide to brief therapy.* New York: Norton.

Califano, J. A. (1988, Mar. 20). The health-care chaos. *New York Times Magazine,* pp. 44, 46, 56–58.

Campbell, B., & Jaynes, J. (1966). Reinstatement. *Psychological Review, 73,* 478–480.

Carpenter, G. C., Tecce, J., Stechler, G., & Friedman, S. (1970). Differential visual behavior to human and humanoid faces in early infancy. *Merrill-Palmer Quarterly, 16,* 91–108.

Chamberlain, L. (1994). Psychopharmacology: Further adventures in psychology's Jurassic Park. *Psychotherapy Bulletin, 29*(3), 47–50.

Chase, R. A. (1969). Biologic aspects of environmental design. *Clinical Pediatrics, 8,* 268–274.

Chasin, R., & Roth, S. A. (1990). Future perfect, past perfect: A positive approach to opening couple therapy. In R. Chasin, H. Grunebaum, & M. Herzig (Eds.), *One couple, four realities: Mutliple perspectives on couple therapy* (pp. 129–144). New York: Guilford Press.

Chasin, R., Roth, S. A., & Bograd, M. (1989). Action methods in systemic therapy: Dramatizing ideal futures and reformed pasts with couples. *Family Process, 28,* 268–274.

Combs, G., & Freedman, J. (1990). *Symbol, story and ceremony.* New York: Norton.

Cousins, N. (1989). *Head first: The biology of hope.* New York: Dutton.

Cummings, N. A. (1979, Jan.). The general practice of psychology. *APA Monitor.*

Cummings, N. A. (1986). The dismantling of our health system: Struggles for the survival of psychological practice. *American Psychologist, 41*(4), 426–431.

Cummings, N. A. (1991, Spring). Out of the cottage. *Advance Plan,* pp. 1–2, 14.

Cummings, N. A. (1995). Behavioral health after managed care: The next golden opportunity for professional psychology. *Register Report, 20*(3), 29–33.

D'Agostino, D., McCabe, J., & Sclar, B. (1995). A psychiatric day program in an HMO. *HMO Practice, 9*(2), 79–83.

Daley, B. S., & Koppenal, G. S. (1981). The treatment of women in short-term women's groups. In S. Budman (Ed.), *Forms of brief therapy* (pp. 343–357). New York: Guilford Press.

de Shazer, S. (1985). *Keys to solution in brief therapy.* New York: Norton.

de Shazer, S. (1988). *Clues: Investigating solutions in brief therapy.* New York: Norton.

de Shazer, S. (1991). *Putting difference to work.* New York: Norton.

de Shazer, S. (1994). *Words were originally magic.* New York: Norton.

de Shazer, S., & Berg, I. K. (1985). A part is not apart: Working with only one of the partners present. In A. S. Gurman (Ed.), *Casebook of marital therapy.* New York: Guilford Press.

Doan, R., & Bullard, C. (1994). Reflecting teams: Exploring the possibilities. *Dulwich Centre Newsletter,* No. 4, 35–38.

Donovan, J. M., Bennett, M. J., & McElroy, C. M. (1981). The crisis group: Its rationale, format and outcome. In S. Budman (Ed.), *Forms of brief therapy* (pp. 283–303). New York: Guilford Press.

Duncan, B. L., & Moynihan, D. W. (1994). Applying outcome research: Intentional utilization of the client's frame of reference. *Psychotherapy, 31*(2), 294–301.

Duncan, B., Solovey, A. D., & Rusk, G. S. (1992). *Changing the rules: A client directed approach to therapy.* New York: Guilford Press.

Durrant, M., & Kowalski, K. M. (1990). Overcoming the effects of sexual abuse: Developing a self-perception of competence. In M. Durrant & C. White (Eds.), *Ideas for therapy with sexual abuse* (pp. 65–110). Adelaide, Australia: Dulwich Centre Publications.

Durrant, M., & Kowlaski, K. M. (1993). Enhancing views of competence. In S. Friedman (Ed.), *The new language of change: Constructive collaboration in psychotherapy* (pp. 107–137). New York: Guilford Press.

Efran, J. S., Lukens, M. D., & Lukens, R. J. (1990). *Language, structure and change.* New York: Norton.

Elms, R. (1986). To tame a temper. *Family Therapy Case Studies, 1,* 51–58.

Epston, D. (1994, Nov./Dec.). Expanding the conversation. *The Family Therapy Networker,* pp. 30–37, 62–63.

Epston, D., & White, M. (1992). *Experience, contradiction, narrative and imagination.* Adelaide, Australia: Dulwich Centre Publications.

Epston, D, White, M., & "Ben" (1995). Consulting your consultants: A means to the co-construction of alternative knowledges. In S. Friedman (Ed.), *The reflecting team in action: Collaborative practice in family therapy.* New York: Guilford Press.

Erickson, M. H. (1954). Pseudo-orientation in time as a hypnotherapeutic procedure. *Journal of Clinical and Experimental Hypnosis, 2,* 261–283.

Esler, I. (1987). Winning over worry. *Family Therapy Case Studies, 2*(1), 15–23.

Fisch, R., Weakland, J. H., & Segal, L. (1982). *Tactics of change: Doing therapy briefly.* San Francisco: Jossey-Bass.

Fiske, D. W., & Maddi, S. R. (1961). *Functions of varied experience.* Homewood, IL: Dorsey Press.

Foerster, H. von (1984). On constructing a reality. In P. Watzlawick (Ed.), *The invented reality* (pp. 41–61). New York: Norton.

Follette, W. T., & Cummings, N. A. (1967). Psychiatric services and medical utilization in a prepaid health plan setting, *Medical Care, 5,* 25–35.

Fraenkel, P. (1995). The nomothetic-idiographic debate in family therapy. *Family Process, 34*(1), 113–121.

Frank, J. D. (1974). *Healing and persuasion. A comparative study of psychotherapy.* New York: Schocken Books.

Frankel, R. M., Morse, D. S., Suchman, A., & Beckman, H. B. (1991). Can I really improve my listening skills with only 15 minutes to see my patients? *HMO Practice, 5*(4), 114–120.

Freeman, J., & Lobovits, D. (1993). The turtle with wings. In S. Friedman (Ed.), *The new language of change: Constructive collaboration in psychotherapy* (pp. 188–221). New York: Guilford Press.

Freud, S. (1937). Analysis terminable and interminable. In *Collected papers,* (vol. 5, no. 30) (pp. 316–357).

Friedman, S. (1984). When the woman presents herself as "the patient": A systems view. *Women and therapy, 3*(2), 19–35.

Friedman, S. (1990). Towards a model of time-effective family psychotherapy: A view from a health maintenance organization. *Journal of Family Psychotherapy, 1*(2), 1–28.

Friedman, S. (1992). Constructing solutions (stories) in brief family therapy. In S. Budman, M. Hoyt, & S. Friedman (Eds.), *The first session in brief therapy* (pp. 282–305). New York: Guilford Press.

Friedman, S. (1993a). Does the "miracle question" always create miracles? *Journal of Systemic Therapies, 12*(1), 71–74.

Friedman, S. (1993b). Escape from the Furies: A journey from self-pity to self-love. In S. Friedman (Ed.), *The new language of change: Constructive collaboration in psychotherapy* (pp. 251–277). New York: Guilford Press.

Friedman, S. (1993c) Possibility therapy with couples: Constructing time-effective solutions. *Journal of Family Psychotherapy, 4*(4), 35–52.

Friedman, S. (1993d). Preface. In S. Friedman (Ed.), *The new language of change: Constructive collaboration in psychotherapy.* New York: Guilford Press.

Friedman, S. (1994). Staying simple, staying focused: Time-effective consultations with children and families. In M. Hoyt (Ed.), *Constructive therapies* (pp. 217–250). New York: Guilford Press.

Friedman, S. (1996). Couples therapy: Changing conversations. In H. Rosen & K. T. Kuehlwein (Eds.), *Constructing realities: Meaning making perspectives for psychotherapists.* San Francisco: Jossey-Bass.

Friedman, S. (Ed.). (1993). *The new language of change: Constructive collaboration in psychotherapy.* New York: Guilford Press.

Friedman, S. (Ed.). (1995). *The reflecting team in action: Collaborative practice in family therapy.* New York: Guilford Press.

Friedman, S., & Fanger, M. T. (1991). *Expanding therapeutic possibilities: Getting results in brief psychotherapy.* San Francisco: New Lexington Press/Jossey-Bass.

Friedman, S., & Ryan, L. S. (1986). A systems perspective on problematic behaviors in the nursing home. *Family Therapy, 13,* 265–273.

Furman, B. & Ahola, T. (1992). *Solution-talk: Hosting therapeutic conversations.* New York: Norton.

Gaines, J. (1995, Mar. 12). Battered women finding fewer insurers. *The Boston Globe.*

Garcia-Preto, N. (1982). Puerto Rican families. In M. McGoldrick, J. K. Pearce, & J. Giordano (Eds.), *Ethnicity and family therapy* (pp. 164–186). New York: Guilford Press.

Gergen, K. J. (1985). The social constructionist movement in modern psychology. *American Psychologist, 40*(3), 266–275.

Gergen, K. J. (1991). *The saturated self: Dilemmas of identity in contemporary life.* New York: Basic Books.

Gilligan, S., & Price, R. (Eds.). (1993). *Therapeutic conversations.* New York: Norton.

Goleman, D. (1994, May 11). Seeking out small pleasures keeps immune system strong. *The New York Times.*

Griffith, J. L., & Griffith, M. E. (1994). *The body speaks: Therapeutic dialogues for mind-body problems.* New York: Basic Books.

Griffith, J. L., Griffith, M. E., Krejmas, N., McLain, M., Mittal, D., Rains, J., & Tingle, C. (1992). Reflecting team consultations and their impact upon family therapy for somatic symptoms as coded by Structural Analysis of Behavior (SASB). *Family Systems Medicine, 10*(1), 53–58.

Gudeman, J. E., Dickey, B., Evans, A., & Shore, M. F. (1985). Four-year assessment of a day hospital-inn program as an alternative to inpatient hospitalization. *American Journal of Psychiatry, 142,* 1330–1333.

Gurman, A. S. (1992). Integrative marital therapy: A time-sensitive model for working with couples. In S. Budman, M. Hoyt, & S. Friedman (Eds.), *The first session in brief therapy* (pp. 186–203). New York: Guilford Press.

Haley, J. (1973). *Uncommon therapy: The psychiatric techniques of Milton H. Erickson, MD.* New York: Norton.

Haley, J. (1976). *Problem-solving therapy.* San Francisco: Jossey-Bass.

Haley, J. (1984). *Ordeal therapy.* San Francisco: Jossey-Bass.

Haley, J. (Ed.). (1967). *Advanced techniques of hypnosis and therapy: Selected papers of Milton H. Erickson, MD.* Boston: Allyn & Bacon.

Hare-Mustin, R. (1994). Discourses in the mirrored room: A postmodern analysis of therapy. *Family Process, 33*(1), 19–35.

Hargens, J., & Grau, U. (1994a). Cooperating, reflecting, making open and meta-dialogue—outline of a systemic approach on constructivist grounds. *The Australian and New Zealand Journal of Family Therapy, 15*(2), 81–90.

Hargens, J., & Grau, U. (1994b). Meta-dialogue. *Contemporary Family Therapy, 16*(6), 451–462.

Hebb, D. O. (1946). On the nature of fear. *Psychological Review, 53,* 259–276.

Heinssen, R. K., Levendusky, P. G., & Hunter, R. H. (1995). Clients as colleague: Therapeutic contracting with the seriously mentally ill. *American Psychologist, 50*(7), 522–532.

Held, R., & Hein, A. (1963). Movement produced stimulation on the development of visually guided behavior. *Journal of Comparative and Physiological Psychology, 56,* 872–876.

Herron, W. G., Eisenstadt, E. N., Javier, R. A., Primavera, L. H., & Schultz, C. L. (1994). Session effects, comparability, and managed care in the psychotherapies. *Psychotherapy, 31*(2), 279–285.

Hobbs, N. (1966). Helping disturbed children: Psychological and ecological strategies. *American Psychologist, 21,* 1105–1115.

Hoffman, L. (1981). *Foundations of family therapy.* New York: Basic Books.

Hoffman, L. (1989, Oct.). *Partnership therapy.* Workshop presented in Portsmouth, NH.

Hoffman, L. (1991). A reflexive stance for family therapy. *Journal of Strategic and Systemic Therapies, 10,* 4–17.

Hoffman, L., & Davis, J. (1993). Tekka with feathers: Talking about talking (about suicide). In S. Friedman (Ed.), *The new language of change: Constructive collaboration in psychotherapy* (pp. 345–373). New York: Guilford Press.

Holder, H. D. & Blose, J. O. (1987). Changes in health care costs and utilization associated with mental health treatment. *Hospital and Community Psychiatry, 38*(10), 1070–1075.

Hoyt, M. F. (1993). Group psychotherapy in an HMO. *HMO Practice, 7*(3), 127–132.

Hoyt, M. F. (1994a). Promoting HMO values and the culture of quality. *HMO Practice, 8*(3), 122–126.

Hoyt, M. F. (1994b). Single session solutions. In M. F. Hoyt (Ed.), *Constructive therapies* (pp. 140–159). New York: Guilford Press.

Hoyt, M. F., & Austad, C. S. (1992). Psychotherapy in a staff model health maintenance organization: Providing and assuring quality care in the future. *Psychotherapy, 29*(1), 119–129.

Hoyt, M. F., Rosenbaum, R., & Talmon, M. (1992). Planned single session therapy. In S. Budman, M. Hoyt, & S. Friedman (Eds.), *The first session in brief therapy* (pp. 59–86). New York: Guilford Press.

Hunt, J. M. (1965). Intrinsic motivation and its role in psychological development. In D. Levine (Ed), *Nebraska symposium on motivation* (vol. 13). Lincoln: University of Nebraska Press.

Imber-Black, E., Roberts, J., & Whiting, R. (1988). *Rituals in families and family therapy.* New York: Norton.

Jacobson, N. (1995, Mar./Apr.). The overselling of therapy. *The Family Therapy Networker,* pp.40–47.

Janowsky, Z., Dickerson, V., & Zimmerman, J. (1995). Through Susan's eyes: Reflections on a reflecting team experience. In S. Friedman (Ed.), *The reflecting team in action: Collaborative practice in family therapy.* New York: Guilford Press.

Johnson, L. D., & Miller, S. D. (1994). Modification of depression risk factors: A solution-focused approach. *Psychotherapy, 31*(2), 244–253.

Jones, K., & Vischi, T. (1980). Impact of alchohol, drug abuse and mental health treatment and medical care utilization: A review of the literature. *Medical Care, 17,* 1–82.

Kaplan, S., & Greenfield, S. (1993). Enlarging patient responsibility: Strategies to increase patients' involvement in their health care. *Forum, 14*(3), 9–11.

Keeney, B. (1993). *Improvisational therapy.* New York: Guilford Press.

Kelman, H. (1969). Kairos: The auspicious moment. *American Journal of Psychoanalysis, 29,* 59–83.

Kiesler, C. A. (1982). Mental hospitals and alternative care: Noninstitutionalization as potential public policy for mental patients. *American Psychologist, 37*(4), 349–360.

Kiesler, C. A., & Morton, T. L. (1988). Psychology and public policy in the "health care revolution." *American Psychologist, 43*(12), 993–1003.

Kiresuk, T. J. (1973). Goal attainment scaling at a county mental health service. *Evaluation, 1*(2), 12–18.

Kiresuk, T. J., & Sherman, R. E. (1968). Goal attainment scaling: A general method for evaluating community mental health programs. *Community Mental Health Journal, 4*(6), 443–453.

Kiresuk, T. J., Smith, A. & Cardillo, J. E. (Eds.). (1994). *Goal Attainment Scaling: Applications, theory and measurement.* Hillsdale, NJ: Erlbaum.

Koestler, A. (1964). *The act of creation.* New York: Macmillan.

Kowalski, K. & Durrant, M. (1991, Oct.). *Foolish Constructions: Co-dependent vs. competent.* Workshop presented at American Association of Marital and Family Therapists, Dallas, TX.

Kowalski, K., & Kral, R. (1989). The geometry of solution: Using the scaling technique. *Family Therapy Case Studies, 4*(1), 59–66.

Kreilkamp, T. (1989). *Time-limited intermittent therapy with children and families.* New York: Brunner/Mazel.

Lambert, M. J. (1992). Psychotherapy outcome research: Implications for integrative and eclectic therapists. In J. C. Norcross & M. R. Goldfried (Eds.), *Handbook of psychotherapy integration* (pp. 94–129). New York: Basic Books.

Langer, E. J., & Rodin, J. (1976). The effects of choice and enhanced personal responsibility for the aged: A field experiment in an institutional setting. *Journal of Personality and Social Psychology, 34,* 191–198.

Lankton, S. R. (1990). Just do good therapy. In J. K. Zeig & S. G. Gilligan (Eds.), *Brief therapy: Myths, methods and metaphors* (pp. 62–77). New York: Brunner/Mazel.

Lankton, S. R., & Lankton, C. H. (1986). *Enchantment and intervention in family therapy.* New York: Brunner/Mazel.

Lax, W. D. (1992). Postmodern thinking in clinical practice. In S. McNamee & K. J. Gergen (Eds.), *Therapy as social construction* (pp. 69–85). Newbury Park, CA: Sage.

Lax, W. D. (1995). Offering reflections: Some theoretical and practical considerations. In S. Friedman (Ed.), *The reflecting team in action: Collaborative practice in family therapy.* New York: Guilford Press.

Levinson, W. (1994). Physician–patient communication: A key to malpractice prevention. *Journal of the American Medical Association, 272*(20), 1619–1620.

Lewin, T. (1996, May 22). Questions of privacy roil arena of psychotherapy. *The New York Times,* pp. 1,020.

Lipchik, E. (1988, June). Brief solution-focused therapy in inpatient settings. Paper presented at American Family Therapy Association, Montreal, Quebec, Canada.

Lipchik, E. (1992). A reflecting interview. *Journal of Strategic and Systemic Therapies, 11*(4), 59 74.

Lipchik, E. (1994, Mar./Apr.). The rush to be brief. *The Family Therapy Networker,* pp. 34–39.

Lipchik, E., & de Shazer, S. (1986). The purposeful interview. *Journal of Strategic and Systemic Therapies, 5,* 88–99.

Lobovits, D., Maisel, R., & Freeman, J. (1995). Public practices: An ethic of circulation. In S. Friedman (Ed.), *The reflecting team in action: Collaborative practice in family therapy.* New York: Guilford Press.

Madanes, C. (1981). *Strategic family therapy.* San Francisco: Jossey-Bass.

Madigan, S., & Epston, D. (1995). From "Spy-chiatric gaze" to communities of concern: From professional monologue to dialogue. In S. Friedman (Ed.), *The reflecting team in action: Collaborative practice in family therapy.* New York: Guilford Press.

Maturana, H. R., & Varela, F. J. (1987). *The tree of knowledge: The biological roots of human understanding.* Boston: New Science Library.

McGoldrick, M., & Gerson, R. (1985). *Genograms in family assessment.* New York: Norton.

McNamee, S., & Gergen, K. (Eds.). (1992). *Therapy as social construction.* Newbury Park, CA: Sage.

Menses, G. (1986). Therapondulitis and theraspondence: The art of therapeutic letter writing. *Family Therapy Case Studies, 1*(1), 61–64.

Meredith, R. L., & Bair, S. L. (1995, June). Hi Ho . . . Myrt's riding the INFO HIGHWAY. *Register Report, 21*(2), 1, 14–18.

Miller, S. (1992). The symptoms of solution. *Journal of Strategic and Systemic Therapies, 11*(1), 1–11.

Miller, S., Hubble, M., & Duncan, B. (1995, Mar./Apr.). No more bells and whistles. *The Family Therapy Networker,* pp. 52–58, 62–63.

Miller, W. R., & Rollnick, S. (1991). *Motivational interviewing: Preparing people to change addictive behavior.* New York: Guilford Press.

Minuchin, S. (1974). *Families and family therapy.* Cambridge, MA: Harvard University Press.

Mittelmeier, C. M., & Friedman, S. (1993). Toward a mutual understanding: Constructing solutions with families. In S. Friedman (Ed.), *The new language of change: Constructive collaboration in psychotherapy* (pp. 158–181). New York: Guilford Press.

Mittelmeier, C., & Meyer, B. L. (1994). Building social skills in school age children. *HMO Practice, 8*(1), 46–47.

Mould, D. E. (1994). A call to arms: But is managed care the dragon? *Psychotherapy Bulletin, 29*(4), 42–44.

Mumford, E., Schlesinger, H. J., Glass, G. V., Patrick, C., & Cuerdon, T. (1984). A new look at evidence about reduced cost of medical utilization following mental health treatment. *American Journal of Psychiatry, 141,* 1145–1158.

Nichols, T., & Jacques, C. (1995). Family reunions: Communities celebrate new possibilities. In S. Friedman (Ed.), *The reflecting team in action: Collaborative practice in family therapy.* New York: Guilford Press.

Noble, H. B. (1995, July 3). Quality is focus for health plans. *New York Times,* pp. 1, 7.

Novak, D. H., Goldstein, M. G., & Dube, C. (1993). Improving medical history taking skills. *Forum, 14*(3), 3–6.

Nurcombe, B. (1989). Goal-directed treatment planning and principles of brief hospitalization. *Journal of the American Academy of Child and Adolescent Psychiatry, 28*(1), 26–30.

Nyland, D., & Thomas, J. (1994, Nov./Dec.). The economics of narrative. *The Family Therapy Networker,* pp. 38–39.

O'Hanlon, W. H. (1993a). Possibility therapy: From iatrogenic injury to iatrogenic healing. In S. Gilligan & R. Price (Eds.), *Therapeutic conversations* (pp. 3–17). New York: Norton.

O'Hanlon, W. H. (1993b). Take two people and call them in the morning: Brief solution-oriented therapy with depression. In S. Friedman (Ed.), *The new language of change: Constructive collaboration in psychotherapy* (pp. 50–84). New York: Guilford Press.

O'Hanlon, W. H., & Weiner-Davis, M. (1989). *In search of solutions: A new direction in psychotherapy.* New York: Norton.

O'Hanlon, W. H., & Wilk, J. (1987). *Shifting contexts: The generation of effective psychotherapy.* New York: Guilford Press.

Papp, P. (1983). *The process of change.* New York: Guilford Press.

Parry, A., & Doan, R. E. (1994). *Story re-visions: Narrative therapy in the postmodern world.* New York: Guilford Press.

Patterson, J., & Scherger, J. E. (1995). A critique of health care reform in the United States: Implications for the training and practice of marital and family therapy. *Journal of Marital and Family Therapy, 21*(2), 127–135.

Postman, N. (1976). *Crazy talk, stupid talk.* New York: Delacorte.

Prochaska, J. O., DiClemente, C. C., & Norcross, J. C. (1992). In search of how people change: Applications to addictive behavior. *American Psychologist, 47*(9), 1102–1114.

Rifkin, J., & O'Hanlon, W. H. (1989). The tape recorder cure. *Family Therapy Case Studies, 4*(2), 33–36.

Rodin, J., & Langer, E. J. (1977). Long term effects of a control-relevant intervention with the institutionalized aged. *Journal of Personality and Social Psychology, 35,* 897–902.

Rosen, S. (1982). *My voice will go with you: The teaching tales of Milton H. Erickson.* New York: Norton.

Rosenhan, D. L. (1973). On being sane in insane places. *Science, 179,* 250–258.

Rosenthal, E. (1995, Mar. 25). As HMOs rise, New York is catching up with others. *New York Times,* pp. 1, 26.

Roth, S. A., & Chasin, R. (1994). Entering one another's worlds of meaning and imagination: Dramatic enactment and narrative couple therapy. In M. F. Hoyt (Ed.), *Constructive therapies* (pp. 189–216). New York: Guilford Press.

Ryle, G. (1949). *The concept of mind.* New York: University Paperbacks.

Sabin, J. E. (1978). Research findings on chronic mental illness: A model for continuing care in the health maintenance organization. *Comprehensive Psychiatry, 19*(1), 83–95.

Sabin, J. E. (1991). Clinical skills for the 1990's: Six lessons from HMO practice. *Hospital and Community Psychiatry, 42*(6), 605–608.

Sabin, J. E. (1994). A credo for ethical managed care in mental health practice. *Hospital and Community Psychiatry, 45*(9), 859–860.

Sargent, J. (1986, May/June). Psychopharmacology and family therapy. *The Family Therapy Networker,* 17–18.

Sawatzky, D. D., & Parry, T. A. (1993). Silenced voices heard: A tale of family survival. In S. Friedman (Ed.), *The new language of change: Constructive collaboration in psychotherapy* (pp. 405–427). New York: Guilford Press.

Schnitzer, P. K. (1993). Tales of the absent father: Applying the "story" metaphor in family therapy. *Family Process, 32*(4), 441–458.

Schulz, R. (1976). Effects of control and predictability on the physical and psychological well-being of the institutionalized aged. *Journal of Personality and Social Psychology, 33,* 563–573.

Seikkula, J., Aaltonen, J., Alakare, B., Haarakangas, K., Keränen, J., & Sutela, M. (1995). Treating psychosis by means of open dialogue. In S. Friedman (Ed.), *The reflecting team in action: Collaborative practice in family therapy.* New York: Guilford Press.

Selekman, M. D. (1993). *Pathways to change: Brief therapy solutions with difficult adolescents.* New York: Guilford Press.

Selekman, M. D. (1995). Rap music with wisdom: Peer reflecting teams with tough adolescents. In S. Friedman (Ed.), *The reflecting team in action: Collaborative practice in family therapy.* New York: Guilford Press.

Seligman, M. E. (1975). *Helplessness: On depression, development and death.* San Francisco: Freeman.

Sells, S. P., Smith, T. E., Coe, M. J., Yoshioka, M., & Robbins, J. (1994). An ethnography of couple and therapist experiences in reflecting team practice. *Journal of Marital and Family Therapy, 20*(3), 247–266.

Sleek, S. (1995, May). Wanted: Practitioners who keep costs in line. *APA Monitor*, p. 33.

Smith, T. E., Sells, S. P., & Clevenger, T. (1994). Ethnographic content analysis of couple and therapist perceptions in a reflecting team setting. *Journal of Marital and Family Therapy, 20*(3), 267–286.

Smith, T. E., Yoshioka, M., & Winton, M. (1993). A qualitative understanding of reflecting teams. *Journal of Systemic Therapies, 12*(3), 28–43.

Stroebe, M., et al. (1992). Broken hearts or broken bonds: Love and death in historical perspective. *American Psychologist, 47*(10), 1205–1212.

Stromberg, C., & Ratcliff, R. (1995, June). A legal update on provider credentialing. *The Psychologist's Legal Update*, No. 7, 1–12.

Talmon, M. (1990). *Single session therapy*. San Francisco: Jossey-Bass.

Tomm, K. (1990, June). Ethical postures that orient one's clinical decision making. Presentation at American Family Therapy Academy, Philadelphia.

Varela, F. J. (1989). Reflections on the circulation of concepts between a biology of cognition and systemic family therapy. *Family Process, 28*, 15–24.

Wall, S., & Arden, H. (1990). *Wisdomkeepers: Meetings with Native American spiritual leaders*. Hillsboro, OR: Beyond Words.

Wangberg, F. (1991). Self-reflection: Turning the mirror inward. *Journal of Strategic and Systemic Therapies, 10*, 18–29.

Waters, D. B., & Lawrence, E. C. (1993). *Competence, courage and change: An approach to family therapy*. New York: Norton.

Watzlawick, P. (Ed.). (1984). *The invented reality*. New York: Norton.

Weick, K. (1984). Small wins: Redefining the scale of social problems. *American Psychologist, 39*(1), 40–49.

Weiner-Davis, M., de Shazer, S., & Gingerich, W. J. (1987). Building on pretreatment change to construct the therapeutic solution: An exploratory study. *Journal of Marital and Family Therapy, 13*, 359–363.

Whiston, S. C. & Sexton, T. L. (1993). An overview of psychotherapy outcome research: Implications for practice. *Professional Psychology: Research and Practice, 24*(1), 43–51.

Whitaker, C. A. (1976). The hindrance of theory in clinical work. In P. Guerin (Ed.), *Family therapy: Theory and practice* (pp. 154–164). New York: Gardner Press.

Whitaker, C. A., & Bumberry, W. M. (1988). *Dancing with the family: A symbolic experiential approach*. New York: Brunner/Mazel.

White, M. (1986). Negative explanation, restraint, and double description: A template for family therapy. *Family Process, 25*, 169–184.

White, M. (1991, Oct.). *Re-authoring lives and relationships*. Workshop at Leonard Morse Hospital, Natick, MA.

White, M. (1995). *Re-authoring lives: Interviews and essays*. Adelaide, Australia: Dulwich Centre Publications.

White, M., & Epston, D. (1990). *Narrative means to therapeutic ends*. New York: Norton.

White, R. (1959). Motivation reconsidered: The concept of competence. *Psychological Review, 66*, 297–333.

Woodworth, R. S., & Schlossberg, H. (1954). *Experimental psychology*. New York: Holt, Rinehart & Winston.

Wright, R. H. (1991, Spring). Toward a national plan. *Advance Plan*, pp. 1, 14–15.

Zimmerman, J. L., & Dickerson, V. C. (1993). Bringing forth the restraining influence of pattern in couples therapy. In S. Gilligan & R. Price (Eds.), *Therapeutic conversations* (pp. 197–214). New York: Guilford Press.

# Index